7.95

D1061885

THE RENEWAL OF
AMERICAN CATHOLICISM

THE RENEWAL OF
AMERICAN
CATHOLICISM

DAVID J. O'BRIEN

New York
OXFORD UNIVERSITY PRESS
1972

MY LORD GOD, I have no idea where I am going. I do not see the road ahead of me. I cannot know for certain where it will end. Nor do I really know myself, and the fact that I think that I am following your will does not mean that I am actually doing so. But I believe that the desire to please you does in fact please you. And I hope that I will never do anything apart from that desire. And I know that if I do this you will lead me by the right road though I may know nothing about it. Therefore will I trust you always though I may seem to be lost and in the shadow of death. I will not fear, for you are ever with me, and you will never leave me to face my perils alone.

THOMAS MERTON

FOR
JOANNE

ACKNOWLEDGMENTS

Portions of this book appeared first as articles, and I wish to thank the publishers for permission to use them here. "American Catholics in an Age of Crisis," *New City* (November 1967) (a monthly formerly published in Chicago) appears in revised form in Chapter 1. The paper "American Catholicism and American Religion" was presented in shorter form to the Duquesne University History Forum in October 1970. In its present form it was published in the Winter (1971) edition of the *Journal of the American Academy of Religion* and is used by permission. "The Ambiguity of Success" was prepared for presentation to the International Historical Congress, Moscow (1970). The last section of Chapter 7 is taken from "Eugene Genovese and the Student Left," *Liberation* (October 1969). Finally, parts of Chapter 8 originally appeared in *The Holy Cross Quarterly* (January 1971); later this was revised for *The Berrigans* (New York, 1971), edited by Philip Nobile and W. V. E. Casey, S.J.

This is also the occasion to thank the Society for Religion in Higher Education for a cross-disciplinary fellowship which enabled me to spend the year 1970–1971 studying theology at the Boston Theological Institute's member schools. This was a rare and valuable experience for one whose training had been in American political history. A faculty fellowship from Holy Cross College also assisted in the preparation of this manuscript. Many friends read portions of the manuscript and many more helped in ways large and small. My family continues to be my constant source of encouragement and support. In particular my wife, Joanne, bears patiently my preoccupations with the past and gently nudges me to confront the present and the future. To her this book is gratefully and lovingly dedicated.

PREFACE

In the summer of 1968 I left Montreal's Loyola College to teach in the summer session at Marquette University in Milwaukee, Wisconsin. Having been away from the United States for four years, I took the opportunity to learn as much as possible about the political and religious currents agitating the country in the middle sixties. In addition to talking and working with students and faculty at Marquette, I traveled to Chicago to see friends and attend the second annual convention of the National Association of Laymen. My scholarly and personal interest in American Catholicism was sharpened by the visit, and I was led to undertake this book. The possibility of writing a series of essays on contemporary issues confronting American Catholics had long been in my mind, but the sense of deepening crisis and enormous potential that I derived from my stay in Milwaukee stimulated me to begin.

The fall brought severe conflicts at my home campus in Montreal and these, together with new demands on my time in these abnormal days for university men, forced postponement of the project. The following year I left Montreal to accept a permanent post at Holy Cross College in Worcester, Massachusetts. There again new academic demands occasioned by regular contact with American students, plus the enormous burdens placed on us all by the war in Viet Nam, absorbed my time and energy. Only in the fall of 1970, did I return to the project, begun almost two years before, with my sense of the depth of the national crisis and the importance of the Catholic response even more sharply etched on my mind than it was that remarkable summer in Milwaukee.

I hope that what follows will contribute in a positive and constructive way to the discussions going on among all Americans and among Catholics in particular. It will be clear to the reader that I have no intention of making detachment or objec-

tivity the hallmark of this study. Rather I would like to help
sharpen the issues in such a way that my words will eventually
contribute to actions I think are necessary and desirable. Peter
Maurin and Dorothy Day used to talk of "clarification of
thought," regular and often interminable discussion of what
Christian commitment should mean in social and political life,
which brought inspiration and renewed confidence to them and
their Catholic Worker colleagues. If this book helps to "clarify
thought" it will be a success.

The book derives its focus from my interest and training in
American history and the history of the Catholic Church in the
United States. I have written professionally on the latter subject, and my study in the field is the major basis for my
confidence in undertaking the present work. I think the essays
that follow are historical essays, for the writing of history need
not imply a sharp separation of past and present. The purposes
of historical study are related to our own needs here and now.
History must justify itself in terms of our desire to act in a
meaningful way in regard to our most pressing problems. Historical consciousness enables us to understand our situation and
to act with perspective, deepened sensitivity and humility. If we
lack historical awareness we will deserve the reproach of H.
Richard Niebuhr: "the evil habit of men in all times to criticize
their predecessors for having seen only half of the truth hides
from them their own partiality and incompleteness."[1]

The thesis, which is the basis for all that follows, can be
simply stated. American Catholics are passing through a period
of crisis, a common enough statement. But the crisis is more
profound than most commentators have suspected. The surface
manifestations of apostate priests (a quaint term now), rebellious nuns, independent layment, liturgical chaos and a thousand other items reflect a severe strain upon the American
Catholic consciousness. The roots lie in the two major determining factors of any religious situation: theology and social structure, or, if you prefer, theory and practice. On the one hand
American Catholics are for the first time in their history aware
of theological controversies that touch the most basic doctrines
of Roman Catholicism and explode cherished notions of the
church and the faith. On the other hand American Catholics

have "come of age" in their society: they are no longer a minority in an alien country, and they know it. At last they have the respectability and power they have yearned for since Lord Baltimore planted the banner of King Charles on the banks of the Chesapeake.

Pope John XXIII and President John F. Kennedy, those two idols of my generation, unwittingly shifted the fulcrum of Catholic life and permanently altered the Catholic conception of allegiance to God and country. "What does it mean to be an American Catholic?" is now an open question, open, in poker player's parlance, at both ends. The reforms of Pope John made it difficult to know what it meant to be a Catholic; the election of John F. Kennedy added the problem of defining the American Catholic. Tragically Kennedy's successors have opened up the question of what it means to be an American. Whether we look at the nation: war, violence, racism, disorder in the citadels of American life or at the church: celibacy, birth control, nationalism, intransigence, the picture is one of deepening division, intellectual confusion and moral outrage.

To those who still think in the categories of the 1930s or the 1950s the situation is depressing; to those who long for liberation to a brave new world of harmony and freedom it is exhilarating. For the rest of us the contemporary situation arouses our hopes while it nourishes our fears; it promises a better church and a better world even as the threat of spiritual isolation and physical annihilation hover in the background. We are where Christians should be, poised on the razor's edge between present and future, aware of the possibilities for good and evil which open out in front of us. Knowing the reality of sin and the possibility of failure, men must nevertheless push on, relying on the love of God and their own talents, seeking to build a Kingdom that will be God's because it will be man's.

D.J.O'B.

College of the Holy Cross
Worcester, Massachusetts
June 1972

CONTENTS

THE RENEWAL OF
AMERICAN CATHOLICISM

1

AMERICAN CATHOLICS IN AN AGE OF CRISIS

On January 20, 1961, John Fitzgerald Kennedy, Irish, American, Catholic and President of the United States, proclaimed the advent of "a new generation of Americans—born in this century, tempered by war, disciplined by a hard and bitter peace, proud of our ancient heritage—and unwilling to witness the slow undoing of those human rights to which this nation has always been committed and to which we are committed today at home and around the world."[1] The high hopes and unselfish dedication aroused that day stood in sharp contrast to the apathy of the previous decade. Young activists for peace and civil rights began to look upon politics as perhaps an honorable vehicle for the attainment of moral ends while others, less active, began to question the complacent disdain for public issues that characterized what had been called "the silent generation." Kennedy's unique blend of rhetorical idealism and tough practicality inspired a new concern for the quality of American life and a new desire to participate in the work of completing what the president called "the great unfinished business" of American democracy.

Almost two years later, in October 1962, a man of another generation stood before the Roman Catholic bishops of the world, assembled in St. Peter's in Rome, and opened a new era in Christian history. Pope John XXIII offered to the Vatican Council no outline of a new church or a new Christendom, only the possibility of relevance through freedom and a personal example of humble faith. He gave Catholics back their church, hoping they would fashion it into an instrument of witness to the saving presence of Christ by dedicated service to mankind. In the short run the disposition of that church lay with the Council fathers; in the long run it lay with the "people of God" themselves.

At first glance the inauguration of a president and the con-
vocation of an ecumenical council are connected only inciden-
tally, but in this case there was a profound relationship. For one
thing it is clear now that the impact of these men went beyond
the confines of church and nation, that both came to symbolize
ideals of hope, reason, justice and peace, which cut across such
boundaries. Each narrowed the yawning chasm between profession and practice that had become the despair of men of
good will everywhere and, for a time, made it appear possible
that the American dream of personal liberty, independent self-
government and shared affluence had not been invalidated by
habitual betrayal and the Christian vision of love and brotherhood had not been irretrievably smothered by ecclesiastical and
personal hypocrisy.

For American Catholics the lives of Pope John and President
Kennedy converged in more immediate ways. The election and
successful tenure of a Catholic president all but destroyed the
traditional Catholic sense of being a beleaguered minority in
constant danger of persecution and repression. Kennedy demonstrated the falseness of most non-Catholic fears while educating
his fellow Catholics to a more mature sense of their civic
responsibilities. Together with the popularity of Pope John and
the respectful attention of the media to the affairs of the
council, the Kennedy years brought an end to the isolation and
aloofness long characteristic of American Catholic life. The
council further cemented Catholic respectability by ratifying
freedom of conscience and separation of church and state, while
its positive response to modern society eased Catholic doubts
and insecurity about their own participation in secular life. The
importance of these events only becomes clear when it is
realized that for over a century Catholics in the United States
had struggled to reconcile the demands of church and society
by refuting charges that Catholicism was incompatible with the
American way of life. The results were complex, for the church
accepted and sanctioned many features of American life and
thought, but it rejected others as "secularistic" and "materialistic." Despite the efforts of men like Isaac Hecker and John
Ireland to make the church fully American, the general con-

scious response to minority status was negative and defensive until the events of the 1960s shattered forever the social and psychological bases of "ghetto Catholicism."[2]

The effort to be loyal to church and nation took many forms, not all of them admirable, but in the hands of the church's best leaders it meant a creative reconciliation of the ideals of democracy, personal liberty and constitutional government learned from the American tradition with the demands of justice and love preserved in the Christian heritage. With the coming of a Catholic president and an ecumenical council it appeared to many that such a synthesis was finally possible. Michael Novak, a young theologian who personified the new era, echoed President Kennedy's proclamation of "a new generation," this time one that was fully "American and Catholic," while another young scholar-journalist, Daniel Callahan, called for reforms that would remove the tension between the values of self-reliance, independence and initiative taught the Catholic as American and the docility and obedience expected of him as a Catholic.[3] Novak, Callahan, Donald Thorman and other young Catholic leaders demanded reforms in the church that would give the newly educated and self-confident laity a larger voice and would motivate them to participate with other men of good will in fulfilling the goals of American society.

To an extent few would have thought possible at the time their program was realized during the council. A new theology of the church emphasized the role of the laity, religious liberty was sanctioned, new structures that appeared more representative were established in Rome and at home, Catholics achieved new prominence in political life and many joined vigorously in the drive for civil rights.

Yet things did not work out as expected. By 1970 the old gap between pretence and practice appeared more impassable than ever, and the high hopes of 1961 seemed in retrospect romantic and utopian. American cities became battlegrounds between the armed forces of white America and a Negro population verging on revolution, unsure any longer whether it cared to be American, certain that it would die rather than continue to aquiesce in injustice and indignity. On the other side of the world American young men fought and died for 8 years in a cause which was for many of them politically confusing and morally dishonorable.

The Black revolution and the Viet Nam war posed severe challenges to the American conscience. For some sensitive Americans an almost apocalyptic vision of the death of traditional ideals and dreams seemed to become a bleak reality in the decade of the 1960s. It is hard to sustain devotion to democracy as blacks are denied it, and whites adopt it as a slogan to justify the murder of Asians. Liberty ceases to have meaning for people who hear it from the lips of men who assist in its destruction. The people seem to know democratic responsibility only as a part of a pre-organizational past, and their vague sense of loss is smothered in the pillow of affluence. Unable to understand how the crisis came about, given little leadership in solving their problems, many Americans seem certain only of failure, explicitly the failure of their leadership, secretly the failure of themselves. The American dream of shaping the course of history, leading the world to material sufficiency, personal liberty and popular government gives way to apathy and despair, to a sense of impotence and frustration before the rush of events over which men appear to have no control.

For Catholics the American crisis comes at a particularly important moment in their own history. From the flood of Irish immigration in the 1840s until World War II American Catholicism was the church of immigrants and workers. Only with the cumulative impact of the New Deal, the CIO, wartime wages and taxation and the G.I. Bill of Rights did American Catholics in large numbers enter the middle class. Gradually the old concern for acceptance and respectability faded, long standing anti-Catholic emotions subsided and, in 1960, American Catholics entered a new phase of their history, a phase that was no longer marked by minority self-consciousness and that inevitably brought profound changes in the structure and character of the American church. The Vatican Council came in the midst of these profound social changes in American Catholicism. The popularity of Pope John and the respectful and intense interest of the secular press in the affairs of the council reinforced the conditions that were destroying Catholic minority consciousness. No longer could Catholics assume the latent hostility of Protestants and secular liberals, no longer could the church shape ecclesiastical policy in response to outside challenges. Catholics would be forced to define their role in American society on the basis of something other than survival, the goal that the sense of being a beseiged, threatened minority had always dictated.

The second effect of the council was to make that self-definition more difficult, for it challenged some of the most cherished ideas and some of the most secure certitudes of the Catholic population. Sensitive to the fact that they were "strangers in the land" both as immigrants and as Catholics, the church's leaders and people had concentrated their attention on those features of Catholicism that most distinguished them from Protestants. Friday abstinence, compulsory worship, a fixed moral code including clear rules on sexual, marital and medical ethics, these features of Catholic life came to seem not merely important but indeed essential to the identity of Catholics in a Protestant land. For both Catholic and non-Catholic the bishop symbolized other distinctive features of Catholicism: to the non-Catholic he represented the foreign, authoritarian, and consequently un-American, aspects of the Church; to the Catholic their religious loyalty, ecclesiastical unity and cultural identity. Everything in Catholic life seemed to accentuate the need for these organizational qualities of discipline, order and unity, and to de-emphasize the explosive potential of Christian ideals when they are taken seriously.

The council called all of this into question. It stressed the freedom of the people of God, a Christian vocation embracing both the laity and their clerical servants, personal responsibility and the integrity of the individual conscience, an ethic of love rather than simple abstract moral laws and numerous other elements of Christian tradition that the church universal had lost sight of in the years since the Reformation and that social conditions in the United States had further obscured. The Council weakened the *de facto* authority of the bishops by rediscovering the laity; the bishops' role was further diminished by their inability to grasp the significance of the changes taking place at home. The council undermined the fixed and unchang-

ing moral code on which Catholics had long relied by emphasizing the primacy of conscience and the complexity of the
application of abstract principles of justice and charity to varying and dynamic historical conditions. The moral code was
further weakened by the inability of the church to deal with the
birth control issue, made increasingly pressing by the growth of
the Catholic middle class. The council reduced the place of the
organized institutional church in the lives of Catholics by abandoning the old cry of secularism in favor of a vague blending of
the church and the world, stressing the fellowship of Christians
and blurring the distinction between Catholics and "others,"
and refusing to deal frankly with the issues of war, racism and
population growth that most disturbed the conscience of mankind. Again this was accentuated in the United States by the
reduction of ethnic boundaries and by the increasing questioning of the need for the schools, hospitals and benevolent agencies that had long been symbols of Catholic power and sources
of Catholic allegiance.

Before the council the issues had been relatively clear, as they
were for example in Donald Thorman's *The Emerging Layman*
or John Tracy Ellis's groundbreaking 1954 essay on Catholics
and the intellectual life.[4] For liberal Catholics of the postwar
generation the major question was the traditional one of choosing between aloofness to or participation in American life. In
1959 John Cogley wrote in criticism of American Catholics:
"We content ourselves with standing in judgment on our age as
if *its* problems were not our problems, as if *its* failures were not
our own, as if the challenges confronting *it* were not confronting us."[5] For Cogley, and for most Catholic liberals of a decade
ago, the enemy was the narrow, prejudiced, self-righteous
Catholicism of the ghetto. The Catholic Worker movement and
the Social Action Department of the National Catholic Welfare
Conference had begun hammering at the walls in the 1930s; in
the 1950s Monsignor Ellis launched an explosion that shook the
ghetto to its foundations; Kennedy, Pope John and the Second
Vatican Council finished the job. But during the 1960s the
alternative of assimilation, of creative participation in progressive democratic America that Archbishop John Ireland,
Monsignor John A. Ryan and John Cogley had championed,

suddenly began to crumble. A disintegrating America was not such an attractive alternative after all. Perhaps America was not the land of freedom, democracy and justice that Ireland had seen; perhaps it was not peopled by the free, independent spirits others had imagined. To many America now appeared instead as a vicious society, which necessarily excluded the poor from power and inadvertantly but necessarily devoured men's souls. As Catholics began to question their nation, the liberals among them had to reassess the myth of the ghetto. Behind its walls adaptation had always taken place. While rejecting some aspects of American life as "materialistic" and "secularistic" Catholics had easily adapted to machine politics, to economic opportunity and mobility, to America's obsession with education, to patterns of racial discrimination and to many other features, good and bad, of American life. The products of the combination of assimilation and aloofness were seen as the crisis of the 1960s deepened, when nuns and priests joined picket lines to receive insults and rocks thrown by Catholic laymen.

The Catholic crisis broke open American Catholicism and laid bare its divisions, its paradoxes, its contradictions. The American crisis broke down the old alternatives of Americanism and the ghetto and left American Catholics adrift, uncertain and leaderless. At the same time the American church continued to possess enormous energy and vitality. The contrast between tremendous potential and possible disaster can be illustrated by almost any controversy of the last ten years. While Los Angeles' Cardinal McIntyre unsuccessfully ordered the sisters of the Immaculate Heart of Mary to retain their traditional wearing apparel, the IHMs and hundreds of other nuns went ahead exploring heretofore forbidden areas of the secular city from pop art to nonviolent direct action. In 1968 the American bishops published guidelines on theology that insisted on retention of traditional doctrine on authority, sacraments and birth control; also in 1968 2500 enthusiastic Catholics in a Chicago ballroom cheered excitedly while an English priest-theologian who had left the church (Charles Davis) and a Notre Dame Jesuit (Rev. John L. McKenzie, S.J.) agreed that the church was irrelevant, most doctrine was outmoded and traditional authority was unnecessary. At about the same time the president of a Catholic university informed alumni and parents that his administration would not tolerate student demonstrations nor countenance "student power" while the young people, led by theology students, discussed strategy and tactics for bringing about a drastic restructuring of the university community. The instances of contrast between puzzled and even frightened leaders and enthusiastic and dedicated nuns, priests and lay people can be multiplied one-hundredfold. Demands for change have gone far beyond the wildest dreams of the cautious reformers of a decade ago, driving many of them into a conservative stance, while the worst fears of conservatives that discord, division and even disintegration would inevitably follow the least reforms seem to be coming true before their horrified eyes.

In 1960 the suggestion that perhaps some of the liturgy of the church might be translated into English stamped one as a "kook" in Catholic circles. By 1970 not only had the entire liturgy been transferred to the vernacular, but laymen were demanding drastic reforms in the parish structure and free experimentation in the Mass. Singers and dancers appeared, and guitars, brass ensembles and bongo drums sounded forth from beneath dusty organs in neo-Gothic churches. Small groups of suburban Catholics followed their teen-age children to services in the inner city church that had become a center for community action, liturgical excitement and general religious and social nonconformity, while other ghetto churches stood nearly empty. Suburban churches no longer bulged with people and expanded their plants, and dissatisfied laymen began their own "floating" or "underground" parishes, meeting in private homes, club rooms or storefronts for community religious celebration, discussion of social and theological problems and development of *avant garde* sunday schools for the young.

Perhaps an event in 1968 can serve as a point of reference for the crosscurrents of change. On the weekend of June 28-30 in Chicago, the year-old National Association of Laymen (NAL) held a convention attended by delegates, members and interested individuals from all over the United States. The NAL was founded at a meeting in St. Paul, Minnesota a year before by a small group of Catholic laymen who believed that the time was ripe for a new association, independent of the formal ecclesiastical structure, that could develop lay consciousness and serve as a pressure group within the church. The existing bodies, the National Councils of Catholic Men and Women, seemed to the NAL organizers to be too closely tied to the hierarchy and, like the Rosary Sodalities, Altar Guilds and Holy Name Societies, which served as their local units, to be essentially under clerical direction and to carry on only the most innocuous activities. The NAL hoped to anticipate the formation of parish and diocesan councils, already in the works in many dioceses, and to continue to serve as a vehicle for specifically lay action after these were organized. The initial success of the NAL could be seen in the fact that the two hundred who attended the founding meeting in 1967 had grown to over a thousand by the 1968 convention.

The scope of the convention revealed the diversity of currents at work in the church. The first two days were devoted to workshops on such subjects as Women and the Church, Racism in America, Student Power, Parish Councils, Experimental Communities, War and Peace, Spanish-Speaking Catholics, the Church and the Urban Crisis. The session on racism featured two priests closely associated with the newly formed Association of Black Priests, whose initial statement charging the church with racism and demanding drastic changes in the church's relations with the Black community had created a sensation only a few weeks earlier. Their message was clear: whites have to get out of the ghetto, church activities must incorporate black people and black leadership, the church must be willing to make a transfer of wealth and energy from rich suburbia to the poverty sector while vesting control in the hands of the poor themselves. Only such drastic changes, they argued, could prevent the church from "dying in the slums." It was significant that the comment of a fellow panelist that such "withdrawal" was both unrealistic and retrogressive, promoting the very segregation that was the root of the problem, excited almost no comment or agreement from the audience. Rather the mood was assent to the propositions made by the black clergy regarding the direction the church should take, and troubled exploration of what they—middle-class, concerned, white Christians— could do to help. The only answer they could find that day was the need to educate their fellow suburbanites to the problems and needs of black Americans, to explain to them the reasons for welcoming and supporting the development of black power. White racism is the cause, one member of the audience argued, and black power cannot change that; it must be fought by white men acting through white organizations in white society.

A second session, on war and peace, exhibited the same preoccupation with what individuals and groups of concerned laymen should do rather than with the stance of the church hierarchy and clergy. Again, too, there was a willingness to accept a radical message: draft resistance, condemnation of American militarism and imperialism, even pacifism. The loudest applause was reserved for a member of the Catholic Peace Fellowship whose argument was similar to that of new left Christians in England: that Christianity is essentially a political faith that necessarily drives its members to unending struggle against social and political power. Two social scientists on the panel took issue with the radical argument, but it was supported by a spokesman for PAX, an international Catholic peace group, and, less unequivocally, by an editor of the *Bulletin of Atomic Scientists*. Bitter criticism of the bishops, so outstanding a feature of such meetings a few years before, was notably absent here. Instead all devoted their attention to methods of action whereby committed people could have a significant impact on the arms race and the Viet Nam war.

While few resolutions came out of the convention, probably because of the lateness of the general session, the drift was clear. The housewives, professionals and business people represented in the National Association of Laymen (academics and writers so frequently present at such affairs were notably outnumbered) were anxious to share in church policy and administration, but their attention was gradually shifting from demands for a more positive posture of the church on public issues to demands for independent lay initiative and action. Joined by rebellious priests and nuns, these "new layman" were going to be a lot tougher to control—the days of the monolithic church bent upon harnessing and channeling lay energies were over. Christianity was something they were defining for themselves in action, whatever efforts the bishops might make to define it for them. Even the birth control debate, which had always diverted lay attention from other issues, no longer enjoyed much prominence. One could only assume that the position of many young priests that couples must exercise their own judgment, considering their responsibilities to themselves, their children and the community, had effectively settled the issue. Any attempt to enforce the renewed condemnation of artificial contraception, which came several weeks after the convention, would undoubtedly widen and formalize existing divisions and drive a large number of these dedicated priests and laymen to sever their already tenuous ties to the institutional church.

There was in all this both a promise of tremendous energy directed to the alleviation of social and economic injustice and serious danger that an unstructured and disorganized Christianity might gradually lose its dynamism and be dissipated by outside forces. In the "debate" between Charles Davis and John L. McKenzie, which highlighted the convention, almost all the commentators who spoke from the floor expressed their sympathy with Davis and their acceptance of much of his critique of the church. Yet several stated that they were held back from following him because of their fear that the unorganized and vaguely defined Christian "movement" to which he gave his allegiance offered neither the spiritual sustenance more and more Catholics were finding in the underground communities nor the social effectiveness potentially contained in organized denominational groups like the NAL. Davis regarded ferment such as that revealed at the convention as evidence that the Spirit was moving in the Christian people. The less transcendentally oriented may see in it forces of social and political change: the arrival of American Catholics to middle-class respectability at a time when Catholic identity has been shaken by the council and its attendant theological revolution. For Davis the concern, honesty and independence evident among the awakened minority is a hopeful sign. For the bishops it seems to foreshadow trouble, even schism. For American society, badly in need of commitment, idealism and active acceptance of social and political responsibility by the suburban middle class, it offers hope that the nation may yet be reformed and its ideals redeemed.

American Catholics stand then at a critical moment in their

history. The best of the church's leaders in the past called for full, free participation in American life, confident that, whatever its faults, the nation was open and progressive. Once American Catholics had overcome the social and political barriers Protestant America had erected to exclude Catholics from positions of power, prestige and influence, any sense of isolation, of persecution or of exclusion they continued to feel was the result of a false consciousness, to be eliminated by taking to heart the message of the council and its major American interpreters. If the "ghetto mentality" was overcome, the road to full Catholic participation in the American experiment would lie open.

It may be that, as this liberal image suggests, Catholics are not at a crossroads but a junction, where two hitherto parallel roads labeled Catholic and American merge into a single American Catholic highway. The religious bigotry and nativism of Americans and the ethnic exclusiveness and religious conservatism of Catholics having been exposed and discredited, little remains but to continue the journey. Unfortunately, few historical struggles have such unambiguous results. Thesis and antithesis may bring synthesis, but it in turn contains the seeds of further disjunction. Human goals and aspirations when achieved seldom seem as satisfying as expected: "Don't ever want anything too much," a father told his son, "for you might get it." Part of our humanity, it seems, is expressed in unrealistic utopian hopes and dreams. When these are concretized, they guide our activity, laying the basis for plans and actions. When attained, the concrete goals never seem to fulfill the original hopes, which are sometimes reborn as criticism, alienation and further action but are also sometimes interred in cynicism and despair.

Nowhere is this more evident than in the history of Christianity. When Hans Kung revises the Reformers slogan into *ecclesia semper reformanda,* he means that the church contains within itself a faith that calls for expression in concrete forms yet constantly stands in judgment on those forms.[6] Catholicism, with its emphasis on universality, has usually sought to permeate all phases of cultural life, yet it has fostered contrary

values and attitudes that challenge Christian culture at every
state of its development. It is hardly surprising then that when
American Catholics achieved the accepted and influential role in
American culture which had long been their goal, the result
seemed to many less than satisfying. From several different
critical perspectives it appeared that in accomplishing Americanization the church had come close to losing its soul, surrendering its historical claims and betraying its most basic functions. If
this is at all true then American Catholics confront at least two
paths, sometimes running parallel to each other, sometimes
turning sharply apart, at still other points joining together for a
time. This is only to say that the claims of America and of
Christianity upon the conscience are strong, even compelling,
and both are complex, merging and blending as well as separating and challenging. American Catholics must journey on
their own, personally and with their brethren, trying to plot a
course which will fulfill their real destiny and yet allow them to
remain open in service to those about them.

A decade ago, in a book of essays on the theme of Catholicism's role in a free society, Gustave Weigel saw the issue that
would become central in the lives of American Catholics in the
1960s. Most of the contributors to that symposium argued at
length about separation of church and state, financial aid to
parochial schools and the more general problem of Catholicism's
compatability with America's most basic freedoms. Weigel took
issue with the tone of the discussion, contending that it made
the major question the church's contribution to society. Weigel
suspected that the state, failing itself to foster the virtues of
democratic citizenship, now looked to the churches to mold the
citizens it needed for the preservation of its own order. This was
not the proper role of the church, Weigel argued, for the church
must be itself, doing those things proper to the church, fostering a spirit of austerity, prayerfulness and love. The church
must worship God and proclaim his Gospel, serving as a prophet
in society. "If society is pursuing a virtuous goal, the church
will spontaneously pursue the same goal," Weigel wrote. "If
society pursues a sinful objective, the church must refuse cooperation. And it will be the church which will make the

decision as to the goodness of the goal."[7] The church must reject society's offer to "cover it with honor" in return for its support and must instead be true to itself.

The "church being itself," then, is the alternative to Catholic Americanism. In 1960 Weigel's argument seemed less dramatic because few felt any basic disagreement with American society or government; to most people a church true to itself offered no fundamental challenge to the nation. Today events have transformed the picture, and few would feel such an uncritical attachment to America. While it is difficult to decide exactly what is meant by a church "true to itself," such a church surely could not relax comfortably in the America of the 1970s.

If it is true that American Catholics must choose between faithful discipleship and uncritical Americanism, then indeed they are in the midst of crisis, with its dangers and opportunities. Perhaps the community will divide into irreconcilable factions, and its future will be decided by social and political forces it neither understands nor controls. The divisions in American society, of black and white, of young and old, of rich and poor, could well tear the churches apart, as they threaten to destroy so many other institutions. But these very dangers are also opportunities, for men are face to face with fundamental issues: What does it mean to be a Christian? What should be the church's mission? What kind of judgment should Christians make about America's present and future? Such questions can give rise to division or to renewal. They can clear the way for history and society to remake the church for its own purposes, but they can also act to release the history-making potential of men reborn in Christ. All men today, including Americans, desperately need the faith, the hope and the love given to men by Jesus. If what Peter Maurin used to call "the dynamite of the Gospel" is to explode with history-making force, Christians must try to face these questions more seriously and intelligently than they have in the past.

The age-old quest for a synthesis of Americanism and Catholicism was intended to answer these questions and resolve the tensions that plagued churchmen at all levels, but that quest rested on often little recognized assumptions about the church and about American society. Reformers hoped to replace the

old church with one based on the vernacular liturgy, lay participation and democratic structures, and they were likely to be
particularly shaken if these things brought not new vitality but
discord and irrelevance. An ambiguous outcome was probably
inevitable, however, for most Catholics found identity in a
church based on fixed theological and disciplinary propositions.
Description of these things as mere "historical accidents" and
the message that "being a Catholic" could be a far less tangible
thing than it had been could easily threaten the whole structure
of organized Catholicism in the United States. It was naive to
believe that the doors the council opened would lead to a
church remade in the American image. Many are no longer sure
they should, for it is becoming clear that this view not only
contained inadequate ideas about the church but distorted
interpretations of America. Both conservatives and liberal
Catholic leaders had always believed that the church could and
should identify itself with American values, ideals and practices.
While professing devotion to their version of Americanism,
conservative church leaders at the same time argued that only
discipline and unity could preserve the immigrant church
against nativist anti-Catholics who were both un-Christian and
un-American. Their better-educated and more assimilated colleagues played down these fears and urged cooperation and
dialogue with their fellow citizens based on the conviction that
all Americans shared a set of principles regarding man and
society that were fully compatible with Catholic doctrine. As
John Cogley put it after a pioneering ecumenical dialogue in
1959, all sides found that "the 'enemy' now had a face and it
was a face not very different from anyone else's."[8] Denying
basic differences and insisting on the fundamental identity of
Christianity and Americanism, comfortably situated within the
liberal consensus on domestic and foreign policy, experiencing
few doubts that in general America was a good place for
Christians to live, Catholic reformers of the late 1950s were the
true heirs of the "Americanist" tradition.

Today these assumptions have been shattered; Christianity as
such offers no model of society as it ought to be, and neither
does Americanism. Both uphold liberty and equality, human
rights, social justice and the general welfare, without providing a

final synthesis or clear, definite guidelines for realizing them in practice. Both can command enthusiastic commitment, which provides a basis for recurrent self-criticism and reform. Untempered by a pragmatic realism, a sense of irony or an awareness of the inelastic quality of man and institutions, however, these same ideals can appear so far removed from the actual behavior of the institutions dedicated to their realization that reformers are always tempted to turn away in despair, to fatalism or to violence, either of which corrupts the values they cherish.

It is hard to avoid seeing something of this sort happening today when the ideals reawakened by Pope John and President Kennedy appear frustrated by the conservatism of the institutions they so briefly led. Individual Catholics increasingly see themselves standing in opposition to the immobility, even the corruption, of their church, a polarization of person and organization paralleling developments in American society generally, as informed and sensitive citizens experience a crisis of conscience over a war seeming to lack intellectual or moral justification and a domestic crisis touching the most basic foundations of their society. Like the Catholic who feels compelled to abandon the church to retain his integrity, the citizen must ask himself whether or not the war and the reaction to urban and campus unrest have not destroyed the validity of American institutions to the degree that he must refuse to participate in the normal processes of American life.

Posing the problem in this way reflects a concern with personal values and individual fulfillment long characteristic of reform thought. The goal of a fully American Catholicism was to be achieved by reforming Catholicism, for American society seemed to need only a few minor adjustments. Kennedy's liberalism marked the limits of whatever Catholic left existed a decade ago, aside from a few fringe groups of pacifists. Reform was to be ecclesiastical, freeing the Catholic of the tensions that beset him by confirming his positive response to secular America, recognizing his dignity by structural democratic procedures and vitalizing his community and personal religious life by liturgical changes. The early liturgical reformers of the depression years had regarded the liturgy as a school of social justice which would communicate a sense of human solidarity which in turn would strengthen the drive for Christian social reconstruction outlined in *Quadragesimo Anno.* Latter-day liturgists paid lip service to hopes for Christian social action flowing from the liturgy, but their real concerns were with personal and group spirituality and were only secondarily related to social and political change.[9] This became increasingly clear as some reforms were frustrated and those achieved proved illusory. Once begun, self-criticism and demands for reform multiplied dramatically, exposing the conservatism of the institutional church but revealing as well the escalating power of Christian ideals defined in individualistic, personal terms.

It is a serious mistake, as Father Andrew Greeley continually insists, to regard renewal as the liberation of religion from the confining grasp of organizations and institutions, to call for a non-institutional church or a prophetic Christianity freed of the influence of nation, class, ethnic group or neighborhood.[10] In one of the most perceptive pieces to appear in recent years, John P. Sisk pointed to the twin dangers of the "sweet dream of harmony" and the "sweet dream of liberation."[11] Many bishops, priests and laymen, frightened by the ferment and consequent insecurity fostered by change, hold fast to the hope for an eventual restoration of consensus and unity, qualities deemed essential to the functioning of any institution and particularly necessary for the church. The dream of harmony is not confined to conservative nostalgia for the good old days but even touches many who see the present as a transitionary stage to a new harmony based on the liturgy and voluntary religious association.

The dream of liberation is most marked among men and women long frustrated by the pressures of ecclesiastical conformity. But it infects as well many advocates of personalism, fired by a high dedication and nourished by the realization of the extent to which Catholicism has become encrusted with features having more to do with nationalism, class interest or race consciousness than with the Gospels. Dorothy Dohen's muckraking portrayal of the super-patriotism of American Catholic bishops whose identification with the national cause often contradicted the values they professed is a good example of the shocked righteousness and critical honesty of younger American Catholic intellectuals.[12] Miss Dohen and dozens of others stand aghast at their church's surrender to what Will Herberg called the "idolatrous new religion of Americanism." [13] These young Catholics may have little else in common with Herberg or with the late Christopher Dawson, a long-time critic of American religion, but they share with these older men a determination that for the Christian religious values, however defined, come before national or class values. Paraphrasing a popular question of a decade ago, they are Christians who happen to be Americans, rather than Americans who happen to be Catholics.

Their difficulty is that in the absence of meaningful community life in the church it is hard to determine what being a Catholic or a Christian means. Thirty years ago Dorothy Day and Peter Maurin denounced Catholic acquiescence in American bourgeoise culture in terms unmatched by today's radicals, but they were certain that they possessed a secure basis for building a truly Christian culture and society. By today's standards they were theologically conservative, for they found in the liturgy a basis for community and a model of society, the Mystical Body of Christ. Today's Catholics have been greatly influenced by the Catholic Worker's insistence on personal responsibility, but they are less able to regard the liturgy as central to their social and political concerns, even if many find it crucial for their religious life. Equally important they have been unable to transcend the polarization of the individual and the state the Catholic Worker fostered by its hostility to welfarism and its doctrinaire pacifism. Maurin's personalism led him to dream of a liberation of the individual from the complexities of modern society. Today's young Catholics are unable to accept his simplification of the social problem, though they remain convinced of the relevance and utility of personalist categories, which they frequently transfer into a dream of liberation from an ambiguous and compromising church.

The problems raised by the opposition of person and institution were presented most clearly in England when Charles Davis left the church. The radical Catholics of the *Slant* group rejected Davis's "liberal" opposition of his personal values to the institutional church in favor of their own "radical" demand for the "necessary social structure of Christian belief" through which the church can "challenge a corrupt society and change it."[14] In this context America's Catholic intelligentsia has been liberal rather than radical; its members have emphasized personalism, the need to reform the church as an institution in order to foster and encourage personal Christian growth and fulfillment, rather than structural changes designed to broadcast the message of social revolution the *Slant* group feels is essential to Christianity. In their personalism Catholics have shared the perennial preoccupation of the American reform movement with individual morality, a phenomenon described by historians like Stanley Elkins and Richard Hofstadter.[15] While one might disagree with the *Slant* emphasis on the theological imperative of social revolution, their awareness of the need to organize and institutionalize the energies generated by religious reform might well be taken seriously as American reformers seek a method whereby the church might become an effective agency for promoting change that encompasses society as a whole.

In the past the personalist inheritance of Catholic intellectuals in the United States has inhibited their attempt to define a Christian response to American society, with the result that the American church has failed to produce a creative leadership attuned at once to the needs of a Catholic people passing through a period of profound social change and to the demands of a revitalized Christianity. This weakness can be illustrated by contrasting the enthusiastic reception given by many to Harvey Cox's optimistic portrayal of urban middle-class America with the demands for vaguely defined "basic," "fundamental," even "revolutionary" change that punctuated discussions of American society in the same period. Inconsistency and ambiguity in Catholic thought in America is probably inevitable, given the rapidity and scope of changes affecting the Catholic community, but the goal of a vital, reforming church in America necessitates an attempt to understand American society by listening to economists, sociologists, historians and others who study the factors that make this highly complex society work.

Such an effort is at least as important as the theological speculation and liturgical tinkering, which have so far received far
greater attention.

Given this situation it may be a healthful sign that several
commentators have referred for guidance to Max Weber's
famous essay on "Politics as a Vocation." Weber's distinction
between the "politics of ultimate ends" and the "politics of
responsibility" surely has relevance for political developments
in the United States as the opposition of conscience and government sharpens. Similarly its applicability to Catholics who object in principle to the war in Viet Nam or who despair of
effective government action to alleviate racial injustice is also
clear. What may be less apparent is that these categories may be
applicable to the relation between the individual and any institution, particularly when the problems facing it are not simply
religious, social or political. Only ignorance of the historical
evolution of the contemporary Catholic dilemma has obscured
the interrelationship of all these factors in the present crisis.
The large-scale entry of Catholics into the middle class during
and after World War II, the opportunities for higher education
opened to Catholic veterans by the G.I. Bill of Rights, the
election of a Catholic President and the work of an ecumenical
council all helped shape the problems, and the ideas, of today's
Catholics. Similarly the work of understanding and alleviating
their problems must encompass all dimensions of the life of
their church and their society.

What the *Slant* group realized is that there is no escape, no
secure haven, from politics, nor should there be. This should
now be clear in the United States where the comfortable assumption of the 1950s that aloofness from politics would not
affect the harmonious functioning of American life has crum-
bled beneath the rush of events. In such a situation the tendency to see personal moral integrity and realistic political
action as incompatible, to insist with Thoreau that "the only
obligation I have a right to assume is to do at any time what I
think is right" is particularly harmful. As Weber saw, any man
not "spiritually dead" recognizes that the point might come
when he must say "Here I stand; I can do no other," but
adherence to principle and concern for effectiveness are supple-

ments, not absolute opposites, and "only in unison constitute a genuine man." When every action has political consequences, when every institution is politically involved and responsible and when despair is an ever-present danger, hard-headed, realistic, informed action is morally imperative. All men then must have the "calling for politics." "Certainly all historical experience confirms the truth that men would not have attained the possible unless they had reached out for the impossible," Weber concluded.

> Even those who are neither leaders nor heroes must arm themselves with that steadfastness of heart which can brave the crumbling of all hopes. This is necessary right now or else men will not be able to attain even that which is possible today. Only he has a calling for politics who is sure that he shall not crumble when the world from his point of view is too stupid or too base for what he wants to offer. Only he who in the face of this can say "In spite of it all!" has a calling for politics.[16]

By such a measure, the failure of the 1960s was one of blindness, of loss of faith. Catholics demanded of their church and their politics what they will always be unable to provide. Faith, courage, reason and love, these things men must supply. Pope John in a very real way gave Catholics back their church. No longer can they blame others for its failure; they can only blame themselves. They must demand of its leaders no more than they demand of themselves. The breakdown of the American image of Catholicism has been a destruction; it should have been a liberation, not of individuals, but of a people. Peter Maurin, who with Dorothy Day founded the most vital lay movement American Catholicism has produced, once said of his fellow Christians that men would say of them not "see how they love one another" but "see how they pass the buck." After the council every Christian must say with Harry Truman: "The buck stops here."

In politics the situation is more hopeful, for the resistance of young people to the war offers eloquent testimony to the fact that responsibility begins with the citizen. The lesson of recent American history is not the failure of democracy, but its passive abandonment. No president will appear to give government back to the people because no one ever took it away. Until recently no Catholic believed that he was responsible for the actions of the pope or the bishop; the individuals duty was to follow, not to share, responsibility. Men spoke of Catholic Action as "the participation of the laity in the apostolate of the hierarchy," valid only when initiated, approved and directed by the bishop. But American democracy always asserted that the individual shared responsibility and power; that he was implicated in decisions by his support or by his silence. If he disagreed he was, at least in theory, free, and indeed bound, to register his dissent. Ultimately Thoreau and Frederick Douglass, Eugene Debs and Norman Thomas became enshrined in the American pantheon. The draft evaders, the picketers, the protesters, can refer to a central, indeed a fundamental American tradition. If by silence most Americans fail to accept their responsibility, if they respond that there is nothing they can do about the events which overwhelm them, they have abandoned democracy by loss of faith.

For it is faith after all that is the alternative to despair; not an irrational acceptance of whatever seems to answer emotional needs but a conscious and deliberate commitment to goals and values that convince men's intellects and move their wills. The American faith was that of Jefferson, who responded to charges that men could not govern themselves by asking who, then, could govern them, lacking available angels. Only an enlightened, responsible and benevolent people could make a society worth living in; and faith in the ability of Americans to be such men was a faith that could resist the drift of events and make history. And it was a faith not far removed from that of Pope John, who rejected the counsels of the prophets of doom, who opened the windows of the Church to the fresh air of freedom and of reason because he sensed what no one else in his sphere could sense: that the alternatives were un-Christian because they were irrelevant and stupid. Confident that men could reason together and could find a common humanity, Pope John called on men to humbly take charge of history, shaping it to their purposes, refusing to submit to violence and destruction. The message of Pope John, like that of Jefferson, still lives for those who will listen. "Pope John's optimism was really something new in Christian thought," the late Thomas Merton wrote in 1964, "because he expressed the unequivocal hope that a world of ordinary men, a world in which many men were not Christians or even believers in God, might still be a world of peace if men would deal with one another on the basis of their God-given reason and with respect for their inalienable human rights."[17] Perhaps the new mission of the Catholics of America is to spread *that* good news so they and their countrymen may be an example to mankind of what men of reason, of courage and of faith can do in shaping a just and humane society.

2
HISTORY
AND THE PRESENT CRISIS

American Catholicism requires a serious re-examination of its heritage and a clear recognition of the complex interaction of social and religious factors in its historical development.[1] The present ferment in the church has its roots both in the dramatic changes in Catholic life and culture initiated by Pope John XXIII and the Second Vatican Council and in the tumultuous events that have punctuated American society in the last decade. Even superficial familiarity with articulate Catholic radicals should demonstrate the importance to them of the shocks administered to American ideals by confrontation with the manifest deficiencies of national policy and institutions and their equally significant experience of deepening Christian commitment associated with the broad social vision of the council and the new theology. Who can say whether Daniel Berrigan, for example, has been more influenced by his contacts with militant Christians in France, eastern Europe and Latin America or by his first-hand experience of domestic alienation and repression and foreign war? Equally difficult questions arise concerning Catholic conservatives, offended both by the changes in the church and by the raucous revolt in the nation. Obviously it is impossible to assign exact proportions to distinctively Catholic and American elements, now or in the past, but it is also obvious that some effort must be made to sort out these elements and examine their interaction in the life of the church and its people.

Efforts have been made before to clarify the relation of church and society, to discern the Christian impact upon the world and worldly intrusions upon religious life and practice. Ordinarily such interpretations rest upon assumptions about the nature of the church and the characteristics of the particular society under discussion. Today the problem is complicated because we realize that the interpretive constructs of ecclesiology and sociology are themselves part of the historical process. When men recognize the historical basis of their own normative models, then theology and the social sciences are subsumed under history. Yet the historian himself is stranded in the raging current of time, unable to speak meaningfully of its origins and ends. While he confines his attention to providing a detailed reconstruction of the course of the stream's movement, men yearn for some sense of its direction and goal. This dilemma, which expresses both a liberation and a new captivity, only gradually dawned on the consciousness of Catholics in the rapid changes of the last decade, but has long been a preoccupation of non-Catholic intellectuals.

In his recently published memoir, Czech theologian Josef L. Hromadka recalled how the events of the 1930s forced Eastern European churchmen to question Western theology and to examine their own traditions. The living history of those years became primary material for theological reflection as men sought to understand God's will for them in their unique historical situation. "I emphasize the significance of the historical situation," Hromadka wrote, "not so that history might transform the message of the Bible, of the prophets, and of the apostles, but rather so that we might more deeply understand the meaning of the fact that God has come into our lives in the body of a particular man at a particular time and place, that he is the Lord not only of the Church but of the whole world around us, and that we thus may undertake our work with joyous hope of his final victory."[2] For the theologian in Czechoslovakia, deep commitment and involvement in the history around him was part of a lifelong effort to understand God's purpose in and through historical events. Theology, history and politics were inseparable in this quest, as active responsibility in history brought them together in a life of action and reflection. A similar experience marked the lives and thought of men as diverse as Dietrich Bonhoeffer, Albert Camus and Martin Luther King.

Some theologians have attempted in recent years to build a positive understanding of this new-style historical consciousness, and their work is characterized by the same pattern of active encounter with the world, continual reflection on past and present and hope for the future. "The revelation of God and the corresponding knowledge of God are always bound up with the recounting and recalling of history and with prophetic expectation," Jürgen Moltmann writes. Because men do not know God at the end of history but in its midst, "this knowledge must constantly remain mindful of the promises that have been issued and of the past experience of God's faithfulness, and at the same time be a particularly hopeful knowledge." The implications for historiography are clear and startling, drawing the scholar from the dead past to the living present and hoped-for future, for the knowledge of which Moltmann speaks "must be a knowledge that does not merely reflect past history—as a mental picture of the completed facts of history—but it must be an interested knowledge, a practical knowledge, a knowledge that is upheld by confidence in the promised faithfulness of God."[3]

This suggests that scholarship requires an activist stance and an examination of public role and responsibility, tasks particularly incumbent upon historians. It is therefore of interest to note that many American historians are now addressing themselves to the pressing problems of their own day. At the American Historical Association Convention in Washington in December 1969 almost 500 votes were cast for a resolution calling for immediate withdrawal from Viet Nam, end to the harassment of the Black Panthers and release of all political prisoners. The resolution contained these words: "We must renew our commitment to one of the great historic tasks of independent historians in a time of crisis: we must expose to critical analysis and public attack the disasterous direction in which our government is taking us."[4] The so-called radical historians were defeated in this effort as the majority of their colleagues preferred to say nothing as historians on the issues of the day. It was ironic that the chairman of the meeting, standing as the symbol of the professional establishment, was C. Vann Woodward. Ten years earlier Woodward had called upon the historical profession to embark upon an "age of re-interpretation." "What is required is an answer to the questions about the past and its relation to the present and future that the accelerated process of history raises," Woodward said in 1960. "If historians evade such questions, people will turn elsewhere for the answers and modern historians will qualify for the definition that Tolstoi once formulated for academic historians of his own day. He called them deaf men replying to questions that nobody puts to them."[5]

The difference between the Woodward of 1960 and the young radicals of 1970 is simply the activism of which Moltmann speaks, for the radical scholars are determined to unify their politics, their scholarship and their lives. They rebel at the comfortable assumption of Woodward and most historians that historical and political judgments and activity must be separated. The rigid segregation that traditional leaders of academic life make between their profession, their politics and their lives is wholly abhorrent. "For a long time the historian has been embarassed by his own humanity," Howard Zinn has written. "Touched by poverty, horrified by war, revolted by racism, indignant at the strangling of dissent, he has nevertheless tried his best to keep his tie straight, his voice unruffled and his emotions to himself. True, he has often slyly attuned his research to his feelings, but so slyly, and with such scholarly skill, that only close friends and investigators for Congressional Committees might suspect him of compassion."[6]

Because Woodward's warning of 1960 was not seriously heeded the conflict between the historically minded and the young became particularly acute, and, as the challenge of radicals gradually emerged, historians all too eagerly accepted the role they had officially assigned themselves years before as "guardians of the cultural heritage of mankind," now against the assaults of teeny-bopper barbarians.[7] Such a stance should not surprise any serious observer of American cultural history for historians, even when actively participating in movements for reform and social change, have characteristically been the high priests of American democracy. Failing in general to apply their sophisticated historical tools to the analysis of their own profession and its intellectual and political role, historians have always been the bearers of the sacred flame of American uniqueness and destiny, supplying the usable past, which crucially affected the making of modern America. That is not to say that historians have not been willing, even eager, to redirect their research and rephrase their message to meet changing times. It is to say that they have done so as enthusiastically patriotic and increasingly professionalized Americans, more and more integrated into the organized institutional structures of this country, sympathetic to democracy but suspicious of the people, responsive to the needs of the structure rather than to the call of truth and the responsibility of intellectuals. Incredible as it may seem, when Staughton Lynd stated simply "we are men as well as historians," the words became a battle cry.[8]

Yet the realization that historical work requires faith and commitment was clear to such earlier historians as Frederick Jackson Turner, Carl Becker and Charles Beard. By 1934 Beard had concluded that written history required "an act of faith," which meant in practice a search for motive, responsibility and freedom in history and firm commitment to a humane vision of the future. "If history is nothing except a 'chain of causes' and individuals are merely atoms in the flow of things, then all of us, students and teachers alike, are mere puppets in a mechanical play. If, on the other hand, history-as-actuality is made in part at least by thought and purpose,—by ideas—then there is room in the world for will, design, courage, and action, for the thinker who is also a doer," Beard wrote. "This does not mean that the individual is emancipated from all conditioning circumstances, that he can just make history out of his imagination, but it means that by understanding the conditioning reality revealed by written history, as thought and description, by anticipating the spirit of the coming age, he may cut new paths through the present and cooperate with others in bringing achievements to pass."[9]

Such a definition of the moral and political responsibility of the historian should receive a positive response from Christian scholars who have been profoundly influenced by the experience of twentieth-century man. Again Hromadka draws the lesson clearly.

> Every historical event and personality must be fully understood in the perspective of subsequent historical development. . . . History is not just a procession of favorable events which can be ascertained and described from the memory of contemporary men or on the basis of written documents in archives. History is

only history when events are constantly transformed in the minds, hopes, decisions and actions of individuals, nations, or cultural and social units. What matters is the comprehension, the understanding, the agreement or criticism of the actions or desires of the generations which follow . . . whenever we talk about historical epoch or years, we are not just passive observers of that which has been; we do not accept historical events and personalities as fatefully determining our present beliefs, decisions, and goals. We struggle with every event and personality on the basis of our own responsibility. And we carry on their meaning and content as they were creatively transformed by our struggle, creative thought, and by practical decisions.[10]

Adoption of such a point of view would mark a true revolution in historical scholarship, heretofore preoccupied with objective, detached analysis and fixed categories. This has frequently made the task of the historian of American religion quite difficult, for, at least until recently, most such men were convinced that the American religious experience was unique. Some deplored the distinctive qualities of American religious life that departed from European norms; others concluded that the categories of earlier Christian history were inapplicable to the American situation. Yet in either case these interpreters of American Christianity were forced to utilize models of church life and social relations drawn from Scripture and the Christian tradition. Their conclusions necessarily rested upon assumptions about church and society strongly influenced by the Christian tradition and open to challenge from within as well as from without the Christian community.

The contemporary Catholic who would understand the dynamics of religion and society in America is in a similar position. In the past Catholics have firmly believed that their church possessed an authoritative, clear self-definition, which provided a standard against which other churches could be judged. They believed as well that there was an ideal structure of relations between the church and the broader culture, a theoretical and historical "Christendom," which provided an authoritative norm for shaping judgment and action. This conviction that the church possessed a divinely revealed model of itself and of society fostered self-righteous criticism of other churches and considerable misunderstanding of the interplay of religious and cultural forces in the historical process. Rigidity of ecclesiastical dogmas inhibited the development of a viable historiography and had a good deal to do with the general weakness of American Catholic intellectual life. "The American Catholic tends to find something like a Golden Age in medieval times, which he imagines as 100 per cent Catholic," Father Walter Ong wrote a decade ago, and he described at length the harmful impact of that static model on American Catholic understanding of the church and of American society.[11]

One of the most significant achievements of the Second Vatican Council was the reintroduction into Catholic orthodoxy of a more dynamic and humble conception of history. In his opening speech to the council, Pope John XXIII decried the "prophets of gloom, who are always forecasting disaster, as though the end of the world were at hand." "In these modern times they can see nothing but prevarication and ruin," the Pope continued, "They say that our era, in comparison with past eras, is getting worse, and they behave as though they had learned nothing from history, which is, none the less, the teacher of life." That the council took this message seriously became clear as its work proceeded. Its discussion of the church broke with the static categories of canon law and drew instead on the mysterious and dynamic images of Scripture. The "Pastoral Constitution on the Church and the Modern World" was more explicit, insisting that in carrying out its mission, "the church has always had the duty of scrutinizing the signs of the times." One of those signs was historical consciousness: "the human race has passed from a rather static concept of reality to a dynamic, evolutionary one."[12]

This revived sense of history has many roots but its overall effect has been to modify dogmatic absolutism, release pastoral energy and encourage searching re-examination of long-accepted doctrinal formulations, church practices and hierarchial responsibilities. As a result it stimulated powerful opposition from those whose outlook had been shaped by a traditional Roman ideology, which Michael Novak characterized as "non-historial orthodoxy."[13] This position, which derived from the Catholic response to the Reformation, placed great emphasis on the juridical structure of the church and the timeless categories of medieval theology. Lack of historical consciousness had long ago eroded the older vision of the church as the Mystical Body of Christ. The gradual objectification of the sacraments and the identification of the church with the broader culture drove out eschatological expectation and obscured the distinction between the church and the Kingdom of God. Reaction to the challenge of the Reformers easily produced a triumphalistic ecclesiology: the church was a "perfect society," never in need of serious reform or development. The felt need to defend the integrity of the deposit of faith, later combined with the isolation of the church from the political and intellectual revolutions of the eighteenth and nineteenth centuries, intensified the tendency toward "a fortress mentality" closed to the influence of changing patterns of life and thought.[14]

It was this legacy that shaped the encyclicals of so many modern popes and the polemics of scholars and writers serving the church. The modern world, originating in revolt against God and his constitution, could be saved only by conscious and sincere recognition of the moral law and return to the fold of the one true church. When churchmen of earlier generations scrutinized "the signs of the times," they found evidence of unmitigated disaster. "It is very true that disorder in human life has resulted from the rejection of universally valid moral norms," a typical passage reads. "That has occurred progressively: first, the Reformation destroyed the faith in the true church, then deism and rationalism rejected faith in Christ, and finally atheism came and chased God from public life. . . . For, without faith in the Church, there is no true faith in Christ, and without faith in Christ, there is no true faith in God. And where faith in God has disappeared, the moral order itself is compromised. Religious agnosticism leads to moral and juridical agnosticism; incredulity prepares the way for social anarchy. The chaos of present day [1956] western civilization must be attributed to the progressive dimunition of Christian influence in public life. . . ."[15] Such a historical vision was hardly conducive to service to mankind or effective proclamation of the Gospel.

Against this point of view Pope John offered an alternative emphasis on historical change and development, a pastoral spirit and insistence on close attention to concrete reality. In doing so he recognized that, as Novak put it, man "must enter the stream of history and work within it, conscious that his words and his concepts are conditioned by it . . . and that his theories must meet the test of concrete facts, movements, and events."[16] According to exponents of this view, reform of the church, the ministry, ecclesiastical institutions and discipline and forms of fellowship and service were permanent requirements of "the people of God" enmeshed in the uncertainty and ambiguity of human history.

The Christian church has always been torn between its need to preserve itself, objectify its work and organize itself to influence and shape the lives of men and the radical demand for perfection, which was an equally authentic part of its tradition. In the classic exposition of this dualism in Christianity, Ernst Troeltsch wrote of the tension between "church" and "sect." "Whereas the church assumes the objective concrete holiness of the sacerdotal office, of Apostolic succession, of the *depositum fidei* and of the sacraments and appeals to the extension of the incarnation that takes place permanently through the priest-hood, the sect, on the other hand, appeals to the ever new common performance of the moral demands of Christ."[17] Even before the Second Vatican Council, theologian Karl Rahner predicted that Catholicism, long considered the embodiment of Troeltsch's church-like qualities of universalism and objectifica-tion, would increasingly take on sectarian characteristics: volun-tarism and continual renewal. Reading the "signs of the times" to indicate that the church was a minority in society, living now in a "diaspora situation," which was a "must" of history, Rahner had predicted, even prescribed, a radical shift in the character and style of Christian life.[18] Whether right or wrong, Rahner's thesis made clear that historical-mindedness could seriously threaten the security and harmony of a church whose formulations and structures were considered exempt from the erosion of history.

While the church-sect typology may be an inadequate tool for understanding the changes that have swept the Catholic church in the last decade, there can be little doubt that a pervasive dualism is one of the realities of Christian history, that it affected both the church's definition of itself and its relation to the world, and that in the 1960s a definite movement took place from one pole to the other. This dualism was described by Cardinal Suhard of Paris in the wake of World War II as a tension between an evolutionary adaptation of the church to the world and an opposing tendency to reduce the church "to her 'out of time' and unchangeable aspect."[19] The church, while always insisting that neither pole was acceptable, that the church and the Christian could neither totally reject the world nor totally surrender to it, had nevertheless tended in recent centuries to adopt the conservative position, illustrated most dramatically in the condemnation of Modernism in 1907.

Pope John was conscious of this ever-present tension between adaptation and aloofness, but he courageously sought to correct the imbalance that was the legacy of the post-Reformation era. He was fully aware of the need to preserve the integrity of doctrine, but he was even more concerned with its proclamation in a manner conducive to a response from modern man. "The substance of the ancient doctrine of the deposit of faith is one thing, and the way in which it is presented is another," he wrote. "And it is the latter which must be taken into great consideration with patience if necessary, everything being measured in the forms and proportions of a magesterium which is primarily pastoral in character." In the same spirit he called for involvement in modern social life. Christians "should not foolishly dream up an artificial opposition—where none really exists—between one's own spiritual perfection and one's active contact with the everyday world . . . ," but should instead take up "the immense task of giving a human and Christian tone to modern civilization."[20]

To carry out this task the church requires at the very least a clear understanding of the historical situation in which it finds itself. Interpreting the "signs of the times" is a historical effort as well as a theological one, for it requires not only a sense of the Christian criteria of evaluation but a feeling for the complexity and the subtlety of the historical forces shaping modern civilization, including the very church that aims to serve it.

Indeed, as Pope John's distinction between the "substance" of faith and the "way in which it is presented" indicates, the new historical awareness was limited, stopping short of some basic, unchangeable "essence" of faith and dogma. But historical consciousness is corrosive and as conservatives had long recognized, the opening of the windows of *aggiornamento* might easily result in disaster. Predictably, scholars did begin to question the foundations of things regarded as essential and exempt from change and development, such as the definition of the Eucharist. The result was a reaction most notable in Pope Paul VI's statement that the sacred formulas of ancient doctrine are "adapted to men of all times and all places." Moving sharply away from the conclusions many drew from Pope John's historical distinction, Pope Paul broadened the area believed exempt from history: "For those formulas, like the others which the Church uses to propose the dogmas of faith, express concepts which are not tied to a certain form of culture, not to a specific phase of human culture, not to one or another theological school."[21]

Historical consciousness thus became a two-edged sword, initially generating a new openness to those outside the church and a new spirit of reform within the church but soon threatening the identity and the faith of Catholics themselves. Gradually men in the church have come to recognize the crucial issues of human life and thought raised by a consistent, honest commitment to history. Historical awareness, experienced at first as a liberation from the confines of a rigid authoritarian heritage, rapidly threatened to erode all stable values and institutions. Cut adrift in a sea of change, men confronted a reality long shrouded by reactionary Catholic mythology, a reality of drift masquerading as progress, a reality seemingly indifferent to man's feelings and immune to his actions. History, in all its stark, bleak force, caught up with the Catholic church.

The result is what Herbert W. Richardson calls a "cultural crisis" in which "the matrix of meaning that undergrids and unifies the various dimensions of man's life breaks down and, with it, all inherited institutions and habitual modes of thought and action. That we are in the midst of such a cultural crisis

today is evidenced by the fact that we face not a single problem, but a problem syndrome. There are no sure criteria and
method in one realm which we can 'borrow' to solve problems
in another. The matrix of meaning itself has broken down."[22]

In this situation it would be a serious mistake to seek an
escape from history, to deny the realities of change and historicity. There are no ideas and no institutions that can be insulated
from history. Not only must the church and the Christian adapt
to "the signs of the times," it must recognize its own profound
involvement in the historical process. Efforts to escape can only
bring new idols, new oppression, new burdens on man's freedom and hope. Consequently the church and the Christian must
find new ways of relating the promise of the Christ-event to a
world in flux. It must recognize and endorse man's quest for
liberation from the ambiguity and oppression of history while
at the same time calling men to their responsibility for human
history itself. The church must recognize that its claims rest
finally upon its promise of such a release from the burdens of
history to the freedom and unity of the Kingdom of God and
proclaim that promise from the middle of the historical stream
with the humility and sensitivity which this position dictates.

For the church lives within history calling men forward to its
promised goal. "The decisive relationship between the Church
and the world is not spatial but temporal," Johannes Metz
writes. "The golden age lies not behind us, but before us: it is
not recreated in the memories of our dreams, but created in the
desires of our imagination and heart."[23] The search for truth
for man in history "will mean discovering that the world can be
changed and nothing has to remain as it has been."[24] In a world
in which historical awareness can easily eventuate in despair,
Christian faith "should strive so that men 'keep their heads up'
in a world which is extremely involved, that they can recognize
meaningful goals and find the courage to make human as well as
material investments for this purpose."[25]

In the vision of the new history man is "man becoming,"
open to the past and the future in his own experienced present,
able if he will to resign himself to the absurdities of the chaos
around him or to forge his life in an effort to shape the world

with others to the realization of his deepest hopes and aspirations. Man in history "is challenged and questioned from the
depths of his boundless spirit," Metz writes.

> Being is entrusted to him as a summons, which he is to accept and
> consciously acknowledge. He is never simply a being that is
> "there" and "ready-made", just for the asking. From the very
> start he is something that can Be, a being who must win his
> selfhood and decide what he is to be. He must fully *become* what
> he *is*—a human being. To become man through the exercise of his
> freedom—that is the law of his Being.[26]

If this perspective has merit, it suggests that historians must
devote at least as much concern to the future as to the past.
Rather than telling the story of the past for its own sake, they
must tell the present and the future as history. Theirs must not
be the stance of Tocqueville's generation, placed in a rapid
stream, gazing back at the ruins on the shore left behind, while
the current hurried them away and carried them backwards
toward the gulf. Rather men must turn around; they must make
clear that the present is the result of a complex interaction of
impersonal forces and human decisions in the past; that all
things change, but the character and shape of change is subject
to human action. Many today, in the deepest recesses of their
being, believe, in Tocqueville's words, "that men are not their
own masters here below and that they necessarily obey—I do
not know what—some insurmountable and unintelligent forces
arising from anterior events . . . —These are false and cowardly
doctrines," Tocqueville believed, "which can never produce
anything but feeble men and craven nations. Providence didn't
create mankind either entirely independent or completely in
servitude. It traced, it is true, around every man a fatal circle
that he cannot leave, but within that vast confine man is
powerful and free, and so are nations."[27]

It is part of the task of historians to induce in men an
awareness that present conditions are always in part a product
of specifically human choices, which can be changed and altered
in significant degrees. It may well be that the great task was laid
out in the report of the Harvard University Center for the Study
of Technology and Society. The researchers acknowledge the

promise and the threat of rapid technological change, which broadens out the range of possible human choice, providing the first real historical possibility for that freedom from want that is the prerequisite for individual liberty and collective self-government. On the other hand, they emphasize even more emphatically the individual's loss of control over his destiny, the erosion of traditional democratic structures and the isolation and despair of lonely men and women. The bureaucratic centralization, which goes hand in hand with technological expansion, necessitates an enlightened, dedicated, interested citizenry acting through radically new institutions to shape the goals and control the mechanism of the emerging technocratic society. Instead of the cheerful robots who could be the population of this fearsome yet alluring society, men are needed who, in the words of the report, can strike a balance "between their commitment to private goals and satisfactions and their desires and vastly expanded responsibilities as public citizens."[28] If men lack understanding of themselves and their society, and if they lack the will to make history, then history, in the form of technology and bureaucratic structures, will make them, and make them more directly and more completely than ever before seemed possible.

Those who take seriously the life of the mind must believe in the possibility of human reason and the potentiality of human freedom, for without freedom, reason cannot function, and without reason, education is absurd. These are values that must inform the work of scholars and teachers, and others have the right to insist that they stand behind those values, are not neutral to them and will fight to preserve and extend them. "Our interest in history," C. Wright Mills has written, "is not owing to any view that the future is inevitable, that the future is bounded by the past. That men have lived in certain kinds of societies in the past does not set exact or absolute limits on the kinds of societies they may create in the future. We study history to discern the alternatives within which human reason and human freedom can now make history."[29] The making of history, that is the final justification of the work of the historian and the theologian. The deepest commitments of Christianity and of man as intellectual coalesce finally around a vision of the future as the reign of God in which man is able to be fully himself.

If the object of historical thought is the making of history, then, for American Catholics, a deeper awareness of the concrete historical background of their present situation is indispensible. While providing no final answers to the question "how have we come to our present state?," such knowledge remains an indispensible prelude to intelligent action. Each generation must rewrite its past to provide answers to its peculiar questions or to gain perspective for dealing with its characteristic problems, so that powerful contemporary movements invariably force a re-examination and revision of the accepted historical record. The Negro revolution, for example, has done just this: it has all but destroyed the complacent American historiography of the postwar years by challenging its confident belief in America's record of progress through free enterprise and democratic politics. Under the impact of the 1960s, attention is now directed to hitherto obscure features of racism, violence and oppression that were as much a part of American life as movements for reform and a steadily improving standard of living.

To be sure, the association of the "new history" with the aspirations of a particular group has intensified the dangers of myth-making inherent in all historical revisionism, as the passionate debate over William Styron's *Confessions of Nat Turner* indicates. But that problem is paralleled by the amoral detachment of a historiography that ignores present and future in the name of the dead past. The ever-present demand for a meaningful explanation of change makes "new history" inevitable; the crucial importance of historical consciousness in shaping man's future makes an honest and authentic "new history" imperative. The conflict and confusion within the Catholic Church of the United States in particular offers a promise of vitality and dedication that could have tremendous impact both on the church and on American society, but it offers as well the possibility of failure, dissipation of energies and gradual erosion of institutional relevance and personal commitment. Many Catholics today are experiencing profound uneasiness over such things as guitar Masses, youth rebellions, sermons on social issues, debates about birth control and clerical celibacy and simultaneous demands for obedience and commitment. These personal troubles are in reality symptoms of broader changes the character of which is shrouded by ignorance and confusion, even for more informed Catholics. Until personal, ecclesiastical and social problems are seen as expressions of a single, complex reality, until, that is, the personal and institutional aspects of American Catholicism are integrated in terms of history, the American Church and its members will be able to exert little control over their future.

It is not necessary to accept Karl Rahner's "diaspora" or Harvey Cox's "secular city" as adequate descriptions of modern conditions to agree that rigid adherence to the categories and assumptions relevant to the 1930s or the 1950s will no longer serve the cause of scholarship in areas related to Catholicism or to Christianity generally. History, like all facets of the life of the mind, must be based upon a consciousness of contingency and must address itself to problems meaningful to each generation. "Because the questions of a period grow out of that period's interests," Sidney Mead writes, "the questions asked by historians change with changing times. The history of one era may not interest the people of a following era because they are no longer interested in the same questions. And in history as elsewhere, nothing is as useless as the answer to an unasked question. . . . People want to know how they 'got that way' in order to understand their present situation in such fashion as to suggest what they can and ought to do."[30]

An understanding of historical forces can free a man for truly responsible faith and action. "Only insofar as one is consciously aware of the dynamic forces within the culture in which he has been nurtured, as a fish is in water, is he free to make intelligent choices regarding them."[31] If this is true, the historian's role becomes a particularly crucial one in a time of rapid change when those "dynamic forces" are no longer taken for granted or unrecognized but are pushing men from their old moorings and into uncharted seas. The contemporary situation in American Catholicism reflects the general "cultural crisis" described by Richardson, when men's sense of identity, their sense of "that element of permanence in the series of momentary selves which

together constitute a person" has been severely shaken by
events. The re-establishment of identity requires "a conscious
intellectual effort to interpret the meaning of . . . habitual
modes of thinking and acting," so that an informed awareness
of the historical structure of the communities in which men
were nurtured is indispensable.[32]

Unfortunately, with a few exceptions like Daniel Callahan,
most Catholic reformers lack such historical sensitivity. Yet the
responsibility is not entirely theirs, for until recently there was
very little available work on the history of Catholicism in
America. Lacking the stimulus of secular interest and theological vitality, Catholic historical writing long occupied an area
considerably removed from the major interests of American
historians. From their point of view it remained denominational
history, often superbly done, but denominational history nonetheless. This assessment was reinforced by the dominant characteristics of that historiography: heavy emphasis upon episcopal biography, intense concern with internal controversies; lack
of interest in non-Irish Catholics and in "conservative" groups
and their bishops; and neglect of Catholic thought and of the
period since World War I. Of equal significance, many works
were unoriginal, avoiding all but the most cautious and judicious interpretations, a result deriving from a church history
orientation which emphasized documentary collection and exposition with only the most limited critical commentary.[33]

In a review of a collection of John Tracy Ellis's essays Robert
D. Cross once wrote that "American Catholic history makes
sense only to one who is familiar with America in its peculiari-
ties, with European Catholicism in its continuing themes, and
with the church in its essential timelessness."[34] No doubt this
statement evokes an immediate consensus but perhaps these
words should be regarded as a challenge rather than an axiom,
for clear understanding of America, European Catholicism or
the church can at best be tenatively reached and then only
through prolonged effort.

In each of these three areas American Catholic historians
have generally accepted a set of assumptions common to their
religious community. These ideas united historians with their
subjects and with the audience for which they wrote, expressing

the unity of American Catholic self-consciousness and reinforcing a conservative temperament by indicating that the problems faced by previous Catholic leaders, their goals and their
most fundamental attitudes coincided with those of the historian's own generation. Because the historian and his audience
felt no real dissatisfaction with their church's institutional arrangements neither questioned the conservative character of
historical efforts. The storm of controversy unleashed by Ellis's
1954 essay "American Catholics and the Intellectual Life"
indicated that the old situation was changing, that the intellectual underground of self-critical dissenters was becoming confident and assertive and that the old felt need for unity was no
longer strong enough to prevent public controversy. The fact
that the essay appears moderate and restrained today measures
the depth of the social and intellectual changes of recent years.

What were the assumptions that dominated American Catholic thought and found expression in historical writings down to
the present day? One, perhaps the most important, was the
assurance that there was no fundamental incompatibility between the demands of full Americanism and loyal Catholicism.
"To understand the Catholic Church in America," Peter
Guilday wrote, "one must see how naturally and integrally the
spiritual allegiance of its members knit into the national allegiance so as to round each other out."[35] Another closely related
assumption was the notion that American Catholics have constituted a minority in a nation whose people often regarded
them as foreign, hostile and subversive.[36] The big problem for
the church's leaders was to retain the allegiance of millions of
immigrants, not by shaping the nation's culture or politics, but
by voluntary action. Because the Catholic Church taught the
essential need for grace dispensed through the sacraments, the
problem was uniquely important for Catholic leaders, for the
institutional identification had to extend to regular attendance
at church as well as considerable financial support. The characteristic policies of the nineteenth century: non-interference in
politics, adjustment to the social and economic norms of the
new community, effective abandonment of roles still regarded
as intimately related to clerical responsibility in Europe, extensive charitable endeavors, prevention of indiscriminate Vatican

condemnations, neutrality toward labor unions, all were seen as the shrewd responses of church leaders to minority status.

The third area with which Cross held the historian must be familiar is the church itself. Protestant historians have recognized that the basic problem of church history is contained in the question, What is the church?[37] Instead of regarding an answer to this question as a goal of study, Catholic historians have tended to assume an answer in terms of the existing structure of the institutional church, emphasizing its hierarchical, juridical character. While few would deny the essential role of the laity, historians have tended to define the church in terms of the episcopate and clergy and to think of it as an actual historical institution, united under the Pope of Rome, governed through the bishops and marked by unity and discipline. The history of the church has been told in terms of the hierarchy, and episcopal biography became the typical mode of study. The major themes were unity and loyalty; the heroes were those who supported the bishops and dug into their pockets to pay for schools and social services themselves designed to perpetuate Catholic unity. The villains were those who disrupted the community: foreign bishops who overrode Irish sensitivities; recalcitrant priests who rebelled against ecclesiastical jurisdiction; critical layman and apostates whose pride and greed led them to desert their people. While Father Thomas T. McAvoy's essays provide a basis for understanding the problems of the laity, it was only with the publication of Daniel Callahan's *The Mind of the Catholic Layman* that an attempt was made to place the layman in the center of the picture, to see in his problems the practical working out of Catholicism in the United States, to deal with his need to reconcile the demands of his society with those of his church.

The changes taking place in the Catholic world today should lead to the recognition that these assumptions were themselves shaped by the historical experience of American Catholics. The position that America and Catholicism were fully compatible required a de-emphasizing of the role of non-Irish groups and of the supposedly conservative nineteenth-century bishops and neglect of the period since World War I. By the 1930s divisions among American Catholics on social and political issues indicated the difficulties in adjusting the demands of church and society. The strident nationalism and anti-communism of Father Charles E. Coughlin drew much of its strength from the need felt by many Catholics to prove their Americanism, a need accentuated in later years by severe "status anxieties." At the other extreme, the Catholic Worker movement, led by Dorothy Day and Peter Maurin stressed a perfectionist ethic, condemned important features of American society and denounced Catholic acquiescence in social abuses. Fighting anti-Semitism, promoting racial justice, ministering to the poor, the Catholic Worker's activism and its utter contempt for those who cared about acceptance by American society posed a profound challenge not only for Coughlinites but for "liberals" who saw the essence of the Catholic experience in the drive to overcome the implications of minority status and Americanize the church.

The assumption of compatibility required a simplified interpretation of American history as well. In recent years Walter Ong, Daniel Callahan, Andrew Greeley and others have argued that the American experience has particularly relevance for contemporary Christianity. Unfortunately, Catholic historians tended to describe and interpret American society from the point of view of the Catholic minority. A full history of American Catholicism or a theological understanding of the American experience will necessitate greater attention to the work of those seeking to evaluate the American experience as a whole. Louis Hartz's thesis of America as a liberal society, Richard Hofstadter's delineation of a consensus on capitalist values, David Potter's study of economic abundance and the American character, each of these works suggests insights for the study of American Catholic history.[38] Did Catholic attitudes differ from those of native Americans and did the increased power and influence of Catholics force any modification in American political or social attitudes and practices? What effect, if any, did American mobility and affluence have upon Catholic immigrants from traditional societies? The history of American Catholicism must give at least equal attention to the American context as to the Catholic heritage and its adaptation if the life of the Church and its members in America is to be more completely understood.

This suggests the importance of immigration history. The role of the church in immigrant society, the complexities of the assimilation process, the limitations of the idea of the melting pot, the relationship between the church and ethnic self-consciousness and nationalist organizations, all deserve more study than they have received. Andrew Greeley has pointed out that one-half of American Catholic adults are immigrants and children of immigrants. The church and the faith can hardly be understood apart from the life history of the nation's ethnic communities, which, while apparently now fully at home in America, nevertheless continue to exert a significant and distinctive impact on national life. Like them, the church has hardly reached the end of the assimilation highway for, as Greely notes, "American Catholicism, now a full if still junior partner in the American experiment, stands with one foot in the old neighborhood in the central city, and the other foot in the college-educated suburbs."[39]

Professor Henry F. May, in his study of "the revival of American religious history," attributed great importance to the influence of H. Richard Niebuhr's suggestions that "religious impulses are never fully embodied in religious institutions, and the unity to be found in American church history must be found in a cycle of renewal and decline." Catholicism's failure to participate in the revival of religious history may be due to its inability to take exactly that point of view, May suggests, but he hopes that in this period of new openings, "an analogous point of view may be found from which American Catholics can look freshly at their own church and at American religious history in general."[40] Several years before the council Walter Ong noted that church history did not adequately deal with the relation of the church to the secular world. Rather than a story of the modern church standing static and rigid in resistance to modernity, he predicted that the truly profound effect of the modern world upon the church would be seen not as the loss of the papal states but in "the slow, and sometimes exceedingly painful, elaboration of a more profound understanding of herself and her role in God's design."[41]

Certainly none of the developments of the council was more significant than the constitution on the church, which departs drastically from the juridical and hierarchical emphasis of such great importance in American Catholic thought. The document stresses the essential mysteriousness of the church, which is discussed in terms of the people of God traveling through history attempting to witness to the truth. It is a servant church, not simply dispensing grace to those who come in the door, but searching for Christ wherever he manifests himself. Some of the implications of this are obvious: the sharp distinction between spiritual and temporal might be questioned; concentration on the hierarchy and on church organizations may not give a complete history of the church. That history is not mainly a story of individual pursuit of holiness or collective pursuit of power and influence. It is most importantly the history of the church in the world, the people of God trying to live out their lives with their fellow men. The historian must search out not only the evidence of the preservation of dogmatic truth or internal unity and discipline. He must look for evidence of the Christian impact on society, for "when men become Christians," as Pope John wrote, "they feel bound to work vigorously for the improvement of institutions in the temporal environment, trying to prevent them from debasing the dignity of man or to eliminate all obstacles in the way of a wholesome life or multiply incentives to its attainment." [42] Social and political action, rather than being mere addenda to real church history, may be essential to it.

Professor Mead has described the work of the great University of Chicago historian William Warren Sweet in terms that in fact describe the current needs of American Catholic history. According to Mead, Sweet saw it as his task "to remind secular historians of the religious factors which have helped to shape America; and to remind denominational and other historians of religion of the significance of other religious groups and the secular forces in shaping their particular groups." Whatever the merits of a largely ecclesiastical focus in historical writing, it is clear, as Mead suggests, that Sweet "was right in supposing that the history of Christianity in America cannot be comprehended simply by pouring it into the mold of traditional church history studies." [43] This emphasis on a social history approach to American religion became dominent in the field under the impact of

Sweet and his students, some of whom are now going beyond
his method. It had its limitations, which will be explored in the
next chapter, but it did assist powerfully in fostering a deepened understanding both of American Protestantism and American culture generally. American Catholic history would benefit
enormously from such a broad social history approach to its life
and culture, a need endorsed by the new theology of the
church. "If the church is truly 'the people of God,' a 'pilgrim
church' properly active in the world as Vatican II has proclaimed," Frank H. Littell writes, "how much more must
church history be set in the context of the whole believing
people and even of humanity as a whole."[44]

This need for a more meaningful religious history is further
illustrated by the developments of recent years. In 1960 Msgr.
John Tracy Ellis called upon American Catholics to abandon
their narrow concentration on group interests and concerns. "It
is now asked of us," he wrote, "that we learn to look beyond
the narrow interests of our Catholic body to the interests of
those around us. . . . What is demanded is a broader understanding of the society of which we are a part and the world in
which we live."[45] The absence of such understanding had
always plagued American Catholic scholarship; the inability of
Catholic scholars to respond to Msgr. Ellis's plea is one reason
for the present confusion in thought and policy in the American
Catholic community. Today, when Catholics generally are looking at the nation with a more critical eye, perhaps the time is
ripe for the kind of "understanding of the society" that America and the church so desperately need.

In the 1950s, when Catholic intellectuals were primarily
concerned with overcoming Catholic exclusiveness and the so-
called "ghetto mentality" they naturally looked with favor
upon the enthusiastic endorsement of America and its ideals by
earlier Catholic liberals like those of the 1890s, calling attention
to their ecumenical activities, their concern with social problems, their love of democracy and their passion to make Catholicism a relevant and meaningful feature of American life. In
short, their aims were the same as those of Catholic reformers
of more recent vintage, and the enthusiasm of historians was
natural. Today, other features of their thought that were then

overlooked seem equally obvious: their confidence in free enterprise and their failure to give serious consideration to labor
unions or legislative reform; their identification of religion and
Americanism; their lack of concern with the problem of the
Negro; their strident nationalism; their failure to alter significantly the direction of American Catholic life. As Henry J.
Browne writes, the bishops, for all the controversy of the
1890s, entered the twentieth century fully Americanized and
fearful of social upheaval: "the sanctity of private property was
about their social philosophy and the fear of Modernism their
school of thought."[46]

Realization of this might indicate how sharply contemporary
views differ from those of the 1890s or the 1930s. While noting
continuity, the historian must also point to differences so that
men might realize that the American Church developed in
conditions different from their own through the efforts and
decisions of men sincerely dedicated to the welfare of the flocks
entrusted to their care. Catholics today might define that welfare differently. The viewpoint of the Catholic Worker may
seem to many a more truly Catholic one than that of those
prelates who were great because they emphasized the fundamental compatibility of Catholicism and Americanism. As
Dorothy Dohen has demonstrated it could lead to a nationalism
indistinguishable from that of the most zealous patriot. The
concern may express with the hierarchy's position on the Viet
Nam war certainly is based upon a view of the church's responsibilities quite different from that of earlier American bishops
who from the War of 1812 through World War II hid any
reservations they might have had about the justice of America's
wars and urged Catholics to support the government. "The ideal
of universal peace is very good," John Ireland once said, "but to
make it a gospel is a mistake." Insisting that American civilization was fundamentally Christian Catholic historians sometimes
failed to recognize the gap between American practice, where
religion came early to be regarded as instrumental in nature and
indispensable for national welfare, and church teachings, whether of the nineteenth century or the Second Vatican Council. [47]
Conscious of that gap and prepared to draw upon the social
sciences for tools of analysis and upon the revived theology for

guides to interpretation, American Catholic historiography may experience a vitalization similar to that experienced by Protestant history in the last generation and in so doing become an effective component in the new effort to make history in days to come.

3
AMERICAN CATHOLICISM
AND AMERICAN RELIGION

Those who profess history in America frequently argue that this is a particularly anti-historical age. Youthful radicals and their most vigorous opponents appear as opposite sides of a coin; both engage in historical myth-making, manifesting a common abhorrence for the uncertainty, ambiguity and conflict that are the fruits of historical consciousness. Worse, some of our most respectable scholars seek to correct the situation with a pseudo-historical realism which mocks human purpose and contemporary man's efforts to master his destiny. Fortunately Americans have always rejected such fatalism and ignored the supposed demands of an impersonal and inexorable history. Instead they have continually manufactured for themselves new and hopeful histories to underpin their truly religious faith in the nation, its ideals and its mission.

This American aversion to a history that seeks to confine men's hopes to the obviously possible and to debunk their deepest yearnings and aspirations has considerable significance for contemporary Christians. In *The Search for a Usable Future*, Martin Marty contends that men act in the light of futures they envision or project, futures the raw materials for which are things remembered, the usable past.[1] Similarly Sidney Mead argues that "what one sees as important in the past depends upon what he wills to prevail in the future."[2] In theology, as hinted earlier, it is the theologians of hope who are reorienting history and theology within the horizon of the future. "Modern man is not interested in the past," Carl Braaten writes. "Only as it has any bearing on his future will he bother with his past."[3]

If these scholars are right, then perhaps what American religion in general and American religious historiography in particular need is less a revision of the record than a rebirth of vision. A usable past makes sense only in relation to a desirable future; both require a rending of past and future, of what has been and what should be. They require specifically a truly critical view of America. "Knowing God through his promises, revealed in the past and made full in the future, man is drawn to active involvement in the world without surrendering to it," Jurgen Moltmann writes. "Knowledge of the Kingdom of God thus does not give rise to powers of accommodation but sets loose powers that are critical of being."[4]

A critical stance toward American life and culture in turn requires a clear recognition that many cherished notions of American Christians rest on unexamined assumptions about America itself. Whatever the merit of these assumptions and of the American civil religion which they define, American Christians are going to have to deal with their problems within the American framework that continues to shape their awareness and response long after they believe they have "come of age."

"While the past itself has been almost entirely an old-world possession," Henry Steel Commager writes, "Americans have resolutely studied themselves as if they were an isolated chapter in history and exempt from the processes of history."[5] From the very beginning America was somehow beyond the history that men knew. The novelty of the new world infused thought about America long before the first settlers arrived. Once here, those same settlers needed an explanation of who they were and where they were headed. To unify a diverse, fluid, uneasy populace, to legitimize and pass on to the young a sense of corporate responsibility, the nation required a usable past, one which could both bind the people together and confirm their hopeful expectations. Americans thus looked to the past to learn that they were free of its burdens.

History became a major vehicle through which Americans learned what it was to be American.[6] As the nation grew in space and numbers and complexity, its history had to be written over and over again, updated and invigorated, assuming new shapes and contours for a mobile and polyglot people. The story had to be woven around highly symbolic and abstract themes: Providence, Manifest Destiny, the American Way of Life, the American Dream, to suit these diverse peoples and subsume their very real economic, racial, ethnic and religious conflicts. While the central question was always Crevecour's; "What then is the American, this new man?," the answer changed to reflect the nation's changing needs and fears and hopes.

With a future of self-improvement and corporate greatness taken for granted, the historian's task was largely conservative. He helped preserve the American community by reminding its people of their origins and their shared objectives. Puritan clergymen who carried on "God's Controversy With New England," reminded men of their covenant with the Lord and their failure to abide by its terms. By the middle of the nineteenth century the covenant had been secularized, but George Bancroft could still recall his readers to the Lord's lofty expectations for them. Frederick Jackson Turner and Charles Beard used a more academic and scientific terminology but their message was equally clear: the meaning of America was to be found in its origins, and its destiny remained unimpaired. Beneath the superficialities of the most dramatic changes, the national story was a tale of eternal changlessness.

History, then, was a major component of national self-consciousness, a source of common understanding of the meaning of the continual process of movement and settlement. Yet America's was a history oriented to the future rather than the past. Somehow the past was given; a new start had been made by man and had been ratified in the sacred covenant of the Puritans to which every immigrant adhered by his journey. The revolution and the constitution confirmed the transaction by binding men together in the new order American demanded. The past was notable for this gift to men of escape from the old way—it was closed. Only the future was open: to be sure, its ultimate goodness was guaranteed, but its shape and contours were in men's hands. Individually and collectively they had the responsibility to build and to grow, to become what they could in a land that made hope truly possible. American history, then, was America's theology of hope as the historian recorded both the good news of man's resurrection in escape from Europe and pointed toward the future as the location of the completion of man's quest for liberation and fulfillment.

The parallels between American self-consciousness and Christian faith are appropriate, for, throughout most of their history, Americans have blended religious and national identities. Perry Miller demonstrated that Protestant Christianity provided the English settlers, even those whose explicit motives were far more secular than those of the Puritans, with the symbols that explained and justified what they were about.[7] Thereafter Christian and secular models and images interacted creatively to generate a national consciousness that was truly religious and religious attitudes that were distinctly American. As numerous historians have noted in recent years, categories of sacred and secular merge and blend in America, on the one hand producing churches preoccupied with secular affairs and on the other "a nation with the soul of a church." In both cases the result was welcome for, unlike many European nations, America experienced little polarization of church and state. Rather the state praised the church as the agency of civic virtue and the church praised the state as the embodiment of the nation's highest aspirations.

Of course, to the outside observer, the situation was distressing. Was not Christianity a historical faith, bound to the past, to traditions? How could it adapt to a nation that exalted novelty, innocence and nature? If the churches turned their back on Europe, and the past, how could they preserve the Christian heritage? Generations of churchmen and church historians rejected the dilemma. They promoted and defended the Americanization of Christianity, arguing, indeed, that the apparent chaos and disorder of America were marks of the approach of Christ's kingdom.

The dilemma of American Christianity should have been particularly acute for Roman Catholics. "Roman Catholicism has continually come under suspicion because it habitually acts as the true bearer of history's meaning," John E. Smylie has written. But in America, "only the nation bears ultimate universal purpose and has continuing historic meaning."[8] Indeed many Protestant leaders long believed that the Catholic Church, with its strong institutional controls and its reactionary view of history, could never adapt to American conditions, and many a Catholic visitor from Europe agreed. The American religious scholar has been able to develop his work within an almost entirely Protestant framework, secure in the assurance that the possible contradictions that might be raised by the Catholic's experience of America were confined to a small, insignificant portion of the population. "Doubtless Roman Catholicism had made important contributions to American life," H. Richard Niebuhr wrote, "yet both history and the religious census support the statement that Protestantism is America's 'only national religion and to ignore that fact is to view the country from a false angle.' "[9]

Non-Catholic historians invariably regarded the nation as Protestant; they took little interest in Catholicism and when they did they sought to fit it into their own biased view of the nation, which meant appending a description of the Catholic population as a deviant, still foreign, enclave outside the normal, natural area of American religion. As William Clebsch put it: "In a certain sense the history of Catholics and the history of Jews in America arise precisely as these people are viewed apart from their involvement in American society. . . ."[10]

Religious historians were not unique in this regard. Historical scholarship in America was characteristically a Protestant preserve. In the nineteenth century George Bancroft, James Ford Rhodes, Henry Adams and John W. Burgess dominated the historical profession and in varying ways presented an interpretation of the American past that reinforced the WASP's conviction that the United States was his country, destined to bring about the triumph of Protestant Christianity and Anglo-American democracy. Frederick Jackson Turner revolutionized historical writing at the turn of the century, but he was a nationalist who believed that the American frontier had blended diverse peoples together into a new breed of men. Turner's followers in religious history retained a Protestant focus, adding the traits of frontier Methodists and Baptists to the heretofore dominant Congregationalism and Presbyterianism. Turnerism additionally reinforced a growing intellectual hostility to the city, often seen as an artificial and parasitic growth permeated by European remnants and populated by alien Catholics and Jews, where the assimilating power of the American environment could be felt only indirectly if at all. Both Catholics and Lutherans, William W. Sweet wrote as late as 1939, "were to a large degree direct European transplantations, and neither was modified in any marked degree by frontier influences."[11] The more recent consensus historians similarly stressed the powerful attachment of all Americans to a common creed or faith. Whether its content was the tenets of liberal capitalism, Calvinist Protestantism or Lockean liberalism, it flourished to such a degree that alternative perspectives, conservatism or socialism, Catholicism or Judaism, were blotted out.

The Protestant and Americanist bias of church history comes through clearly in a recent volume of essays written by scholars at one time or another associated with the University of Chicago. Martin Marty, Jerald C. Brauer, Winthrop Hudson and Sidney Mead all discuss the state of American religious history, but not one notes the lack of scholarship on American Catholicism as a serious drawback to a comprehensive picture of American religious life. Hudson, for example, protests against the preoccupation with uniqueness prevalent among American church historians: "Church historians have tended to depict the European heritage in terms of the initial colonial settlements, and largely ignore the continuing interplay of influence, as though there were no larger Christian community to which we belonged."[12] Yet, in response, Hudson suggests that historians recognize the importance of contacts between American and English churches and religious movements. However useful this may be for many branches of the Protestant Church, it has almost no relevance for American Jews and Catholics, whose attention must be focused on other sections of Europe. Jerald C. Brauer comes closer to the point, but in the end still identifies American religion with Protestantism. After examining the historiography of American religion, almost all of which was written by and about Protestants, he concludes that church history must adopt the techniques and tools of the history of religion and comparative religion, a suggestion that could well lead to consideration of the entire spectrum of the religious experience of the American people.[13]

Like Hudson and Brauer, Sidney Mead expresses his dissatisfaction with American church history, but unlike the others he insists on relating the subject more intimately to general American history. Here, as in his other writings, Mead emphasizes the need to see the institutional churches in relation to their ideals and aspirations and to see both in creative interplay with other features of American culture. The peculiar dynamics of this relationship are, in Mead's view, shaped by the ability of America to foster and encourage a critical discontent with the status quo, a discontent frequently embodied in churchmen, which "brings about continuous evolutionary change and periodically creates constructive revolution" in the life of the nation. This in turn derives from the critical decision of the Founding Fathers to "deliberately" shape a form of government "to prevent an unimaginative orthodoxy from ever again gaining control over society."[14] America was thus "a nation with the soul of a church," with a real, although nonsectarian, religion of its own, a religion that, like that of the churches, always contained a tension between its expressed goals and values and their embodied political reality. Instead of a conflict between church and state, America witnessed competing theologies, the particular theologies of the sects versus "the common, universal theology" of the Republic.[15]

Mead's thesis, like the "civil religion" argument of Robert Bellah, confirms the view that America is a religious nation, though its religion is fluid and vaguely defined. The most important feature of this argument is that it expresses a new and critical self-consciousness regarding the Americanist thrust of much Protestant scholarship. Two recently published works, Martin Marty's *The Righteous Empire* and Robert Handy's *A Christian America,* are further signs that Protestant historical scholarship is coming to terms with its past pretensions. [16] Nevertheless, in all these cases, the overall interpretation of the American religious experience remains rooted in the assumption that American Protestantism is both the lock and the key of American religion, that it has provided the framework to which alternative religious systems have had to conform.

These Protestant preoccupations have not been confined to self-consciously Protestant scholars. In 1964 Henry F. May wrote that American religious history, which was of little interest to secular historians twenty years before, had become one of the most fruitful and influential areas of scholarship, so that no serious student of American culture questioned the fact that religion had been a most essential component of American culture.[17] This recovery he attributed to several sources, among them the ecclesiology of H. Richard Niebuhr, whose sharp distinction between Protestantism as order and as movement had enabled scholars to deal both with the church and with the religious dimension of other aspects of American life and thought. Still it was clear that the recovery of American religious history was a Protestant phenomenon. Not that it was brought about by Protestant scholars; on the contrary it was led by secular scholars many of whom had no personal involvement in a Christian church. Rather the recovery was one of interest in American religion as American Protestantism. The articles and books cited by May almost invariably dealt with aspects of Protestantism and the essay reflected the continuing conviction that American religion, American Christianity and American Protestantism were synonymous terms. May noted that Catholics, together with atheists, had made the least contribution to the recovery, not simply by not writing about themselves but, presumably, by not persuading others to write about them.

Invariably, then, American religious history has been Protestant history, resting on the unannounced assumption that Protestantism, particularly in its least authoritarian, least formal expressions, has been the true religious expression of the American people. Sydney Ahlstrom recently confirmed this judgment when he spoke of the "synthesis of American church history," dominant until very recently, as an "uncritical Protestant celebrationism," written from a point of view that was "proud, nationalistic, stridently Protestant."[18]   Similarly, William Clebsch writes of the newer historians of American religion: "They recognize American man as religious—primarily Christian and specifically Protestant—man just as clearly as Charles and Mary Beard have understood him as economic man."[19] This has resulted not from any deep conviction that Catholics and others were not religious, or not Christian, but that in some sense they were not really American. In the non-Catholic world of American religious history, then, history and historiography united around the common ground of unexamined assumptions, even faith statements, about the nation and its meaning.

The dilemmas of American Christian history have been a matter of concern for Protestant scholars like Mead and Marty. They have seldom been part of the consciousness of the intellectual leaders of American Catholicism, even though in the case of their church the dichotomy of religious and national values was particularly severe, as non-Catholic scholars knew. Yet the historians of American Catholicism, and the leaders of the church, affirmed the central features of the American faith and refused to enter any significant Catholic dissent.

In regard to the church, they were "Americanists." Before the 1950s no prominent American Catholic historian admitted that there had been any significant failures in the record of his church or country. Frequently and with regret scholars noted the church's failures in other lands, but in America they saw an unmarred record of growth, prosperity and virtue. By every available criterion the church had been remarkably successful. Of course there had been difficulties, but invariably they were the product of alien intrusions. The "scandal" of trusteeism resulted from the combination of "foreign" priests and congregations and "protestant" notions of church law. The condemnation of Americanism at the end of the century similarly derived from the inability of outsiders to comprehend the genius of the American church. "The American character of the church, not its foreign origins, provided the central themes of Catholic historical writing," Rudolph Vecoli has concluded. [20]

In many ways the work of the major historians of American Catholicism drew strength from points of view common among general American historians. The uniqueness of the American experience, the spontaneity of American institutions and the emphasis upon adaptation to the American situation constituted staple themes for Catholic scholars. Historians saw the experience of the church in this country as unique; they noted the spontaneous development of indigenous attitudes and institutions, and they regarded their church's policy of adapting to the given conditions of America as not only necessary but desirable. While less likely than their non-Catholic counterparts to ignore the European background, Catholic historians distinguished between the roots of the faith in Europe and the special qualities the church developed in America, qualities that gave it a distinctive character. Most articulate ecclesiastical leaders urged the church to become fully American, and the historians sought to ease the process by demonstrating the compatibility, even the identity, of American and Catholic values.

Recent historians of American Catholicism continue to utilize the long dominant motif of Americanization. Andrew Greeley, for example, argues that the church was forced in spite of itself to adapt to American conditions but it did so with little insight or understanding. The great liberal prelates of the late nineteenth century began to articulate a positive rationale for the process, but the condemnation of Americanism ended their premature effort. The result of the unfortunate eclipse of their ideas and policies was not that Americanization ended or even slowed down but that the church and its leaders held fast to old ideals and attitudes while simultaneously struggling to keep pace with the ongoing acculturation of the Catholic people. Intellectually the church remained entrenched in a ghetto largely of its own creation while its people rapidly entered the not-so-secular city. "The Catholic population has become Americanized," Greeley writes. "The ecclesiastical structure has yet to follow suit. It missed the marvellous opportunities presented to it in its past, and Americanizers, whatever their theoretical triumphs, were not always practically successful."[21]

Far more sophisticated and precise is Philip Gleason's description of the church as a highly successful "institutional immigrant," itself caught in the conflicting pressures to conform to American ways and uphold old-world traditions. Today, as in the past, Gleason argues, the Catholic Church, like other institutions, is compelled to change to meet the new needs of its members, while preserving enough of its traditional beliefs and practices to retain its identity and sense of purpose. All institutions must "accomodate to the changes in their clientele" while avoiding betrayal of their heritage, Gleason argues, "for the preservation of the heritage is the fundamental purpose of their existence and the surest ground of their appeal."[22] The church, now as in the past, must understand what is happening and seek to "maintain identity without isolation and achieve relevance without absorption" into the broader society.

The Americanization thesis has many advantages. It insists on close attention to the sociological dimensions of contemporary Catholic life, correcting the overly abstract speculations of the more theologically oriented. Moreover, the concept of Americanization provides an indispensible key to the past, for upward mobility and acceptance into American culture were indeed the objectives of immigrant Catholics and their leaders. The story was one of adaptation to the demands of the American situation and debate over the meaning of what it meant to be an American Catholic. Nothing was scarcer than an admittedly un-American Catholic; nothing was more difficult to prove to Catholics than any belief or practice of theirs was contrary to "true Americanism." This is one reason why, as one scholar notes, Catholics "have been influenced by the American environment to a far greater degree than they have influenced it." [23]

The weakness of the approach is its bias toward the descriptive, toward a model of alien Catholics adapting to a stable culture made by others, and its consequent reliance upon relatively uncritical tools for dealing with American society as a whole. It underrates the impact of the urban-Catholic-ethnic component upon American culture generally and thus tends to give a one-sided view of the processes of assimilation. The "heritage" which for Gleason is the stable core which adaptation was designed to preserve, was itself shaped by national and ethnic considerations. Thus the historian of Italian Catholics finds that " the 'Italian problem' was many things to many people, but to the Italian immigrants themselves it may have been that the church in the United States was more American and Irish than Catholic."[24]

Finally the objective, social science approach to history obscures the extent to which the historian and those he describes utilize America itself as the solid anchor of interpretation, finding in the life of the church the values and style most admired in American society. Today, for the first time, significant numbers of American Catholics are seriously questioning the moral basis of American life. Unless the contemporary crisis in America is understood, the concept of Americanization may continue to provide clues for understanding the past, but it may well confuse and misdirect efforts to shape the future.

It might be constructive in this context to examine American

Catholic liberalism, for in retrospect it appears to have long accepted assumptions about American society that were bound to result in severe disillusionment. Men like Leslie Dewart, Eugene Fontinelle and James Hitchcock have ably exposed the weakness of earlier theological assumptions, pointing in particular to the comfortable belief that the forms of doctrine and discipline could be changed without calling into question "essential" matters of faith and authority.[25] It has been less apparent that there were also prevalent until very recently a set of assumptions about American society that helped support the ideology of reform. In shaping that reform temper, Catholic historians have played no small part.

For almost 175 years Catholics in the United States concentrated their energies and resources on the tasks of survival and personal and collective achievement. When they did look beyond themselves they had to face the fact that many of their countrymen doubted their loyalty. In the eyes of their fellow citizens Catholics symbolized many of those elements Americans most disliked: Catholics were European, they valued tradition, they submitted docilely to the dictates of a hierarchy who spoke the authoritarian language of the past. The fact that their drinking, eating and sexual habits also differed from those of native Americans only accentuated the problem. At the same time, leaders of the Catholic church in Europe had great difficulty comprehending the problems and recognizing the accomplishments of the American church. Catholic leaders were proud of their success in retaining the loyalty of their flocks and constructing from the voluntary contributions of their members an impressive array of churches, schools and benevolent institutions, but they looked in vain at home and abroad for sympathy and recognition. Caught between American modernity and Roman reaction, American Catholics struggled valiantly to prove that they were at one and the same time devoted Catholics and exemplary Americans.

The central tradition of American Catholicism, the tradition personified in the great prelates from John Carroll to Francis Spellman, was contained in the constant and passionate assertion that Catholicism and Americanism blended happily together and rounded each other out. French Catholics might decry the revolutionary tradition, German Catholics might struggle valiantly against Prussian imperialism, English Catholics might withdraw quietly to their drawing rooms, apart from the tumultous multitude, but neither challenge nor withdrawal was the style for American Catholics. Heedless of the difficulties that disturbed more thoughtful nativists and perceptive European visitors, American Catholics loved their Church and their country, insisted upon total allegiance to both, and either ignored criticism or regarded all challenges as wrongheaded and prejudiced.

When Leo XIII condemned the heresy of "Americanism" in 1899, most Catholics denied that it existed in the United States. Nevertheless Leo effectively stifled the efforts of enthusiastic Americanizers, like Archbishop Ireland of St. Paul, who were so enchanted by the prospect of their nation that they urged full and immediate destruction of those ethnic characteristics that separated Catholics from full participation in national life. His opponents shared his nationalism, but they were not prepared to put aside group loyalties that still provided the cement holding many of their flock to the church. Rather they preferred the slower and more difficult path of accommodation through ethnic nationalism, finding that intensification of ethnic identity, while it caused occasional difficulties with native Americans, proved useful in retaining the loyalty of people caught in the complexities of assimilation. Ireland's naive espousal of the melting pot was in their eyes both unrealistic and morally questionable, and they refused to be bullied. They welcomed Leo's encyclical as a vindication of their efforts at Catholic organizational separatism, and in the years that followed they saw to it that Americanism was held within the bounds of continued religious identity and loyalty. Ireland's attempt at dialogue with non-Catholics was abruptly canceled, internal debate and self-criticism ceased, the Catholic University of America stalled in its drive to become the intellectual center of an Americanized church and the symbolic ascendancy and leadership of James Cardinal Gibbons obscured the decentralization necessitated by diocesan autonomy and national division.

However, the defeat of the Americanizers did not impede the

central drive for acceptance as fully American and Catholic. In the years that followed, Catholic spokesmen continued to insist upon the complementary character of their dual loyalties. Revival of anti-Catholic sentiment in the 1920s did not stimulate any serious criticism of American life but was met with the charge that the Klu Klux Klan and other opponents of Catholics were not only anti-Catholic but un-American as well. In the campaign of 1928 Catholics admitted of no conflict between religious and national values. They insisted, as one editor put it, that they were more truly American than those who denied them their rights.[26] A few years later the many Catholics who responded to the nationalist, isolationist message of Father Charles E. Coughlin found in the communist issue the perfect vehicle for Catholic Americanism. The Vatican's accommodation with Fascism and its simultaneous declaration of war on communism in Pius XI's *Divini Redemptoris* in 1937 demonstrated that no cause could be more fully and completely Catholic than opposition to the red menace. Nor was anything more truly American, for Catholics argued persuasively that communism violated basic American tenets and they found support for the argument in the most respectable sectors of American life, even among groups long hostile to the church. The fact that liberal intellectuals, who were usually critical of the church, often flirted with communism only confirmed Catholic suspicion that such people were not truly loyal to America and were hypocritical in their affirmation of religious freedom. In the polemics over Mexico and Spain, in particular, Catholics forged a true integration of religious and national values that provided solid support for the retention of group loyalty as Catholics rose in wealth and status in the years following World War II.

There were exceptions to these generalizations, men like the pro-German Edward Koch who upheld a reactionary criticism of American secularism and called for corporate reform to restore medieval unity and harmony. More significant was the much different stance of the Catholic Worker movement, whose scathing criticism of American society and explicit critique of American Catholic life attracted many young laymen during the great depression. Not all Catholic Workers accepted Peter

Maurin's rejection of patriotic nationalism and Dorothy Day's ardent pacifism, a fact that the exodus of many from the movement in 1940 and 1941 amply demonstrated. Nevertheless the Catholic Worker fostered a radical perspective on American society that, whatever its weakness, stood as a strong dissent from the Americanism of liberal and conservative Catholics alike.

Nevertheless, most Catholic leaders enthuiastically supported American wars and championed the basic tenets of business culture however much they differed over the speed and degree of desirable assimilation and the specific character of the church's adaptation to American society. Generally the better-educated, more Americanized spokesmen championed the uncritical Americanism of the earlier generation. Peter Guilday, professor of American Church History at the Catholic University of America, for example, praised the virtues of America in terms similar to those of John Ireland: "America, to follow the providential guidance which was bestowed upon its great leaders, should become one nation, made up of one people speaking the same tongue, enjoying the same privileges, and living for the same purpose; the glory and prestige of the new Republic." Accepting the contention that there was no fundamental conflict between Catholicism and Americanism, the conclusion he reached was clear: the church should reform itself in the spirit of American democracy. Again Guilday's words were almost identical with Ireland's: "The church in America, to fulfill its destiny as the most compact religious body in the country, must be American in its appeal, American in its sentiments and in its spirit."[27]

Catholic reformers of recent vintage were the true heirs of this Americanist tradition. In the 1950s widespread self-criticism reappeared in the American church for the first time since the 1890s. As Thomas T. McAvoy pointed out, vigorous demands for liturgical reforms and lay participation in church affairs anticipated the advent of John XXIII,[28] and the character of these demands reflected the continuing faith in American society that marked the liberal tradition, now provided with a mass base by the emergence of a new, educated Catholic middle class. Liturgical reform, for example, which in the 1930s had

been advanced as a vehicle for promoting Christian social reconstruction, by the 1950s had been stripped of its social content.
Rather it had become part of a broader movement for a
stronger lay voice in church affairs.

The election of John F. Kennedy climaxed the long quest for
respectability. A Catholic president eased remaining doubts
about Catholic status. All that remained to the task of completing construction of a truly American Catholicism was the reform of the church along American lines. Michael Novak echoed
an old cry when he proclaimed the advent of "a new generation—American and Catholic,"[29] while Daniel Callahan in *The
Mind of the Catholic Layman* described in convincing detail the
conflicts between the values of church and society which laymen had always felt but seldom expressed.[30] The Americanized
Catholic, taught by his society to value individual initiative,
personal liberty and popular participation, was expected to be
silent, docile and obedient in the church. For men like Callahan,
Novak and Donald Thorman, the solution was clear: the church
should officially confirm the validity of American church-state
separation and religious liberty; it should validate the layman's
positive response to secular activity, and it should recognize his
personal freedom and dignity through liturgical reform, democratic structures and an end to paternalism and authoritarianism.

The intellectual monument of these years was John Courtney
Murray's *We Hold These Truths,* whose publication in 1960
earned its author a place on the cover of *Time* magazine.
Murray had, in fact, challenged many of the assumptions that
had prevented accommodation of Americanism and Catholicism
in essays published in the 1940s, but the controversy excited by
those articles reached Rome and Murray ceased publication for
a decade until the changed intellectual climate under John
XXIII encouraged him to present his thesis in book form.
Catholics had long argued that, while the First Amendment was
quite acceptable in the American context, it did not provide an
ideal arrangement of church-state relations. Murray rejected the
expediency of this position, but he wanted nothing to do with
absolutist views of religious liberty and separation either. Instead, he sought to demonstrate that the political system of the

United States accorded fully with Catholic doctrine. In particular he argued that the American Constitution clearly limited governmental power and provided broad exemptions from government's jurisdiction, allowing the church full freedom to be itself and do its work. The combination of limited government and a broad consensus on moral and procedural values eliminated the need for religious establishment, which was, indeed, positively harmful. Murray provided, then, the badly needed justification of religious liberty by approaching the problem not from traditional theological or ecclesiological perspectives but from the viewpoint of political theory, or "western constitutionalism, classic and Christian." His success was measured by the adoption of his main arguments in the Vatican Council Declaration on Religious Liberty.

For Murray, the heart of the American system was a consensus, "an ensemble of substantive truths, a structure of basic knowledge, an order of elementary affirmations that reflect realities in the order of existence."[31] Without such a consensus, true dialogue or conversation, and thus true civil society, was not possible. America had begun with a statement of consensus: "We hold these truths to be self-evident," and its institutions, including its arrangements of church and state, had been based upon it. Unfortunately, Murray believed, the consensus was in danger, for it had been all but destroyed by the naturalist currents of modern thought, which had created "a climate of doubt and bewilderment in which clarity about the larger aims of life is dimmed and the self confidence of the people is destroyed." The inability of America to respond to the postwar crisis in the world positively, its reliance upon a sterile anti-communism as a substitute for a public philosophy, was evidence of the erosion of the American consensus.

Yet, Murray continued, the American creed did live in the hearts and minds of many Americans, most notably American Catholics. The widespread intellectual defection from the American consensus had created the paradox that "the guardianship of the original American consensus, based on the Western heritage, would have passed to the Catholic community." Thus Murray turned things around. With scholarly precision he demonstrated that Catholics who drew upon their intellectual heritage of scholastic philosophy and political theory were not only capable of being good Americans; they were in fact the best and most convinced adherents of America's most cherished propositions. "Catholic participation in the American consensus," Murray argued, "has been full and free, unreserved and unembarassed, because the contents of this consensus—the ethical and political principles drawn from the traditions of natural law—approve themselves to the Catholic intelligence and conscience." The American *ralliement* had been motivated not by mere expediency, as anti-Catholics like Paul Blanshard charged, but by "the evident coincidence of the principles which inspired the American Republic with the principles that are structural to the Western Christian political tradition."

Murray's work was the most successful effort ever made to reconcile the apparently conflicting demands of Catholicism and Americanism. It marked the ultimate intellectual expression of the liberal Catholic Americanism, which had begun with the conversion of Isaac Hecker and Orestes Brownson over a century earlier. Nevertheless, it is important to remember that Murray's interpretation of the church-state problem rested upon an interpretation of the American political process which was characteristic of the 1950s. Shocked by the war and its aftermath, American historians and political commentators turned away from the sharp class and sectional conflicts which Charles Beard and an earlier generation had seen as central to American history. In comparison with European political evolution, the American experience seemed to have been placid, with major issues centering on questions of technique. As one historian put it, Americans shared a set of values that were essentially those of liberal capitalism: respect for individual initiative and private property, insistence on limited government and the pragmatic accommodation and compromise of pressure group politics. There had been no feudalism, no conservatism, no socialism, only a monolithic liberal consensus that obviated the necessity for positive government and made possible peaceful evolution through a selective government intervention that carefully respected traditional civil liberties.[32]

The United States could, in the 1950s, make a virtue of its lack of ideology and discover its "genius" in its processes and institutions, as did historian Daniel Boorstin, whose work Murray cited.[33] Both men contributed to the school of thought which proclaimed "the end of ideology" for both saw America as a non-ideological society which traditionally had avoided sharp division by a common affirmation of consensus. For example, Murray argued that the civil war "was not an ideological conflict but simply . . . a conflict of interests." That this historical outlook might itself be part of a conservative stance, which inhibited radical criticism and efforts at fundamental reform, seldom occurred to its exponents. Even Murray himself, while recognizing that America must ultimately stand under the judgment of Christianity, nonetheless found few political or social evils in American society and politics though he did discover many intellectual aberrations.

In less sophisticated hands than Murray's, his argument easily blended in with opposition to secularism in government and education, for the consensus Murray saw as political and procedural was seen by others as religious, even sectarian. John Ireland had once said that America was "at heart a Christian country" and many who hoped to gain public support for parochial schools or who opposed Supreme Court rulings on religion in public education adapted Murray's thesis without difficulty to such a reading of American history. Equally important Murray had supplied a systematic rationale for attitudes long present in America, attitudes that had fairly clear political implications. Cardinal Gibbons had long before spelled them out:

> I grant that . . . a collision of authority comes within the range of possibility. But the American concept of government and liberty puts the hypothesis outside the range of practical affairs. That concept, as I understand it, is that the Government should leave as large a liberty as possible to individuals and to bodies within the State, only intervening in the interests of morality, justice, and the common weal. There are forces at work in this country, I know, that tend to paternalism and Caesarism in government; but true Americans recognize that these forces would bring disaster on American liberties. So long as these liberties, under which we have prospered, are preserved in their fulness there is, I assert, no danger of a collision between the State and the Catholic Church.[34]

Such a position led to deep suspicion of federal activity in national life and could easily reinforce self-interested opposition to federal regulation of economic life, social welfare and insurance legislation and efforts for a national health and educational policy. While Murray rarely drew such conclusions, his ideas came down squarely on the conservative side.

There was an air of complacency in Murray's work that could not withstand the shocks that lay ahead. It reflected the long-time feeling of Catholics that America, rightly understood, raised no real problem for the Catholic and that Catholicism raised no real problem for the American. After Murray, Catholics could contend with renewed assurance that, while they belonged to the true church, the rights of conscience were guaranteed by both church and state. The only dissent came from a number of conservative theologians at Catholic University, but their voices were gradually stilled as the church moved slowly to the left under John XXIII.[35]

Just as Murray's work marked the culmination of the intellectual reconciliation of church and nation, so the work of the younger laymen brought the drive to reform the church along American lines to a climax. In *The Emerging Layman* Donald Thorman caught the mood of the new breed of articulate, sophisticated Catholics dissatisfied with the church of their fathers.[36] Thorman contended that the laity, now safely established in the middle class, no longer needed or wanted the paternal guidance and direction of the clergy. Catholic Action, "the participation of the laity in the apostolate of the hierarchy" through official lay organizations under clerical control, did not represent a style suitable to a newly confident and responsible generation. The theology of Catholic Action was already under severe attack in Europe, and Thorman drew on this work to support his demand that laymen be granted autonomy in their organizational work, that they be encouraged to participate on equal terms in nonsectarian movements for social reform and that they be given a voice in the operation of Catholic schools and other agencies conducted with their money. Too long had the laity been silent in the churches, Thorman argued. They needed to bring the democratic and participatory experience of their secular life into the church, and such voluntary service would free the clergy for the more energetic pursuit of their distinctive tasks of spiritual guidance, sacramental administration and teaching. A new church, characterized by freedom, openness and cooperation, would be the outcome, a church better able to fulfill its responsibilities and to participate more effectively in the life of the nation.

The layman's newly found independence should manifest itself in the temporal sphere as well, Thorman argued. The widespread belief that the layman's work was inferior to that of the clergy was misguided and should be replaced by a positive conception of common Christian vocation shared by all, whatever their state of life. Rather than trying to organize the laity into a solid phalanx under the direction of the clergy the church should encourage the layman in his creative work and sanction his participation with non-Catholics in social and political action aimed at eliminating social evils and constructing a more decent and humane society. The Christian impact on the world had to be made not simply by the organization, the church, but by men who were Christians. A new role for the layman in a new age, one no longer characterized by the presence of immigrant working-class Catholics in an alien land but by educated, prosperous, Americanized business and professional men who knew America as their own: this was the setting for the emerging layman.

Thorman and Murray both wrote out of a solid liberal tradition in American Catholicism. Both accepted the major and minor dogmatic propositions of the faith. Neither questioned the basic structure of ecclesiastical authority, nor did they call for a re-evaluation of episcopal centralization. The need for Catholic schools, the responsibility of all to remain loyal to the church, the traditional limitations on ecumenical exchange, the church's prohibitions of birth control and divorce, none of these were major concerns of the liberals in the years before the Second Vatican Council. The proposals they did make were not new either. As Father McAvoy asked of Thorman, from what was the layman emerging?[37] In the nineteenth century there had been many argumentative laymen who had not hesitated to engage their bishops in public controversy or to question official church policy. Nor had the church ever overtly placed any roadblocks in the way of the Catholic's political action or ecnomic advancement. Catholic schools had taught civics to the immigrant, and the bishops had repeatedly urged laymen to vote as independent-minded men concerned solely with civic welfare. The schools had likewise inculcated the values of success: hard work, self-discipline, sobriety, punctuality, reliability. The canons of the handbooks on how to succeed were as pervasive in Catholic as in public schools, church-related universities had not hesitated to depart from traditional structures of education to add programs in engineering and business administration, and the church's leaders had honored successful laymen in business and the professions. Catholic learned societies supported by the episcopate were evidence that the church desired its members to value the intellectual life. Thorman advocated no basic changes, as Father McAvoy saw it, but only those reforms that would come naturally as the Catholic minority gained increased affluence and respectability.

The very moderation of the proposals of reformers may explain the remarkable degree to which the Council acted upon them. Murray's defense of religious liberty was incorporated into a conciliar decree; representative structures were established and national episcopal conferences gained real authority. A new theology of the church replaced clerical legalism with a more democratic imagery of the "people of God." The Council Fathers led the way in ecumenical contacts and a wave of self-criticism and reform swept over the universal church. Yet the changes were to prove incomplete and disappointing. Religious liberty for non-Catholics did not necessarily mean freedom of conscience for Catholics themselves. Liturgical reforms, which were to revitalize community life, found few communities and generated no great spiritual or social wakening. Democratic and national structures, when they were established, frequently expressed a point of view at variance with that of their exponents. Yet even these changes occasioned division and reaction. Frightened ecclesiastical bureaucrats and their lay counterparts retreated to the security of old ways and attitudes, while disillusioned liberals often faced crises of faith and conscience more severe than they would have dreamed possible just a few short years before.

The problems inherent in moderate reform in an institution like the Catholic church were magnified for Americans by events at home. If faith in the possibility of a modernized Catholicism was severely challenged by events, faith in the secure assumptions of Americanism was for many all but destroyed. For the first time in the American Catholic experience America itself appeared to have not just a few blemishes, "unfinished business," as President Kennedy had put it, but to be morally questionable in its most basic structures and beliefs. Brutal assassination of the nation's best leaders, a vicious and immoral war, the disaffection and hostility of the country's youth, the polarization of blacks and whites, all helped destroy the consensus view of American society as completely as they shattered the consensus politics of Lyndon Johnson. Adherence to the traditions of American democracy and liberty was increasingly replaced by an apocalyptic vision of America as a land of violence and oppression. A church remade in the American image, the goal of Catholic liberalism for over a century, now seemed to many the basest form of blasphemy.

While it is surely too early to argue that the mass of American Catholics seriously question the moral validity of the nation, it seems true that for many Catholics America can no longer simply be taken for granted. It is events, and the conflicts they occasion, which have brought this about, not the superior wisdom of scholars maturing amid the trials of the 1960s. It must be clear that the Americanist heritage, which seems so sordid today, was a humane and honorable stance that reflected the best aspirations of the Catholic community. Nevertheless it was a position confined in its vision and limited in its critical edge. Expressing as it did the self-consciousness of the Catholic community, it too frequently was shaped by the dialectic of argument with conservative Catholics and anti-Catholic Americans, with the result that it lacked a critical sense of the character of the religious situation in America and of the dynamics of American society itself.

At the risk of vast oversimplification it seems fair to say that the Christian churches of America, including the Catholic church, shared two fundamental aims. One was to bring as many Americans as possible under the saving influence of the church, to church an unchurched people, to evangelize a nation composed of rapidly changing sections and groups. Mobility drew men away from the confines and stability of community, and the churches, profoundly rooted in stable societies, continually adapted to the demands of this mobility, from the development of frontier revivals and mobile missionaries to the crusades of Billy Graham and the television sermons of Fulton Sheen. The second aim of the churches was to exert some influence over the general culture of the nation, to add a godly nation to a holy people. Accepting the value of the first amendment, and recognizing the inevitability of rampaging sectarianism, the best leaders of the churches attempted to keep alive the idea of a common Christian heritage and to find methods consonant with their understanding of the First Amendment through which they could continue to combat secularism and remind the nation of its religious roots. For some this took the form of blatant culture religion, the enthusiastic identification of America as it was with the Kingdom of God, but for others it took a prophetic form, a constantly recurring cry that God expected much from a people he had blessed so well.

Now both of these objectives were fundamentally related to the Catholic origins of Protestantism in Europe, for both were Catholic, universal ideas: the necessity for all men to be within the salvic reaches of the church and the integration of religion and culture. Yet, for Catholics, these ideals seemed incompatible with the sectarianism of the Protestant churches and the liberalism of the First Amendment. If any doubted these points they should have been convinced by the papal stance in the nineteenth century. American Catholics had great difficulty accepting that position in practice, however, for it placed the church at odds with the dominant values held by the majority of Americans. The response of American Catholic leaders was necessarily ambiguous. They adopted these objectives as their own, but as a denomination like the others. Their task was to bring all Catholics within the saving reaches of that church and to dominate as much as possible the cultural milieu in which Catholics lived. Retaining the immigrant's faith and constructing a strong and vigorous Catholic subculture became the central preoccupation of the American church.

Their effort was unappreciated on either side. Other Americans naturally regarded Catholic policy as un-American separatism, manifesting a rejection of America incompatible with civic morality. Heavily concentrated groups of people were left outside the Protestant fold in the hands of European, authoritarian masters, so that construction of the Catholic subculture created serious breaches in the solidity of Protestant America. European Catholic leaders on the other hand were bound to see the Catholic concentration on the task of keeping people Catholic and the church's acceptance of minority status as a retreat from the ideal of total Catholicization of people, culture and nation. So it was that the choice of the church, almost forced upon it by circumstances, was seldom understood by American Protestants, by European Catholics or even by the church's own American leadership.

The common element in American Catholic and American religious history lies in the Americanism of both. Each group found as its major exponents men determined to demonstrate the compatibility of American culture and American religion on the one hand and American religion and world Christianity on the other. They did this in subtly different ways. The Protestant historian, with a few exceptions, accomplished his goal by endowing the nation with religious attributes. Faced with the multiplicity of sects and churches he professed to discern an underlying unity, an American Christianity that was often indistinguishable from the nation. "At the very time the denominations ceased to function as the church, the nation came more and more so to function," John E. Smylie has written. [38] Voluntaristic, respectful of individual conscience while claiming to rest on self-evident truth; able to cut through superficial national, economic, racial and national divisions among men and unite them on the ground of their common humanity; providentially guided to redeem men from the chains of history and sin, the nation became an American church.

While the Catholic historian and intellectual undoubtedly felt a similar impulse to make a church of the nation, and to make it a Catholic church, he was inhibited by several factors. His loyalty to an ecclesiastical authority located abroad raised the danger of heresy or schism. Moreover, his constituency held fast to many old-world ties, which a too complete Americanism might erode. Most important he could not have the same sense of intimacy of his religion and the national culture that was felt by his evangelical Protestant counterparts. In Europe Catholic churchmen could and did endow the state with divine attributes in those countries where they had no need to regard the state as competing for the popular allegiance. In England and Germany where the church was a minority, or in Republican France, Italy or pre-Civil War Spain, where the state was frequently in hostile hands, the church was acutely conscious of the need to stress the temporal, limited character of the state's claims. In Franco's Spain or Salazar's Portugal the situation was different. In America, where Catholics were a minority and where their enemies, real or imaged, exercised great influence, the church would endorse national values while deploring national practice, exhort patriotism while debunking the claims of the state and its leaders. Thus until the social changes of the post World War II years destroyed minority consciousness, liberal Catholic Americanism, as strident as it often was when directed at the Catholic community, had in the end a more pragmatic character than that of many Protestants. This was a stance that might have interacted creatively with Protestant scholarship, were it not for the general problems that inhibited the development of Catholic intellectual life and the additional burdens fostered by the Catholic scholar's training and conception of his role.

The Americanist impulse present in all Christian communions has always disturbed outsiders. Many a foreign observer of American Catholicism deplored the fact that his American brethren so enthusiastically endorsed the nation's materialism, activism and belligerent nationalism. This view had its domestic exponents, who received considerable support by the publication in 1955 of Will Herberg's *Protestant-Catholic-Jew*, a book that persuaded many that the denominations had lost their distinctive faiths and become mere subdivisions of the nation's true religion, "The American Way of Life." "Each of the three faiths, insofar as the mass of its adherents are concerned, tends to regard itself as merely an alternative and variant form of being religious in the American way," Herberg argued. The result was an "American culture-religion" or "civic religion," which was "incurably idolatrous" and which "validates culture and society without in any sense bringing them under judgment."[39]

Herberg was not the first to describe a "religion of America" existing alongside of and frequently becoming integrated into the specific religions of the multitude of churches. Before World War II, for example, Ralph Gabriel had identified a persisting "American democratic faith,"[40] which provided the citizens with a common bedrock of values that shaped their religious and political life.

In the 1960s a number of scholars began serious study of what Robert Bellah called the "civil religion" of America, and their conclusions were far more complex than Herberg's. Bellah, for example, argued that civil religion "has its own seriousness and integrity." It has its prophets and martyrs, ritual and symbols; it has been used as "a cloak for petty interests and ugly passions" but was capable of "growth and new insight." The religion of America was, like other religions, a complex of movement and order that upheld values and ideals, thus serving as a constant source of criticism and reform, providing "a heritage of moral and religious experience" from which Americans still had much to learn.[41]

This new, positive approach to American religion was best developed in the work of Sidney Mead. According to Mead, the equality of religious groups in relation to civil authority and the determination of the Founding Fathers to prevent any new orthodoxy from gaining ascendancy created a truly unique situation in America. The new forms of Christianity, the denominations, contended with one another for members and influence while sharing a common Christian heritage. If, as Paul Tillich said, "religion is the heart of culture and culture the form of religion," then, Mead argued, beneath the diversity of the churches was a common faith, the general statements of ultimate meaning to which the sects gave particular expression. These were never simply a national orthodoxy propagated by the state but a true religion, defined by Durkheim as "a unified system of beliefs and practices relative to sacred things, uniting into a single moral community all those who adhere" to it. While validating the institutions of American society, this creed simultaneously provided a reference for criticism, judgment and reform. "The religion of the Republic is essentially prophetic," Mead concluded, "which is to say that its ideals and aspirations stand in constant judgment over the passing shenanigans of the people, reminding them of the standards by which their current practices and those of their nation are ever being judged and found wanting."[42]

When the America to which the Catholic church and its members were adapting is defined not as an open society of pluralism but as a "nation with the soul of a church," then the argument that American Catholic history is simply a story of Americanization becomes problematic. Father McAvoy contended that the progress of every Catholic group since the Civil War has been directly proportionate to the Americanization of its cultural tradition. Philip Gleason has argued that now that the church is "looked upon as fully belonging in America" its criticism of American society will be "more searching and responsible" and "will be accorded more respect" by others. [43] The "civil religion" argument, however, raises serious questions about McAvoy's assumption that cultural assimilation left the distinctive Catholic faith and tradition intact or Gleason's hope that the now accepted church still possesses the capacity for a distinctive and penetrating criticism.

Recognition of the complexity and limitations of Americanism, evident in the work of Mead, Bellah and Sydney Ahlstrom, is perhaps the beginning of a real possibility of a new ecumenical and critical approach to American religious studies. Certainly there are today signs of a real vitality in American Catholic historical scholarship most notable in the work of Gleason, Timothy Smith and Michael Gannon. The Council, the controversies it has unleashed, the upheavals in the church in this country, and the effect of events at home have combined to open up all phases of Catholic intellectual life while exciting interest in the church on the part of non-Catholic scholars. If these promising developments are to contribute to a new approach to American religious history they will have to take place in a context open to the work of the newly self-critical scholars of American Protestantism and to the changing configurations in religious scholarship generally. Historians of American religion, Protestantism, Catholicism, Judaism, civil religion, the whole variegated religious experience of America, have to face some very serious questions, and they will need help to answer them. They will need the alternative perspectives offered by historians of other periods and other cultures and the challenge of involvement in the ideological controversies now agitating all the learned societies and their constituent departments. Most important they will need theology, general church history, scripture studies and the social sciences, all of which must contribute to the effort to grasp the meaning, significance and implications of religious experience. Amidst the collapse of old assumptions about the church and American society, the historian of American religion is forced once again to ask himself the meaning of history for the Christian and the meaning of Christianity for the historian. American religious history must leave its terms open, relating creatively to American history, to religious studies and to historiographical debate. In the past dialogue between disciplines and denominations in religious studies has been limited at best. Now it must be full and free if scholarship, in general, and religious history, in particular, is to contribute to the resolution of the crisis now wracking the churches and the nation.

4
THE AMBIGUITY OF SUCCESS

The decline of Christianity has long been a staple theme of accounts of the years between the French Revolution and World War I. According to standard interpretations the Christian churches in this period suffered a gradual but steady loss of political and social power and an erosion of moral influence over the lives of individual men and women. In public life the churches no longer controlled education and social services, they could not influence the policy of governments and they lost their economic strength and intellectual predominance. Internally the churches first lost their ability to discipline their members and then lost many of the members themselves. Industrialization and its attendant mobility destroyed patterns of worship and behavior characteristic of village life, and the churches developed no meaningful alternatives adapted to the new urban life style. Wealthier and sophisticated Christians experienced more subtle but no less profound changes in European culture. Material accumulation and political power offered surer avenues to status and respect than did the religious life, while fashionable ideas of art and science undermined long-accepted Christian doctrines and norms. Increasingly Christianity seemed useful as an instrument of social control but was regarded as devoid of spiritual force or cultural significance.

Under steady pressure from within and without, churches and churchmen lost confidence in themselves and in the dynamic elements of their faith. A growing sense of the antipathy of Christianity and culture shaped their response, whether it was the liberal effort to achieve renewal through accommodation or the reactionary movement of withdrawal into a fortress of authoritarian religion and politics. In retrospect it appears to many that those Protestant churches that chose the former course suffered a withering of creedal certitude and moral fervor. As R. R. Palmer puts it:

> Church attendance among Protestants became increasingly casual, and the doctrines set forth in sermons seemed increasingly remote. Protestant laymen traditionally trusted their own private judgement, and regarded the clergy as their own agents, not as authoritative teachers placed above them. Protestants also had always set especial emphasis on the Bible as the source of religious belief, and as doubts accumulated on the literal truth of Biblical narratives there seemed no other source on which to rely.[1]

Trapped by their impulse to identify with a civilization they believed Protestantism had made, the reformed churches opened themselves to becoming the instruments of social and political forces they could neither escape nor dominate.

Historians who hold such a view of the Protestant experience in the nineteenth century often believe, surprisingly, that the defensive strategy personified by the Catholic Church of Pope Pius IX was the wiser course. Palmer, for example, credits Catholicism with greater success than Protestantism in resisting "the disintegrating effects of the era." The negative, reactionary stance of the Papacy, which seemed to contemporaries to isolate the church from the age, for Palmer was a course of action that insulated the church from the crushing disasters of the twentieth century. The intellectual neo-scholasticism of Leo XIII had a similar effect, for it enabled Catholicism "to emancipate itself from science as it did from capitalism and from non-Catholic socialism, marking out instead a way of its own, and never surrendering its ancient position, much battered by the secularism of modern times, that all worldly concerns should be subordinated to a spiritual authority, transmitted from Christ himself, and exercised by the Catholic hierarchy headed by the Bishop of Rome."[2]

Thus, many secular historians, accepting the premise that Christianity and culture truly were incompatible in the nineteenth century, regard the strategy of ultramontanism, however reactionary it might appear, as eminently sensible and astute. Through the trials of the period the Catholic Church, unlike its Protestant counterparts, remained true to itself and occupied a powerful defensive position from which it could reemerge as a political and social force when the energies of modernity had played themselves out in the catastrophes of the twentieth century.

The key to this historical interpretation of nineteenth-century Christianity lies in the definition of success, the criteria by which the church and the Christian are to measure victory and defeat, progress and retrogression. The historian who attempts to give a clear answer to these questions must possess an unambiguous understanding of the ideal form and spirit of the church and the culture of which it is a part. Yet Palmer's argument that Christianity and nineteenth-century culture were necessarily at odds with one another contains no analysis of the nature and purpose of the church and thus no adequate explanation of the sources and character of the conflict. Most of the Catholic participants in the nineteenth-century debate believed they knew what the church was and how its successes and failures could be measured, but the twentieth-century critic can be forgiven his doubt that their definitions were adequate or that their clarity was desirable. In religious history, as in any other, interpretations of such matters are at best ambiguous for, as Cardinal Suhard noted in his famous pastoral letter which raised but did not resolve the problem of "Growth or Decline?" the answer is shrouded in the veil of our transiency and historicity.[3] As a result each new generation, and men at different cultural vantage points, will make their own judgment of yesterday's ideas and actions as their consequences continue to unfold in a never-ending process. "The crown of irony lies in the fact that the most obvious forms of success are involved in failure on the ultimate level," Reinhold Niebuhr writes. "It is the symbol of the potential contradiction between all historic achievement and the final meaning of life."[4]

For the scholar Christian history presents a number of insoluble problems, none more central than the need to define the church. If the church is a visible, hierarchical organization whose purpose is to protect the integrity of the deposit of faith and to directly shape the broad outlines of culture and society, the criteria of its success will be essentially quantitative and easily measurable. If, on the other hand, the church is that of *De Ecclesia* of the Second Vatican Council, the criteria are far more qualitative and elusive. The South American bishop who responded to the charge that there were few real Christians in his country by referring to the purity of doctrine there, illustrates one side of the problem. The would be prophet who castigates the throngs of churchgoers as essentially pagan gives witness to another.

Without touching the depths of theological controversy, it should be clear that even among Roman Catholics, the criteria of success and failure, indeed the very standards of Christian identification itself, are disputable. While historians confine themselves to evaluating the significance of visible social units, the Christian churches, and of people who self-consciously define themselves as Christian, upon the historical process, it should be clear that in doing so they arbitrarily impose an implicit theology upon their historical questions and answers.

The difficulties facing the religious historian who wishes to assess the successes and failures of Christianity in the nineteenth century are compounded if his chosen field of study is the United States. European controversialists of the last century themselves were puzzled by the vitality and dynamism of Christianity in a land in which so many of the apparently antagonistic features of modern life were so radically pervasive. Liberal Catholic dissenters to the intransigent policies of the Roman establishment pointed to the flourishing American Church as evidence of the wisdom of a more flexible response to modernity. Conservatives were forced to rebut these arguments if the policies of the Franco-Italian citadel were not to be undermined, but to do so in such a way as to avoid unduly antagonizing American Catholics. The result was condemnation of "Americanism," the ambiguity of which is manifest in the bafflement of contemporaries and the confusion of subsequent historians.

Surely the American religious experience has differed from the European, although few have been able fully to account for the differences or to endow them with theological meaning. Every serious student of American religion has brought to his European brethren the message that traditional, old-world-centered notions of church and society should be put aside in judging the American experience of Christianity. The pioneer Protestant historian Philip Schaaf expended enormous energy in the effort to convince his continental friends of the unique significance of American religion, and his successors have echoed his views. Similarly Catholic spokesmen from John Carroll to the American bishops at the Second Vatican Council have been acutely aware of the gap between many American ideas and practices and the policies of the Papacy and much of European Catholicism. Always Americans were proud of their remarkable success as measured by growth in members, wealth and influence, but they were ever anxious to demonstrate that these achievements had not been purchased at the cost of any essential article of Catholic faith.

At the same time American Catholic leaders had to fight on another front against the attacks of Protestant critics who were certain that the Catholic church could never be at home in America while it retained its Catholic structure and ideology. While frequently voiced by bigoted nativists and professional Catholic haters, such attitudes were also held by many sincere and decent men who thought they recognized serious and profound contradictions between official Catholic doctrine and semi-official church policies and the values which they believed crucial to the American experiment. There were bigoted Catholics who responded only with diatribes, but most sincerely believed that such non-Catholic fears were unfounded. Native Catholics and Catholics from Ireland and many continental countries had frequently experienced religious and national persecution, so that the image of the repressive, inquisitorial church that dominated Protestant fears seemed not at all just. In response they pointed to their own behavior, their record in America, and honestly felt that argument should end there.

Yet real, substantive differences did exist, not only between Roman and American ideals, but between the patterns of life and thought of Catholic and non-Catholic Americans. These differences might have led to a dialogue fruitful for both sides. Instead of engaging in such dialogue, however, American Catholics generally denounced some elements of American society as "materialistic" and "secularistic" while they overidentified with the more congenial aspects of American life. Richard Hofstadter is but one critic who has noted this:

> One might have expected Catholicism to have added a distinctive
> leaven to the intellectual dialogue in America, bringing as it did a
> different sense of the past and of the world, a different awareness
> of the human condition and of the imperatives of institutions. In
> fact, it has done nothing of the kind. . . . Instead, American
> Catholicism has devoted itself alternately to denouncing the as-
> pects of American life it could not approve and imitating more
> acceptable aspects in order to surmount its minority complex and
> Americanize itself. In consequence the American Church . . . the
> richest and best organized of the national divisions of the Church,
> lacks an intellectual culture.[5]

This situation was no doubt attributable in part to the social
structure of the American church. The limited resources of
Catholic immigrants and workers provided physical facilities,
social services and schools. The church lacked solid, middle-class
families, who usually provided leadership to American cultural
life, while it possessed no counterpart of the old Catholic
aristocracy who served the function in Europe. The clergy, the
largest educated group, received a traditional and rigid training
and, after ordination, were thrust into urban parishes whose
members were in need of pastoral care, material assistance and
religious education, leaving little opportunity for serious intellectual endeavor. The American Church came to be noted for
cultural isolation, hierarchical centralization and institutional
proliferation. "The result has been a paradox still puzzling to
foreigners," Father Walter Ong writes, "a Catholic mentality
which is in many ways the most conservative in the world set in
the midst of a nation whose genius seems to be adaptability and
change."[6]

At the same time European Catholic thought contained little
to assist the American brethren. What contacts America did
have with the European church were usually with the Papacy or
with the more conservative sectors, and what was learned only
reinforced conservative and exclusivist policies. The "siege mentality" of nineteenth-century Catholicism, the stress upon resistance to change and the protection of institutional and group
interests, was the Church universal's reaction to modern life.
The American Church, without some of the problems that
hampered its European counterparts, adapted in many ways to

the political and economic life of the new environment. But social conditions and a rigidly conservative intellectual heritage inhibited the development of thinkers with the training, opportunity and desire to analyze the meaning of this experience for America and for the church. As a result it never developed a convincing explanation of itself out of its controversies with native Protestants and foreign Catholics.

Nineteenth-century European visitors to America frequently noted the sharp contrasts between the Catholic church as they saw it in America and the same church as it existed in their native lands. The differences could perhaps only be seen clearly by the outsider, for American Catholics shared in that myopic view of the world so characteristic of Americans. Beset by immense problems, frequently attacked by their countrymen, immersed in the struggle for ecclesiastical acceptance and social mobility, they were apt to be puzzled if not appalled by the conduct of religious affairs in Europe. From the days of John Carroll to those of the Second Vatican Council, the American Catholic in Rome was an innocent abroad, shocked and scandalized by the life of the Roman court. For the American the politics and diplomacy of Europe were sordid, conspiratorial, flagrantly dishonest, a view that episodes like the XYZ affair served to confirm. For American Catholics the church, and the Papacy, were sacrosanct, but the machinations of churchmen seemed to partake of the same flavor as the intrigues of their secular counterparts.

There was a profound basis for misunderstanding, then, between European and American Catholics, a basis obscured by the natural reluctance of Catholics to supply their domestic enemies with the ammunition which criticism of Roman ways might make available. But all the problems were not on the European side. American Catholics were adapting in diverse ways to the social and religious environment of the United States, often without recognizing that they were doing so. The process was seldom conscious; no more than the people as a whole did Catholics grasp the full significance of their experiment. Such profoundly important questions as church and state and social justice found transatlantic Catholics using the same

words and meaning different things, and they had little opportunity to dialogue about the differences.

In no area was this more important than in the conflicting
definitions of success. Throughout her history the American
church prided itself on its accomplishments; bishops, priests and
laity alike believed that they had succeeded remarkably in
overcoming their problems and doing God's work in the new
world. Criticism was difficult for them to understand and more
difficult for them to accept. Yet the context in which the
church operated in Europe and America was so different that
even the very idea of the church was changed, and with it the
criteria of success.

Yet this is not to say that the church offered no explanation
of its situation. John Carroll, John Hughes, John Ireland and a
number of other Catholic spokesmen did attempt to explain
their church to their European colleagues and to their fellow
Americans. Their arguments contained certain common themes,
repeated so frequently that they became truths taken for granted by the Catholic community. One was the idea, which became
so popular at the time of the Second Vatican Council, that the
church, while holding fast to its central dogmas and discipline,
adapts easily and creatively to any and all cultures and epochs.
"The Catholic religion subsists and expands under all forms of
government and adapts itself to all times and places and circumstances," James Cardinal Gibbons wrote. "This she does without any compromise of principle, any derogation from the
supreme authority of the church, or any shock to the individual
conscience."[7] This argument, repeated endlessly, was designed
to convince Europeans of the American church's orthodoxy and
loyalty and Americans of its readiness to accept and endorse
national practices and institutions. Many on both sides remained skeptical of bridging the gap between the First Amendment and the Syllabus of Errors, but for American Catholics
Gibbons' argument increasingly seemed self-evident.

A second feature of the Catholic argument was its pride in its
material accomplishments and its simultaneous recognition that
these were not the only standards of measuring Christian progress. "One Archbishop and eleven bishops, with so many col-

leges and convents established in so short a space of time ...
presents an arresting spectacle," Bishop John England wrote on
the fiftieth anniversary of the American hierarchy. "But the
truth is," he continued, "that all these things are relative, and to
judge the progress of the missions accurately, it is not enough to
stop with what has been done, but to consider as well whether
all has been done that should have been accomplished."[8] For
England what "should have been accomplished" was a fuller
national organization of the church; for others, like some Ger-
man-American Catholics, the standard was an old-world model
of medieval unity and harmony in marked contrast with American realities. Native American Catholics of English origin questioned the cultural quality of Catholic life; others criticized its
spiritual depth or its influence on national policy. In any case,
despite the apologetic tone and intention of so many Catholic
polemics, rarely were critical voices lacking to raise anew the
question of success and summon the church to new work for
the realization of goals to which at least some of its members
felt committed.

In this light the history of the American church takes on
subtle shadings, as, caught in remarkably rapid change, it sought
in many ways to realize its mission in America, a mission that
was always a challenge but seldom clearly defined.

Although the anti-Catholic sentiments of colonial America
were temporarily submerged by the Revolution, John Carroll,
the nation's first Catholic bishop, was ever mindful of the
minority status of his 25,000 followers. He constantly urged
Roman authorities to exercise care in emphasizing those doctrines that were anathema in the new country. He relaxed the
enforcement of legislation dealing with mixed marriages, allowed the laity wide freedom, maintained extensive contacts
with Protestants and championed religious and civil liberty. The
Maryland Catholics who led the early church were secure in
their economic and social status, and they sought to play down
the religious factor that alone differentiated them from their
neighbors. Their policies of assimilation, lay action, cultural
excellence and quiet dialogue with non-Catholics were supported by highly educated French priests and bishops and were
carried on through the century by such later leaders as Arch-

bishop Martin Spalding, Bishop John Lancaster Spalding, the Kenrick brothers and notable converts from the Protestant mainstream like Orestes Brownson and Isaac Hecker. The story of American Catholicism, then, was never simply one of an immigrant church over against non-Catholic America, for the church the immigrant found when he arrived was already deeply rooted in the American soil. Indeed, Father Thomas T. McAvoy has argued that "the essential characteristic of American Catholic culture were determined by the generation of Catholics in America during the great immigration from 1830 to the Civil War."[9] In these years it was the Anglo-American nucleus who, under the double pressure of immigration and nativism, established a "cultural unity" which "slowly absorbed all the later immigrations since the Civil War." For McAvoy, the original group of English descent, and not the Irish, played the creative role in Catholic history. Despite the mistaken policies of New York's Archbishop John Hughes, the Irish gradually assumed leadership while fully accepting the cultural tradition and values of the earlier generation. Thus James Cardinal Gibbons was able to see in John Carroll at the beginning of the nineteenth century a man who formulated the policies Gibbons and his colleagues were pursuing at its end. "Knowing as he did, the mischief caused by national rivalries," Gibbons wrote of Carroll, "his aim was that the clergy and people—no matter from what country they sprung—should be thoroughly identified with the land in which their lot was cast, that they should study its laws and political constitution, and be in harmony with its spirit, in a word, that they should become as soon as possible assimilated to the social body in all things pertaining to civil life."[10]

Toward this end Carroll had tried to adjust ecclesiastical administration to prevailing American practice by entrusting church property to laymen. The failure of this policy demonstrated the monumental obstacles that had to be overcome to achieve the goal of assimilation and respectability the Anglo-American charter group upheld. The trustee system led to serious abuses, with congregations aided by recalcitrant priests defying the bishops on such matters as clerical appointments. These scandals, combined with the near chaotic conditions created by the large numbers of immigrants, convinced the hierarchy that only a disciplined and orderly administrative structure independent of lay influence could meet the challenges confronting the Catholic church in the United States. The rigid episcopal control that resulted checked lay responsibility for church policy for better than a century. The hierarchy, unable to see any alternative between the lay trustee system and the exclusion of the laity from all responsibility, turned a deaf ear to the pleas of Bishop John England for a moderate system of lay participation and consultation. The immigrants, preoccupied with their own social and economic problems, readily acquiesced in "the development of the church along lines of strict clerical control."[11] Furthermore the almost absolute power of the bishop meant the decentralization of the American church among near autonomous dioceses, which together with continuous and severe ethnic divisions, made development of national Catholic policy and organization extremely difficult.

The tradition of openness to American influence initiated by Carroll nevertheless persisted, however overshadowed by the immigrant tide. Meeting the needs of these newcomers became the church's main preoccupation. Catholic leaders multiplied social welfare agencies and charitable institutions under Catholic auspices and developed an activist spirit that was very apparent to foreign observers. They gave little thought to the causes of poverty, to the faults of the economic system or to the character of the environment, apparently believing that social distress could be solved by personal morality, a Christian upbringing, temperance, private charity and close association with the church.

Highly creative in practice, the church remained rigidly traditional in its thought. While working feverishly to redeem poor immigrant workers, many Catholics looked with a mixture of nostalgia and hope upon life in the countryside. In spite of the overwhelming predominance of city-dwellers, Catholicism produced more than its share of spokesmen who decried city life and urged action to settle Catholics on the land. Colonization projects flourished among Irish leaders before the Civil War; in the latter part of the century Bishop Spaulding recognized the opportunities for cultural creativity the city offered but he argued that the possibility of personal independence, political and economic freedom and Christian nurture made country life preferable to life in the city. Later, in the twentieth century, Bishop Edwin O'Hara's National Catholic Rural Life Conference carried on the tradition. The pervasiveness of the agrarian spirit is seen in a man like John A. Ryan, who devoted his entire life to the consideration of industrial problems and yet often referred to the superiority of life on the farm.

Realists like Bishop John Hughes answered exponents of Catholic colonization. Not only did the immigrant lack the money and training for successful farming, Hughes argued, but colonization was unwise from a religious point of view. Scattering Catholics throughout the West would leave them easy prey to Protestant ministers; the limited numbers of Catholic clergy could best deal with the immigrants in the concentrated urban setting. Still, neither Hughes nor any other Catholic spokesman thought to justify the city for its own sake. While rejecting back-to-the-land movements as impractical, Catholic leaders nevertheless continually demonstrated an attachment to the superior value of the rural environment for Christian living.

The system of Church life and administration that developed in the cities contained inherent problems for the church and its members. It was impossible to isolate Catholics whose economic activity called them into the mainstream of society. Especially in the second and third generation assimilation was inevitable, and this meant that laymen would live a major part of their lives in an atmosphere far different from that of the parish. American secular values of individual initiative, self-reliance, material progress and social mobility contrasted with the concepts of docility, obedience, authority and order emphasized in Catholic schools. In such a situation conflict was sure to arise; that it was not more severe, that more Catholics did not abandon their faith, that lay unrest did not become widespread was due to the unconscious acceptance in practice of the very thing the church's best leaders disliked, the secularization of the lives of individual Catholics, who relegated religion to a category separate and distinct from social and political life.

Nevertheless by the standards and goals it set for itself the Catholic church in the United States was remarkably successful.

Certainly if one accepts the normal criteria for judging these matters and compares the American experience with that of almost any country in the world, Catholicism in the United States was a standing rebuke to the rest of the church. Church attendance declined elsewhere, but in America it rose to remarkable heights. Only in America was there an almost total absence of anti-clericalism. Starting with a tiny band of isolated Catholics, the American church had become the most thriving branch of the church universal in little over a century.

There have been many attempts to explain this success. Certainly the arrangements of church and state in America were of central importance. A major divisive issue elsewhere was removed from the realm of controversy, for the First Amendment offered the Catholic minority full freedom to pursue their group objectives and to combat their opponents. Catholic adherence to the Constitution was full and complete and never wavered. Because the church itself did not possess political power, it could not be the target of political enemies and those fearful of Catholic political influence would have to point to European countries, or later, to the urban machines, and in both cases it was hard to hold the American church responsible for the real abuses that existed. Neither did its enemies directly possess political power, so that only rarely was it necessary for the church to adopt a political stance to ensure its rights. As John Courtney Murray so perceptively noted, only in America was there a liberal solution of the church-state problem, which placed no legal inhibitions on the church's right to be the church, to worship, to teach, to minister. Having achieved this, the hierarchy had no reason to aspire for more, and the resulting reduction of political ambition on the part of the church's leaders was itself undoubtedly an important benefit to American Catholicism.

There were other features of the American political system that were beneficial. The decentralized structure of government meant that the federal government's powers, which might have fallen into anti-Catholic hands, were limited and included few matters of great concern to the church, at least until the twentieth century. Education and social services, on the other hand, were state or, more frequently, municipal responsibilities, which meant that they were more easily influenced by the highly concentrated Catholic population. A minority in the nation, Catholics were frequently a powerful element in many states and even a majority in some cities, able to neutralize actions harmful to their interests and occasionally to persuade the state or city governments to adopt policies they desired.

Certainly the nation's abundance, its vast spaces, its tremendous resources, its preoccupation with mundane matters of material advancement prevented the growth of the political, ideological and national conflicts that wracked so many European countries and disrupted the church abroad. In these circumstances, growth itself was an asset, for, like other institutions in America, the Catholic church had its hands full simply surviving, keeping up with the massive pressures growth forced upon it, so that it had little energy and few resources to expend upon leisure pursuits or upon intensive intellectual controversies. The American church was beset by a good many internal disputes in the nineteenth century, from Trusteeism to Americanism, but they invariably were practical debates over policy resulting from expansion or ethnic rivalries rather than theological or moral issues.

If one had to find a word to describe the policies of the Catholic church in the nineteenth century it would undoubtedly be one of those words so frequently used to describe Americans: pragmatic, practical, adaptive, flexible. And surely what is striking to the American cultural historian is the extent to which the Catholic church in America adapted itself to meet the conditions of the new world. Bishop Carroll fought for national independence, John England for a national policy, Cardinal Gibbons for unity amid diversity. Each gave his primary attention to the needs of the church in this country and each was liberal in the sense that he granted wide scope to the situation and to human responsibility and correspondingly less to the dictates of the past and of authority. Indeed, as Philip Gleason has noted, the Catholic church was an "institutionalized immigrant," forced by the nature of the situation to change in order to survive.[12] Like the immigrant himself, the church could gain success only through such adaptation and would find in the end that not everyone would accept it as fully and completely

American while, at the same time, colleagues abroad would view its success with suspicion and even regard it as betrayal.

The pivot of life in the immigrant community was the parish church. In the Slavic sections of Pennsylvania mining towns, according to Victor Greene, "the Roman Catholic parish offered a common medium; in fact, the words 'settlement' and 'parish' in Polish, Lithuanian and Slovak are identical." [13] While the bishops, with the help of the religious orders, built and maintained a vast array of extra-parochial agencies for social and charitable service, the local congregation, and its affiliated organizations, was the object of the newcomers' loyalty and devotion. The pattern of religious life among the immigrant was never one solely of alienation, for family, ethnic association and religious congregation provided the young and new arrivals a world "where they felt both the security and identity which flow from a structured system of values and relationships." [14]

In many communities, though far from the majority, the parochial school was a central element. Archbishop John Hughes of New York had taken the lead in promoting separate schools for Catholic children after his failure to win public support in the early 1840s. Despite considerable resistance the American hierarchy, under considerable outside pressure, in 1884 adopted the goal of universal Catholic education. This policy accorded well with the desire of many immigrant groups to nurture both religious faith and national identity. "Early in the history of the Catholic church in America," Peter and Alice Rossi write, "the parochial schools became a symbol of the integrity of the church and of the attachment of the immigrant ethnic groups to their national background and to the Church." [15] While church leaders fought, often bitterly, over the policy of Catholic education, many immigrant communities made considerable sacrifices to build and maintain their own schools for their own children. To outsiders the parochial school seemed designed to preserve alien ways and inhibit the beneficent forces of assimilation but to the people themselves "parochial education, like most of the other cultural and social programs which the new citizens from central and southeastern Europe carried on, was from their point of view a nursery of two patriotisms," to the old country and the new, "to both of which the immigrants were fondly attached."[16]

Many immigrants from southern and eastern Europe brought with them to America a tradition of lay initiative and participation in church affairs. In mining towns and city ghettos laymen of Polish, Czech and Slavic extraction soon gathered together as a community, sought out a priest, built a church and often battled fiercely with the bishop for control of church property and pastoral appointments. "Trustee" type controversies remained endemic in the American church, transformed after the Civil War into conflicts between diverse ethnic communities and a predominently Irish hierarchy seeking to control an increasingly heterogeneous church. While the bishops usually succeeded in establishing their power over property and personnel, they did so in part by accommodating demands for foreign language parishes, priests and teaching sisters. Where they failed to do so, there could easily be schism or alienation from the church.

In the mining towns of northern Minnesota, for example, Archbishop John Ireland and his colleagues hoped that "melting pot" parishes would gradually eliminate traits of foreignness among his diverse Catholic flock. However, when vigorous lay action demanded separate churches, Ireland and his successors moved quickly to meet these demands. Elsewhere, in Italian communities, the story was quite different, for there the level of lay interest was low, and so was the willingness to make financial sacrifices for churches and schools. In addition the dominant Irish group looked upon the Italians, with their relatively relaxed attitude toward the sacraments and church discipline, with a distaste they seldom bothered to disguise. As a result the Italian language parishes were slow to develop and many newcomers were lost to the church.

Immigrant religious life involved a complex blending of religious and national traditions. For the Italians loyalty to church and homeland often involved severe conflict, as Italian patriots regarded the church as the major obstacle to national unification and progress. More typical was the close association of the church with national aspirations among the Irish and among many from Eastern Europe. Frequently the early parish and its priest identified religious and national programs, but later sharp competition arose between ethnic associations, which were largely religious in their foundation and composition, and other groups devoted to the national cause and embracing men indifferent or even hostile to the church. For some groups these intra-mural fights were the arena in which real ethnic consciousness was formed.

This interaction of religious and national sentiment in the life of the immigrant community was not an expression of alienation, of being outside the mainstream of American life. Rather it was part of the delicate but quite natural adjustment of men with strong communal loyalties to the requirements of a society characterized by a pluralism of voluntary association. The foreign language parish with its parochial school aided in the complex process of adaptation despite the fears of the Americanizers. The passionate demands for conformity that issued from the citadels of church and society were not simply demands for Americanization and elimination of old-world loyalties, but the expression of the values and ideals of already established groups, at first entirely native but soon augmented by Americanized members of early immigrant communities.

It is extremely important to recognize that this whole process belongs to our very recent history. Indeed ethnic factors remain crucial components of the American "mix" even today. Italian, French, German, even Irish, features remain present in broad sections of the American people, muted by the years but still capable of overt expression in particular situations. Yet, to a great extent ethnic identity has been replaced by religious identity, as Will Herberg noted in the 1950s. Catholicism became the vehicle of identification and group life as the coherent, homogeneous congregation was eroded by time and America's ever-corrosive mobility. The dramatic decline of inter-group conflict among "white ethnic" groups, the equally sharp decline of inter-church tension and the elimination of the clash between religion and the nationalism of the homeland all aided the process. Many Italians, Poles, Slovenes or Germans moved to the suburbs and made little effort to revive ethnic associations, blending easily into the melting pot congregations of the growing suburban communities. When Christian Democratic governments ruled in Western Europe and communist governments in Eastern, Catholic and non-Catholic had little reason to quarrel any longer, for they commonly accepted the one and abhorred the other. Nationality and religion were no longer in tension.

What this may mean is that the loyalty of many Americans, once centered on ethnic-religious institutions of which the parish was the nucleus, came in recent years to be centered on the church itself. "It is a good general rule that except where color is involved as well the specifically *national* aspect of most ethnic groups rarely survives the third generation in any significant terms," Daniel P. Moynihan and Nathan Glazer write. "The groups do not disappear, however, because of their religious aspect which serves as the basis of a subcommunity and a subculture."[17] Certain key issues, like that of public aid to parochial schools, help to sustain their loyalty and provide a focus for common concern and action.

While the recent studies of the church in the ethnic community have added greatly to our appreciation of the role of Catholicism in American life, it would be a mistake to exaggerate the impact of their findings. For example, the pattern of lay initiative remained confined to the congregational level. Even those conflicts that developed between religious and national goals often ended in strengthening clerical control and leadership. In addition, while the bishops showed considerable flexibility in dealing with ethnic tensions and rivalries, they did not allow lay influence to extend to any key areas of ecclesiastical responsibility. An occasional lay editor like James McMaster or Orestes Brownson was able through public opinion or Roman contacts to influence church policy, while the lay congresses at the end of the nineteenth century demonstrated that there was no lack of able and willing lay leaders. Yet, organizationally, the Catholic church retained its structure of extreme episcopal centralization.

This fact became more significant in the twentieth century as perceptive churchmen sought to overcome diocesan and ethnic divisions and create a truly national organization and a distinctive American Catholic culture. Education, social service, war and peace, foreign missions and a dozen other problems seemed to require national mobilization of resources and establishment of national priorities. Exclusion of the laity increasingly seemed to leaders with a national interest and vision a positive obstacle to Catholic progress. It was Father John Burke, later an architect of the National Catholic Welfare Conference, who put the matter squarely in 1906 in words that would be echoed time and again through the 1950s. "The organization of the church at present—whether rightly or wrongly so is not the point just now—makes the layman almost a complete extern," Burke wrote to Father William Kerby, the key figure in organizing the National Conference of Catholic Charities, one of the first solid national Catholic bodies. "Consequently," Burke continued, "the lack of group consciousness on the part of American lay Catholics, significant enough as it is, is, in my mind (and to speak frankly) due, not so much to the lay Catholics themselves, as to the manner in which ecclesiastical authority has prevented them from sharing in that which is a fundamental necessity for group consciousness, namely: an active, personal part in the organization."[18]

The experience of the church in the nineteenth century, with its complex of groups, associations, dioceses and institutions, made generalization extremely difficult. Despite the cost in cultural vitality, national organization and lay participation, Catholic leaders felt impelled to measure their success or failure by the extent to which they succeeded in retaining the loyalty of the immigrant masses and shaping a vigorous set of independent institutions. The first measure of success was the quantitative norm of growth: in numbers of Catholics, lay and clerical, in dioceses, parishes, religious orders and Catholic institutions. Throughout the nineteenth century the dominant objective of church leaders was to bring the benefits of organized institutional Catholicism to all Catholics within the borders of the United States. For John Carroll this meant securing the services of enough priests to administer the sacraments to the scattered Catholics of his huge nation-diocese. This missionary effort remained central until the eastern urban centers were inundated by wave after wave of immigration after 1840 when the focus of attention shifted to retaining the faith of the newcomers by supplying them with priests and churches, but also with a range of educational and social services. The key question then was essentially quantitative—how many men, women and children were baptized, in church on Sunday and contributing to the support of their pastor. Conversely no question was posed more frequently by the church's critics at home and abroad, and none aroused a more intense emotional reaction, than "Has the Immigrant Kept the Faith." The pride in growth was the opposite side of a coin the reverse image of which was the specter of leakage.

A secondary but nonetheless important criterion for success for American Catholic leaders was "respectability," acceptance by the dominant elites of American society as a permanent and beneficial element in national life. As leaders of a minority church forced to defend itself against native hostility and Protestant proselytization, Catholic bishops necessarily focused their primary attention on survival. Yet, whether themselves immigrants or deeply rooted natives, they valued the respect and esteem of their fellow citizens, and they recognized that the support of business and political leaders could reinforce the ecclesiastical loyalty of aspiring and ambitious laymen and serve as a point of pride for status-hungry Catholics.

Many bishops sought to cultivate the friendship of business leaders by serving as a disciplinary agency for the heavily Catholic labor force. From the first waves of Irish immigrants in the 1830s until the rapid entry of Catholics into the middle class during and after World War II, the American church has been predominently composed of workers. The efforts of some early leaders to break this dominance by establishing western agricultural communities proved unsuccessful, and Catholics remained concentrated in the industrial cities of the northeast and middle west. They worked for low wages, they lived in overcrowded and filthy slums, they drank heavily and had less respect for the law than their native-born neighbors. When times were hard, radicalism of word and deed could be attractive and labor violence did occur. Middle-class observers, frightened by the specter of radicalism, sometimes noted the large numbers of Catholics and even associated the church with labor radicalism. Church leaders knew of the European experience of labor agitation and anti-clericalism and they were determined to prevent its appearance in America. Preaching patience and resignation, on the one hand, they added the typically American message of self-help and success on the other. Themselves successful, proud of their personal achievements and those of the church, they could hardly help fighting ideologies and attitudes that seemed to challenge the social order. There was thus a natural alliance of bishops interested in docile, loyal congregations and employers interested in the same qualities among their workers. Archbishop Wood of Philadelphia helped expose and destroy the Molly Maguires; New York's Archbishop Corrigan intervened against Henry George in the 1886 election; John Ireland enjoyed a place in the upper reaches of Mark Hanna's Republican Party. Ireland and Corrigan might disagree over political parties and parochial schools, but they shared a common attachment to private property, free enterprise and faith in American opportunity. They were rewarded with the growing admiration of the nation's leading businessmen and their political allies. Presidents praised the church and James J. Hill built seminaries. Increasingly business leaders referred warmly to the civic and social outlook of the Catholic church.

The conservative views of most bishops can be illustrated in many ways. James Cardinal Gibbons, usually regarded as one of the church's more liberal leaders, believed that the church "renders invaluable aid to the state in upholding the civil law by moral and religious sanctions."[19] He rarely saw any significant evils on the landscape of American society and characteristically looked upon reform as more dangerous than adherence to the status quo. During the Progressive Era he charged that the referendum would "substitute the mob's law for established law," while the recall of judges would make them "habitual slaves of a capricious multitude." When Progressives tried to substitute direct election of senators for selection by state legislatures Gibbons called the latter system "a bulwark against popular encroachments." Although he had earned a reputation as a friend of labor by preventing Vatican condemnation of the Knights of Labor, Gibbons gave little encouragement to the American Federation of Labor or to those Catholics who were organizing support for the unions. "A conflict between labor and capital is as unreasonable as would be a contention between the head and the hands," Gibbons wrote, and on that basis he opposed strikes and looked to employer benevolence as the surest route to justice for the worker. Even after endorsing the highly progressive Bishops Program of Social Reconstruction in 1919, Gibbons continued to fear above all the growth of the power of the federal government.[20] Yet Gibbons was one of the hierarchy's most sensitive and progressive leaders.

Of course there were limits to accommodation, for bishops could not be too overt in their praise of more exploitative business leaders nor could they be too strong in their condemnation of labor activism. Cardinal Gibbons in his successful effort to prevent Roman censure of the Knights of Labor and Henry George, primarily acted to avoid disturbing the laity's warm regard for the hierarchy or arousing nativist hostility. The fact that he recognized that both movements were dying out and offered no real prospect for significant change made his action easier to take. Actually the hierarchy preferred to remain quiet, as it did in regard to the AFL, when it emerged from its silence only to attack extremism, as when socialism began to appear as a real threat after 1910 or when severe depression crippled its members and diminished its resources, as in the 1930s.

The avoidance of controversy was another way in which Catholic leaders sought to win respectability in America. The great divisive issues of the century actually found the church, like the nation, divided. The hierarchy avoided the slavery question and resisted Roman pressure to act positively to assist the free Negro. They rarely commented on the conduct of municipal politics and when they did they privately deplored corruption while publicly avoiding conflict with Catholic political leaders. In the 1890s even those most aware of the injustice of the American war against Spain kept their criticism to themselves. A policy of careful avoidance of controversy and private efforts to overcome those social, political and economic attitudes and practices that deviated from the American norm may have had little relation to implementing social justice and Christian democracy, but it promised retention of an undivided congregation and a reputation for caution and conservatism.

A third means by which the church gained respect as a valuable participant in national life was by its action in regard to its immigrant members. It is a major paradox of American Catholic history that church life was centered on internal and institutional problems, but that Catholicism was at the same time regarded by many as one of the "most effective of all agencies for democratization and Americanization."[21] Church historians have emphasized this in their stress on the need for the Catholic minority to win acceptance from native Americans by assimilating the immigrant. For those who saw America as basically hostile to Catholicism, Americanization was a means to overcome the fears of native Americans by reducing the foreign associations of the church. For the more optimistic leaders like Archbishop Ireland, who believed that America was at heart a Christian nation, assimilation could pave the way to the nation's conversion. Thus conservative and liberal leaders could agree in their opposition to foreign language separatism, while differing markedly in their assessment of American conditions, with the results described above.

A policy of Americanization was far more attractive to the dominant Irish-American wing of the hierarchy than it was to people from continental Europe. The desire of some German Americans for ethnically defined dioceses, and of national congregations for relatively autonomous parishes, threatened the unity of the church and seemed to confirm the nativist charge that Catholicism was essentially a foreign intrusion incapable of full identification with the nation. Yet the opposite extreme of deliberate Americanization was equally dangerous, for it might divide the hierarchy from the masses of non-English-speaking Catholics and bring down the wrath of Rome, succeptible as the Vatican was to pressures from the immigrant's friends in Europe. Thus a middle course was necessary, one which allowed a rhetorical assertion of Americanism but carefully accommodated demands for ethnic congregations and minority representation. Juridical unity and theological consensus coexisted with diocesan autonomy, competing social agencies and educational institutions and a variegated group life. A hierarchy that battled throughout its history for freedom from Roman control and dictation and pioneered the kind of national episcopal conferences so much in vogue since the Second Vatican Council never achieved real unity itself but struggled powerfully to accommodate the multitude of conflicting loyalties within its ranks.

The church's quest for success and respectability was simply a reflection of the aspirations of its members. Timothy Smith has argued persuasively that immigration involved "a process of self-selection" which "turned upon ambition, upon a wish and a will to believe that the future was more real than the past, and upon a readiness to accept change and make adjustments." [22] Earlier historians argued that the newcomer's ambitions were frustrated and that he was left, disappointed, alienated and unhappy in America's burgeoning ghetto slums. But recent scholarship challenges this view, noting among many immigrants a passion for success that was often overwhelming. For some wealth was needed to return to Europe to purchase land; others transferred their land hunger to America. In either case the quest for property was intense, producing "an almost super-human sense of thrift."[23] The concern for success and respectability of the bishops and their followers thus reinforced each other, producing subtle but significant shifts in popular attitudes and church teachings.

One evidence of these changes occurs in the occasional pastoral letters of the bishops in the nineteenth century. In 1829, citing the well-known dictum that it does one no good to gain the world and lose his soul, the bishops urged their people to teach their children "to be industrious, to be frugal, to be humble, and fully resigned to the will of God." In 1840 the bishops modified their stance to urge all "to be content with the moderate acquisition of honest industry." A quarter century later the hierarchy still could not accept with equanimity the scramble for riches, warning against giving children an education fitted less to their needs than to the aspirations of their parents. "Prepare your children for the duties of the state or condition of life they are likely to be engaged in," they instructed the flock. "Do not exhaust your means by bestowing on them an education that may unfit them for these duties. This will be a sure source of disappointment and dissatisfaction, both for yourselves and for them." But, by 1884, the bishops had come to be concerned not with over-education but with the tendency of many to put their children to work at an early age in order to supplement the family income. Do not "hasten to take the children from school," they now urged, "but give them all the time and all the advantages that they have the capacity to profit by."[24]

Given all the conflicting currents that existed in American Catholicism and the varying perspectives foreign and native observers developed in attempting to understand that phenomenon, the Americanist controversy of the late nineteenth century should hardly have been surprising. The controversies that developed within the hierarchy after the Third Plenary, Council of Baltimore covered the whole range of issues, all of which were related to the general problem of the stance that the church should adopt in American society. On dogma, religious practice and loyalty to Rome the hierarchy was united. All the bishops accepted the diocesan framework and agreed that the first priority must be given to the preservation of the faith of the immigrant. Differences developed that involved ethnic rivalries, personality conflicts and differences in spirit. One group, led by Archbishop John Ireland, was enthusiastically and self-consciously American sharing the optimism and confident nationalism of the period. Ireland was an innovator and his enthusiasm for his age and his country was a source of much of the conflict. He believed that America was essentially Christian and he wanted Americans to see the church as the foundation and support of their ideals. Democracy presented a new situation and required revision of traditional attitudes; "The people are the power," he wrote, "and the church must be with the people." The church, which had been truly American in Carroll's day, must eliminate practices which made it appear "foreign in heart and act" Ireland believed. He summed up the need in 1889:

> The church in America must be of course as Catholic as in Jerusalem or Rome but so far as her garments may be colored to suit the environment she must be American. There is danger: we receive large accessions of Catholics from foreign countries. God witnesses that they are welcome. I will not intrude on their personal affections and traits but these if foreign shall not encrust themselves upon the church.[25]

The other faction was more conservative in temper, preoccupied with the problems of immigrant communities and less exposed to the crosscurrents of American life. This group, which included Archbishop Corrigan of New York, Bishop Bernard McQuaid of Rochester and several leaders of the German American Catholics, considered themselves fully American but tended to see problems in terms of the European experience of the church, fearing particularly the growth of liberalism and modernism in the United States. More important, the atmosphere was embittered by the conflicts of nationality. German American Catholics centered around Milwaukee and St. Louis disliked the disproportionate number of Irish bishops and the subordination of German- to English-speaking parishes in some cities. The Germans further resented the Americanizing tendencies of Ireland and Cardinal Gibbons. In the 1880s Catholics in Germany led by Peter Cahensly charged that millions of immigrants to the United States were being lost to the faith because of the American hierarchy's failure to provide national parishes and its insistence on the destruction of national customs and institutions. The nationality question arose again in connection with education in the 1890s. Although the American bishops had in 1886 re-emphasized the importance of Catholic schools, and Rome had held that the public schools contained "evils of the gravest kind" and were "most dangerous and very much opposed to Catholicity," Archbishop Ireland nevertheless suggested the possibility of recognizing and implementing the state's responsibilities in all education. He told the National Education Association in 1890 that he regretted the need for parochial schools and urged the cooperation and possible union of the two school systems. For the German Americans the parochial schools were a central vehicle for the preservation of German language and customs, and they saw Ireland's words and actions as a threat to their cultural existence.

Their anger was intensified by Ireland's support of the proposed Bennett Law in Wisconsin requiring the use of English in all schools. They found an ally in Bishop Spalding who was opposed to state interference in education and hostile to Ireland's educational ideas. The Germans were also joined by Corrigan and McQuaid who disliked Ireland's influence with

Gibbons and had been seeking a basis for attack. McQuaid expressed his feelings in a published letter to the *American Ecclesiastical Review:* "What leads some of our bishops in the United States to fall down before the state in abject slavery for the possible gain of a few dollars and at the same time to sacrifice the best spiritual interests of our children is to me more than a mystery."[26] He went on to denounce "the new liberalism that has of late sprung up among some of our bishops under the leadership of Cardinal Gibbons, with regard to secret societies and parochial schools." The opposition appealed to Rome, which equivocated, but the controversy left a legacy of bitterness, best seen in the alienation of the conservatives and the German Americans from the Catholic University.

These ethnic tensions accentuated by the school question were the basis for serious divisions within the American church. Other issues soon arose, including participation by Catholic bishops in ecumenical religious Congresses, the appearance of Archbishop John Keane at Harvard University, the conduct and policy of Catholic University of America. The issues became world-wide with the publication of a French translation of the life of Isaac Hecker, which stimulated a discussion of the significance of American Catholic experience in Europe. Conservative French commentators accused the church in America as represented by Hecker and Ireland of theological minimism, social liberalism and religious accommodation, and they received support from disgruntled elements in the United States. After several years of intensifying discussion in France, Rome and the United States, Leo XIII in 1899 addressed a letter to Cardinal Gibbons condemning certain tendencies called "Americanism," in effect warning American Catholics against placing greater emphasis on their loyalty to America than on their Catholicism. The pope condemned the proposition that "in order more easily to bring over to Catholic doctrine those who dissent from it the church should adapt itself somewhat to our advanced civilization and relaxing their ancient rigor, show some indulgence to modern popular theories and methods." Further, he denounced the contention "that certain liberties ought to be introduced into the church so that, limiting the exercise and viligence of its powers, each one of the faithful may act more freely in pursuance of his own natural bent and capacity," that, in short, the church should imitate in its internal life the liberty of civil society. Finally, Leo condemned the theories which were attributed to Hecker: the rejection of external religious guidance, the deprecation of passive in favor of active virtues and the dislike of religious vows.[27]

The effect of the encyclical was to deaden the Americanizing impulse of Ireland's followers, though the quest for a full integration of Americanism and Catholicism remained the central theme of liberal and intellectual Catholicism in the years to come. For the time being a great silence fell over the American church, cooperation with non-Catholics was stifled and Catholic leaders labored for years under the threat of heresy. The condemnation of Americanism abruptly killed off the dialogue between church and America that Ireland had tried to promote and dealt a blow to American Catholic self-confidence from which the American Catholic mind never effectively recovered.

Ireland and his supporters had attempted to mediate between the nationalities and the Protestant American establishment. In their desire to purge the church of its foreignness they saw Americanization as a practical problem in terms of nationalities while Rome saw it as a religious question and both were right. In the nineteenth century it was an ethnic problem but in the twentieth century when large numbers of third and fourth generation Catholics were fully absorbed in the population it became a religious question. Increasingly it was clear that the melting pot did not work and that becoming American did not mean the loss of identity and the melting into the general mass of the population. In the middle of the twentieth century concern is felt both over the intellectual rejection of America symbolized by the condemnation of Americanism and the over-identification of Catholics with certain aspects of American life. Ireland's enthusiasm for the America of the 1890s mirrored the general Catholic acceptance of the structure of American life and thought, but his devotion was too complete, too optimistic. To argue as Ireland did that Catholics could wholeheartedly accept America because it was a Christian nation was only a little more of an advance beyond the ghetto than was the exclusivism of his opponents. A mature American Catholicism required recognition of the facts of pluralism and secularism and the interpretations of those facts in a historical and Christian perspective.

Most significantly the condemnation of America reflected the difficulties American Catholics had in taking satisfaction in the successes they achieved. In the years that followed Pope Leo's famous letter to Cardinal Gibbons, the American church would continue on its pragmatic and flexible course yearning for acceptance as American and taking pride in its growing wealth and power. Only in the years that followed World War II would Catholics achieve the respectability and status for which they had striven so long and only then would the rest of the country acknowledge fully and completely their right to be American. Yet, when that happened, as symbolized by the election of John Kennedy in 1960 and the enormous popularity of Pope John in the United States in that same period, American Catholics would find their success less than satisfying. They would develop within themselves the same kinds of criticism of their church and their community that had been leveled at it for years by outsiders: Catholics abroad and non-Catholics at home. Then indeed one would find dissenting Catholics echoing in their assessment of their church's failure thoughts that could have been taken directly from the writings of conservative nineteenth-century Catholics in Europe or nativist anti-Catholics at home. The critiques of many of those younger Catholics who are characterized as the new breed mirror a sudden awareness that the relationship between church and society and thus the assessment of success and failure is an ongoing problem never fully resolved in any historical situation. Each generation's successes frequently seem failures to the next. This often seems a source of agony and tragedy but it is also a reason for rejoicing in the freedom that it brings to each man and to each generation to fulfill as best they can, in the situations they face, the demands of the gospel.

5
CATHOLICS
AND AMERICAN PLURALISM

The American Catholic church that emerged from the Americanism controversy developed with few major changes down through World War II. It was a church that presented an outward appearance of unity, even of monolithic conformity, but that nevertheless contained a great diversity of peoples and cultures, ideals and devotions. Passionately loyal to Rome, it was nevertheless clearly an American church. Unmatched in their affirmations of America, Catholic leaders frequently clashed with others over the meaning of that Americanism. Possessing after World War I a national organization intended to coordinate its wide ranging activities, the church nevertheless remained a loose federation of principalities, with each bishop supreme at home, able, and often willing, to ignore the statements of the national conference and its affiliated agencies. Divided into dioceses, ethnic groups and associations, competitive organizations for youth, charities, missions and higher education, American Catholicism could unite against external attack but could rarely mobilize for positive action in pursuit of common goals.

The most direct impact of the condemnation of Americanism was felt in the area of scholarship, intellectual life and culture. Combined with the official attack upon Modernism a decade later, the conservative counterattack on the Americanizing policies of high church leaders stifled a nascent cultural renaissance and imposed a long era of repression on Catholic scholars, schools and seminaries.[1] Pioneering efforts in theology were all but destroyed, so that for half a century American theologians devoted themselves "largely to canonical, liturgical, and pastoral topics; the field of fundamental theology was more or less ignored."[2] Despite occasional efforts by heroic men to reopen channels for creative exchange with the general culture of the nation, the over-all atmosphere of Catholic life remained dull, drab and defensive. Lacking effective leadership American Catholicism could not overcome the parochialism of its ethnic and regional constituencies. A long list of writers and artists raised as Catholics fled to the freer air outside the ghetto, rejecting the whole complex of institutions, values and ideals that had dominated their youth.[3] Those who remained were forced by circumstances and loyalty to their church and their people to devote inordinate attention to their defense. Several Catholic scholarly organizations were founded after World War I, but it was many years before they pursued as their main objective the dialogue between their religion and their discipline. Instead they provided a focal point for group pride and a defensive bulwark for scholars whose non-Catholic peers re garded them with suspicion if not outright disdain. *Commonweal* magazine, founded in 1921 to promote American Catholic culture, gave over many of its pages to the defense of the church against outside attacks, while such leaders of Catholic social action as John A. Ryan felt compelled to allocate large portions of their time and energy to disputes with those outside the church. Often it seemed that proponents of change within the church, in order to gain a hearing from their fellow Catholics, had to constantly demonstrate their loyalty through vigorous controversy with the presumed enemies of Catholic faith. The effect of all this on the quality, character and depth of Catholic thought can hardly be measured, but it was surely profound.

Yet, as was pointed out in the preceding chapter, the Catholic ghetto was a complex phenomenon, blending ethnic, religious and class considerations and meeting needs that were not only defensive but instrumental to the people's quest for mobility, status and respectability. Pope Leo XIII and Pope Pius X could and did impose sharp limits on the speculations of Catholic scholars, but they could not, if they had wished, stop the drive of the church and its people for acceptance, power and influence. The process of assimilation continued and the hierarchy pursued the middle road between narrow exclusivism on the one hand and headlong Americanization on the other. Schools and social organizations helped preserve the immigrant communities and their ties to the church, but the bishops placed no unnecessary barriers in the way of the social acceptance, economic advancement or political independence of their congregations. As a result there was, as Father Thomas T. McAvoy put it, "a gradual Americanization of the Catholic immigrant without glamor and with little Catholic intellectual leadership for other Americans to see."[4]

In addition, the bishops were compelled by the aspirations of Catholic immigrants, and even more of their children and grandchildren, to accept, indeed, the secularization of life characteristic of modern America. "Catholics should not be the hewers of wood and the drawers of water," a diocesan paper editorialized in the 1930s. "They should lead upright lives, but they should also, if possible, make a big success of life."[5] It was one of the conditions of the church's success in holding the masses in the faith that it was willing to assist this yearning for mobility and status while tolerating many American practices inimical to its teachings, which sometimes meant passive acceptance of racial discrimination, silence in the face of urban political corruption and explicit support for the dominant social and economic values.

Yet, many features of Catholic life were bound to change as the pace of assimilation intensified. Attitudes and institutions established to meet the needs of the nineteenth century were given new life by the large influx of Catholics before World War I. Thereafter the process of change slowly transformed group life until, after World War II, a new situation confronted the American church, generating among many a sense of the growing chasm which separated the received traditions from the needs and aspirations of a new generation. The very success of the church in meeting its old objectives of membership and respectability would provide the occasion for criticism, division and, it was hoped, renewal.

One feature of this conflict between established patterns of Catholic life and the needs of modern America emerges from the realization that the melting pot did not work. Until World War II American Catholicism was clearly a working-class denomination composed of a multitude of ethnic groups, each conscious of its distinctiveness. In the years following the war the social composition of the church changed dramatically as thousands of Catholics increased their incomes, moved to the suburbs and joined new parishes devoid of clear ethnic association, offering the prospect that Catholicism would become a "melting pot church in a mosiac culture." Yet many Catholics were left behind in the city, where they increasingly felt the pressure of urban decay, high taxes and racial tension. By the end of the 1960s the new social diversity of the church would manifest itself in bitter controversy over problems inside and outside denominational boundaries. Those who would grasp the complexity of the present situation would do well to examine these matters carefully.

The experience of the American Catholic church during wartime has sometimes had its ambiguities but on the whole has provided the church with unique opportunities to advance its principal objectives of building internal unity and winning respectability in the eyes of other Americans. Vigorous Catholic participation in the American Revolution, together with the aid given the rebels by Catholic France, contributed to reducing the intense anti-Romanism of colonial America and allowing native Catholics to enter as full participants in the building of a new nation. In the 1840s many suspected that Catholic soldiers would refuse to fight against their co-religionists in Mexico but, despite the efforts of some to demonstrate a high rate of desertion among Catholic troops, the church was able to point with pride to the enthusiastic participation of its Catholic citizens in the war effort. In the agony of the Civil War the Catholic church almost alone succeeded in avoiding sectional division. It participated actively on both sides and emerged from the war united and with its prestige enhanced north and south of the Mason-Dixon line. Although many Catholic prelates tried hard to avoid war with Spain in the 1890s, they endorsed it when it came and joined the national rejoicing over American victories. World War I helped subordinate ethnic conflicts within the church and united it for wartime service, which won wide applause from non-Catholics and laid the basis for permanent national organization after the war.

This record was unchanged by World War II. Although isolationist sentiment had been powerful in Catholic circles before

Pearl Harbor, the circumstances of American entry into the war and the nature of Japanese and German aggression made the transition to war relatively easy, even if abrupt. The only flaw was the *de facto* alliance with the Soviet Union. Throughout the war, most Catholic leaders refrained from overt attacks on Russia while never wholly abandoning their earlier fears. Nevertheless, whatever concern may have been felt about the long-run consequences of Russian success, Catholic efforts to win the war were full and enthusiastic. Interfaith controversies of earlier days were overwhelmed by common desire for victory. Catholic prestige, already heightened by President Franklin Roosevelt's appointment of Myron Taylor as Ambassador to the Vatican, was further increased by the publicity given the world-wide trips of the military vicar Archbishop Francis Spellman of New York and to the pope's efforts to end the war.

Unfortunately the war terminated as well the progress that had been made in the 1930s in relaxing internal conformity and beginning some moderate self-criticism within the church. The Catholic Worker movement, a major source of these changes, became more and more preoccupied in the late 1930s with the moral problems of modern war. In the period that intervened between Hitler's invasion of Poland and the Japanese attack on Pearl Harbor, the pacifist position of the Worker blended well with the isolationist stance of many Catholics. When Archbishop John McNicholas of Cincinnati called for a League of Catholic Conscientious Objectors against the imposition of a peace time draft, Dorothy Day responded positively, although she expressed doubts about the sincerity of much Catholic opposition to war and militarism, which, she feared, was rooted in nationalism and hostility to Russia rather than in strong convictions about the violence of modern war. Once war came, the Catholic Worker was isolated, abhorred by many Catholics and deserted by not a few of its own members. On this question as on many others, the war had the effect of stifling dissent and occasioning a new, more solid consensus on issues in both church and society.

Thus World War II unified the Catholic people and enhanced the prestige of the church in the eyes of non-Catholic Americans. A number of factors ensured that these things would be continued into the postwar years. Internally the major historical divisions of the church had been rooted in ethnic diversity. By 1945 the doors of America had been all but closed to foreigners for almost a quarter of a century and the course of time was eroding ethnic tensions. The renewed wave of anti-Catholicism that followed the war, spearheaded by Paul Blanshard, while a serious attack upon the church, lacked the preoccupation with foreignness and native purity that had characterized earlier movements of this type.

Moreover, the postwar years were marked by a return to religion on the part of most Americans. Church membership and attendance reached all time highs and pollsters found it hard to locate dissenters from basic Jewish and Christian doctrinal and moral teachings. Even among the intellectuals, long leading proponents of secularism and agnosticism, there was a marked resurgence of interest in religious matters. Arthur M. Schlesinger, Jr., a young historian and leader of the Americans for Democratic Action published a book in 1946 that laid out a position of realistic moderation heavily influenced by the thought of theologian Reinhold Niebuhr. *Partisan Review,* a leading organ of the politically involved intelligentsia, came out with a special series on the revival of interest in religion among scholars and political intellectuals.[6] As Edmund Wilson explained, the war, with its technological destructiveness culminating in the unleashing of atomic energy, together with the overwhelming sense of guilt engendered by revelation of the German destruction of European Jewry, ended once and for all the optimistic certitudes of rationality and progress long characteristic of Western liberalism. The mood resulting from this experience was subdued, chastened, even humble, and led men to hearken to long obscured notions of sin, evil and guilt. Such a stance was bound to make intellectuals less dogmatic in their attitude toward the churches and to sharply reduce the emotional intensity of anti-Catholic sentiments among traditionally hostile liberals. While many would decry the authoritarianism and anti-democratic activity of the church and its leaders, few would any longer go beyond this to a passionate assault on Catholicism itself.

An additional factor in the postwar years was the development of the cold war. With almost incredible speed the nation moved from alliance with Russia to a militant hostility to communism at home and abroad. The church, long the world's leading opponent of communism, played no small part in the development of the cold war, and its views now were widely accepted by men beyond the confines of the church. As the anti-communist stance became identified with patriotism and virtue, the prestige of the church was vastly enhanced and its loyalty to America was less and less questioned.

In addition, the new CIO unions and the opportunities for higher education offered by the G.I. Bill of Rights resulted in significant improvements in the social and economic well-being of the Catholic population. Middle-class status seemed to complete the drive for success, but many felt a strong desire that their arrival be registered by the broader community. The new church in the suburbs, with its modern school, the huge rally for the family rosary, massive campaigns against pornography or birth control, all helped impress outsiders with the power and importance of the Catholic population. Any evidence, or apparent evidence, of second-class citizenship was now doubly felt and doubly attacked. The drive for public aid for parochial schools took on a renewed force as in state after state campaigns were mounted for direct financial assistance, school bussing, textbooks and released time from public schools for religious instruction. The courts, while holding firm against direct aid for church-related schools, registered the changing balance of forces by opening the door to varying methods of indirect assistance. The result was a boom in Catholic education unmatched in history, and Catholic parents, proud of their schools, contributed mightily to their support. In 1950 there were over three million children in Catholic elementary and high schools. A decade later 4.2 million children were in grade school alone, while another 844,000 were in secondary institutions.[7] This growth was only one index of the unprecedented progress and prosperity of American Catholicism in the years following World War II.

This prosperity was reflected in the increased self-confidence of the Catholic population, but it excited a good deal of opposition, which in turn reinforced the unity and solidarity of

Catholics. Yet these new inter-group conflicts were subtly different from earlier encounters. While extremists on both sides perpetuated the arguments of an earlier period, the general debate turned upon legitimate questions of public policy and political process. Few non-Catholics denied the right of the church and its members to equal citizenship and almost none saw the problem in nativist terms. On the other hand some Catholics dissented from their church's position or refrained from assaulting the religious views of the church's opponents. These were signs that tensions were declining and that older passions were being replaced by natural and legitimate institutional conflicts arising from the differing interests and perspectives of groups that recognized the other's right to exist in a democratic society.

These postwar arguments about schools, censorship and other issues that divided the nation's religious bodies also provided evidence of the continuing complexity of the assimilation process. Will Herberg contended in the 1950s that the immigrants were being absorbed through the "triple melting pot" of the three great faiths. As men ceased to identify themselves in terms of national origin, they identified even more strongly with their church, so that the dramatic social changes of the postwar years, which opened the door to success for thousands of children of immigrants, were accompanied by an equally dramatic rise in religious affiliation and church attendance. This conclusion was confirmed by the studies of Nathan Glazer and Daniel P. Moynihan, who discovered that ethnic identity, while still alive among residents of New York City, played a secondary role to church affiliation in shaping group behavior. Even if class differences between Catholics and Protestants, still marked in the 1940s, steadily declined, religious differences and conflicts persisted. In the pioneering ecumenical discussions of the 1950s, for example, few participants argued about doctrinal questions, concentrating instead on problems essentially rooted in group interests. On such questions, as long as the participants accepted the processes of accommodation and compromise, conflicts could easily be handled within normal political channels.

However, even these discussions often overlooked some basic political disagreements which existed along religious groups.

Protestant leaders, on the one hand, frequently sympathized with the plight of Catholic parents who supported separate schools while at the same time paying taxes for the public school system. But many who could understand Catholic goals nevertheless disliked Catholic tactics. Again and again non-Catholic spokesmen condemned "pressure," the use of organized political action by Catholics to obtain their ends. Catholics who urged other Catholics to vote as a bloc, or who threatened to inundate public schools with Catholic students, or who refused to approve bond issues or back federal aid to education until justice was provided for their school system, were accused of using political tactics that violated the spirit of American democracy. Some Catholics agreed. "Whoever is responsible," John Cogley wrote in 1959, "the image of the Catholic church which has been created in the American mind, is not that of the church of Christ. It is the image of a power structure."[8]

Such attacks reflected what Richard Hofstadter calls the "Yankee-Protestant" political ethic, which regarded the public arena as a locus of rational discourse in which decisions were reached by disinterested individuals motivated solely by a concern for civic welfare. Many Catholics had long regarded that ethic as hypocritical, voiced by spokesmen of churches whose members had frequently acted in a concerted manner to deprive Catholics of their rights; prohibition, the Oregon school case, organized opposition to an American Ambassador at the Vatican as well as the school question provided ready examples. Convinced that justice was only done to those strong enough to demand it and aware of the function of pressure in the American political process, these Catholics saw no reason why they should not act together to gain what they regarded as justice for themselves.

Differences between Catholics and others, then, persisted in American society long after specifically ethnic consciousness had declined. These differences, as John Cogley's statement indicates, even penetrated into the Catholic community, as individuals and groups within it identified on specific issues with the values of men on the other side. Increasingly it was clear that the church would have to come to terms with internal diversity while, at the same time, recognizing that Americanization did not necessarily bring about the elimination of conflicts with other groups in the society. For better or worse, men's perceptions would be shaped by their differing histories and perspectives, and all would have to accept the demands of a changing sytem of pluralism of faiths, programs and politics.

Perhaps the nature of the new pluralism can be illustrated by reference to Catholic-Jewish relations. Both groups had similar experiences in America, dominated by their minority status in a predominantly Protestant culture. There was a small group of Catholics in Maryland and Pennsylvania at the time of the American Revolution, but the real development of the Catholic population did not come until the two decades before the Civil War, when a flood of refugees from famine in Ireland arrived in Boston, New York, Philadelphia and other port cities of the Eastern United States. They were followed by significant numbers of Catholics from Germany and Canada, and, after 1890, by another huge tide of Catholic immigration from Italy, Poland and the Austro-Hungarian lands of southeastern Europe. The Irish took control of the Catholic hierarchy in the 1840s and held onto church leadership for over a century. Their efforts were directed primarily to maintaining the religious loyalties of the immigrants and fighting off the attacks of nativists and anti-Catholics, from the Know Nothings to the American Protective Association and the Ku Klux Klan.

The nation's Jewish population had a similar evolution. Few Jews were in America before the nineteenth century, when a steady flow of German Jews began entering the country. Establishing themselves in urban centers of the northeast and middle west, the German Jewish community achieved steady advancement in American society and faced relatively little outward hostility or anti-Semitism. In the post-Civil War years, however, the Jewish population began to swell with refugees from the rising tide of anti-Semitism in Central and Eastern Europe. It was the presence of large numbers of clearly "foreign" Jews that stimulated the growth of discrimination, symbolized by the exclusion of Joseph Seligman from a Saratoga resort in 1877. Unable to ignore the newcomers, the Germans instead turned to care for them, assuming a stance of leadership similar to that of the Irish in the Catholic population.

Outright tension between Jews and Catholics was relatively rare before the 1930s. Both groups were heavily urban, both were working class and both felt themselves to be minorities in a Protestant-Yankee country. Their interests often converged, whether in demands for municipal public works in time of depression or in fighting against overt manifestation of Protestant dominance in the public school system. Archbishop John Hughes of New York expressed the common interest of Catholics and Jews in the maintenance of church-state separation: "No matter what sect is assailed, extend to it, in common with all your fellow citizens, a protecting hand. If the Jew is oppressed stand by the Jew. Thus will all be secured alike in the common enjoyment of the blessings of civil and religious liberty, and justly obnoxious union of church and state be more effectively prevented."[9]

Catholics were not prominent in either of the sectors of American life where anti-Semitism flourished before World War I. One of these areas was the agricultural middle west and south, where the Populist movement was strongest. Although there were few Jews in these sections of the country, the Populists often manifested an obsession with Jews, a phenomenon undoubtedly due to their preoccupation with monetary problems and indebtedness, interpreted within an age-old folklore of Jewish financial power. The Shylock symbolism of the Populists was a recurrence of a traditional, if no less vicious, folk tradition, to which was added the American farmer's own suspicion of the city and its immigrant residents.[10]

While Populist anti-Semitism was largely rhetorical, the anti-Jewish discrimination that flourished in the east was real and concrete. In New York, Philadelphia and adjacent resorts and spas, discrimination against Jews became the norm between 1890 and 1900. The whole panoply of practices that constitute American anti-Semitism: restrictive covenants, "no Jews need apply signs" in businesses, discriminatory hiring and promotion policy, developed during these years. The reasons for these developments bring us to a subject which must dominate every discussion of intergroup relations in the United States: the concept of status. What Populists and WASPs had in common in the 1890s was a sense of declining significance and importance

in American society. The farmer, long the hero, the ideal
American, was becoming the rube, the hayseed. The city and
the corporation were the new focal points of success, and the
farmer could not command honor, prestige or government support. He lashed out at the symbols of the forces that oppressed
him: the trust, the banks, the immigrants, the Jews. In more
sophisticated circles of the east a similar process was underway.
Old-line Yankee leaders were being shunted aside, sometimes by
new wealth generated by postwar industrial expansion, sometimes by the manager of the national corporation which
brought out the local small business, sometimes by the machine
politician, often Irish, who with immigrant support, pushed the
Yankees out of civic leadership. Henry Adams was merely the
most self-conscious representative of those old-time families
who were less important and who knew it. And Henry Adams
was an anti-Semite. His kind drew together, they became the
four hundred, the lines of social, as distinct from economic and
political, mobility tightened. There was developing what Digby
Baltzell has characterized as the Protestant establishment. No
longer sure of itself, increasingly self-conscious, increasingly
aware that it too was a minority and deeply disturbed by the
fact, some, though not all, drew up their defenses against
Catholics and Jews.[11]

Not only were Catholics unrepresented in the two groups
who fostered modern American anti-Semitism, they were almost equally important objects of Populist and WASP disdain.
They too were not to apply and not to advance, they too were
foreign and strange. So while Catholics and Jews did not always
live in perfect harmony, they were less aware of each other than
of the common enemy. Yet as every student of such matters
knows, discussions of minorities who are persecuted are often
loaded. Neither Jews nor Catholics were simon-pure believers in
social freedom, and both groups had their own hostile or
status-craving elements. Thus it was to be expected that as time
went on Catholics, gaining power and prestige, would find
reason to join in discriminating against Jews. Catholic anti-
Semitism manifested itself in an overt form during the decade
of the depression.

In the 1930s gangs attacked Jews on the streets of Brooklyn

and other eastern cities with little interference from the police, while organizations calling themselves the Christian Front or the Christian Mobilizers conducted "Buy Christian" campaigns, cheered the Fuehrer and denounced prominent American Jews. The American hero of these groups was a Catholic priest, Father Charles E. Coughlin. Early in the Depression Father Coughlin had emerged as one of the nation's most powerful men, the champion of the common man and the "shepherd of discontent." His Sunday radio sermons on socioeconomic topics had a huge audience; at his call letters and telegrams flooded Congress; and his was generally acknowledged to be the "most persuasive voice in America." He lashed out at the greed and hypocrisy of the old order, its low wages, its unstable farm prices, its financial speculation. Franklin Roosevelt welcomed his support in 1932 and in the early days of his administration. Calling for active government assistance to relieve the distress caused by the Depression, he assisted his listeners in making the transition from the traditional American fear of federal action to the positive government initiated by the New Deal. As a Catholic priest, he did more to popularize knowledge of the social encyclicals than all previous American spokesmen combined. His indictment of the plutocracy and support for inflationary schemes, together with his role as a priest, enabled him to draw support both from western farms and industrial cities, areas sharply divided in the days of Prohibition and the Klan.

Gradually, however, he drifted away from the New Deal and from the sources of his support. Adopting the debtor-oriented schemes of the earlier populists, he became increasingly dogmatic, insisting that drastic fiscal reorganization was a prerequisite for any just and lasting social reform. He identified the monetization of silver and the destruction of the Federal Reserve System with the dictates of Christianity and became increasingly critical of New Deal hesitations and half measures. The Administration's refusal to carry through drastic monetary reforms he took as evidence of its continuing alliance with the plutocracy, while its labor policies and the increased centralization of government he began to denounce as communistic. Intensified by personal slights, these disagreements culminated

in the radio orator's break with Roosevelt and his organization
of a new political party to contest the presidential election of
1936. Father Coughlin challenged his Catholic followers' traditional loyalty to the Democratic party and their gratitude to
Roosevelt for the substantial gains they received from the New
Deal. On the other hand he challenged as well the traditional
suspicion of the church and its clergy among his agrarian Protestant followers. It was a desperate gamble and Coughlin lost;
with the overwhelming defeat of his candidates he retired from
the air, disillusioned with the American people of whom he had
thought himself the spokesman. But several months later he was
back, determined to save the nation from the consequences of
its action in choosing the politicians, the plutocrats and the
Communists over Christian and American principles.

In the late 1930s Father Coughlin became even more desperate, predicting the early advent of a communist society in the
United States and finding indications in the penetration by the
"reds" into all sectors of American life. But there was a new
element in his thought, one that had been implicit earlier and
which admirably served to tie together the twin evils of communism and plutocracy: anti-Semitism. Most, though not all, of
the financial oligarchy were Jewish, he discovered. They controlled the press and propagandized against Christians, most
notably during the Spanish Civil War. They were also the key
figures in the communist movement, having dominated the
Russian Revolution and subsequent party activity. Nazism, like
Fascism before it, was a "defense mechanism" against communism; to prevent a "red" takeover Hitler, Mussolini and
Franco had acted "as patriots rising to a challenge." Fascism,
Coughlin contended through his weekly paper, *Social Justice,*
"was and is Europe's answer to Russian Communism's threat of
world revolution, and it is the bulwark against long active
agencies of destruction."[12]

The Jews were persecuted abroad, according to Father
Coughlin, because of their association with communism and
their lack of patriotism. For the same reasons they would
eventually suffer in the United States, he believed, particularly
if they continued to demand action against Nazism while ignoring the plight of Christians under persecution in Russia, Mexico

and Spain. He reminded them that to destroy Nazism it was first necessary to eliminate its cause, Russian Communism. He denied that he was anti-Semitic; for him it was "not a question of anti-Semitism; it is a question of anti-Communism."

Father Coughlin professed to desire to save the Jews from themselves. "Anti-Semitism is spreading in America," he wrote, "because the people sense a closely interwoven relationship between Communism and Jewry. . . . It is the *duty* of American Christians to aid their Jewish fellow citizens in shaking off Communism before it is too late." He claimed that he was not opposed to "religious Jews," only to those who supported communism. As early as 1936, he called upon the Jews to abandon the law of "an eye for an eye" and to adopt the law of Christ. Later he admitted that the real need was for Jews to "openly profess the divinity of "Christ" and that there would always be a "Jewish problem" so long as they would not accept the "spiritual brotherhood of Christ." In *Social Justice,* Coughlin reprinted the discredited *Protocols of Zion;* invited the contributions of Nazi sympathizer, George Sylvester Viereck; attributed the disasters of modern history to Jewish influence; in sum, conformed to the public image of an anti-Semite. Repeating the arguments again and again, the radio priest became the rallying point for pro-Nazi and anti-Jewish organizations, all the while denying any particular dislike of the Jews or admiration for the Nazis.

As in his earlier economic talks, Coughlin avoided too great an emphasis on specifically Catholic support for his position, instead relying on the general Christian symbols that had proven so effective earlier. His favorite reference was to the work of an Irish priest, Father Denis Fahey, who in turn relied on continental and British Catholic anti-Semitic sources. Coughlin, however, shied away from Fahey's view of the world as a battleground between the mystical body of Christ and a corresponding spiritual union of Satanic forces, for such a framework would have allied him with the visible church rather than with the broad Christian consensus whose fundamentalist wing supplied recruits both for monetary panaceas and anti-Jewish crusades. But the vision of the world as the scene of struggle between good and evil was basic to all Coughlin's rhetoric.

Again and again when distinguishing his policies from those of his enemies, he challenged his listeners to choose between "God's side" or that of "His enemy who goeth about like a roaring lion . . . roaring in the press, roaring on the radio, roaring on the silver screen."[13] Thus, whether the issue was revaluation of gold, the New Deal, the CIO or the Spanish War, the choice was always "civilization or Communism; Christ or chaos."

In addition to Father Coughlin, there was another source of Catholic anti-Semitic propaganda in the United States in the 1930s, less influential but more explicitly Catholic. Edward Koch of Germantown, Illinois, edited a monthly magazine, *The Guildsman,* through which he attempted to spread knowledge of the corporate social thought of the German Catholic social movement. Koch was vigorously anti-capitalist and regularly attacked Catholics who supported labor unions or social legislation, both of which, he believed, only perpetuated the existence of immoral capitalism and delayed the introduction of a social system based on a hierarchy of functional groups. A strong supporter of Franco and an apologist for Fascism, Koch upheld dictatorship as a method of overcoming private interests and introducing the new order. He admired the economic and diplomatic accomplishments of the Third Reich and praised Hitler's *Mein Kampf* for its devotion to German greatness and its concern for the common people. He thought he detected in Hitler's writings the influence of Pius XI's *Quadregesimo Anno* and of the Austrian social Catholics Lueger and Vogelsang. He drew on German and Austrian sources to excuse the persecution of the Jews, who rejected "everything distinctly Christian," controlled the socialist movement, and represented the "money power." He argued that all supporters of the unjust social order were opposed to Hitler and used the defense of democracy as a shield for their exploitation. He denied that the church had everything to gain from democracy and attacked Catholics who combated Nazism or anti-Semitism. After the war had begun in Europe he predicted that, if successful, Hitler and Mussolini would "initiate a new Christian civilization."[14]

Koch's writings were scarcely noticed, but Coughlin's work was a source of division and difficulty for the Catholic community. *Commonweal,* whose editors were regarded as traitors by Coughlin and his supporters because of the magazine's opposition to Franco, from the beginning consistently denounced anti-Semitism, Coughlin and the Christian Front. The *Catholic Worker* likewise was openly opposed to the priest and took the lead in combating anti-Semitism, distributing a press service of news of Catholic opposition to persecution of the Jews. John Ryan and George Shuster both publicly refuted Coughlin's charges against the Jews while Father Joseph N. Moody rebutted the old canards of Jewish financial power and Jewish radicalism. A group of liberal Catholics formed an organization to fight anti-Semitism and published a new journal for this purpose, *The Voice.* Cardinal Mundelein of Chicago stated that Coughlin was not authorized to speak for, and his views did not represent, "the doctrines and sentiments of the Church." Several other prelates, including Milwaukee's Archbishop Stritch and Coughlin's own superior, Archbishop Mooney, spoke out forcefully against anti-Semitism.[15]

For others, repudiation of Father Coughlin was less easy. Coughlin had skillfully tied his anti-Semitism to the issue of communism and to the fears of the Catholic minority of the supposed bigotry of non-Catholic America. Opposition to communism provided him with a convenient point of reconciliation with those Catholics who disliked his earlier activities. Cardinal O'Connell of Boston had deplored Coughlin's appeals to class hatred and his involvement in politics in the first half of the decade. Later Coughlin was denouncing the New Deal and the unions as communistic because they set class against class and declaring that politicians and parties could never come to grips with America's problems. His about-face and his focus on the Communist issue provided a firm basis for alliance with other Catholics who, though they might deplore his anti-Semitism, found little occasion to condemn him by name and undoubtedly welcomed his powerful support in their battle to avoid involvement in a war against Germany, a war which most agreed could only help the Communists.

With very few exceptions, American Catholic spokesmen agreed with Coughlin's major premise that, in the present as well as in the future, communism was a greater menace to the church and to America than was Nazism or Fascism. As Father Parsons of *America* put it, the church opposed the Nazis on political and economic grounds in the name of democracy while it opposed Communism on religious grounds in the name of God. Bishop Noll of Fort Wayne, who had denied support of Coughlin in 1936, later praised his work and endorsed his call for a "Christian Front" against communist penetration in the United States. The bishop's fear, like that of many of his fellow Catholics, was that the nation was being led into war against Fascism while neglecting the communist menace. "There has been such a vigorous campaign against Fascism in the American press and furthered by numerous groups of men and women," Bishop Noll wrote in 1939, "that the attention of the people has been at least temporarily withdrawn from the even greater evil of Communism."[16]

American Catholics were hurt and puzzled by the failure of their countrymen to share their view of events in Mexico, Spain and, later, their view of the war. Widespread indifference to the persecution of the church in Mexico was seen by Catholics as evidence of the continued existence of the bigotry they had witnessed in 1928. The Mexican situation was a sore point in relations between Catholics and other groups throughout the decade and provided a foundation of bitterness on which the intense feelings about Spain could be built. The Spanish Civil War was seen by Catholics as a clear-cut choice between Christianity and communism; opposition to Franco was not only pro-Communist and un-American, it was anti-Catholic as well. When George Shuster abandoned Franco for neutrality, he came under the most bitter and personal attacks. *America's* Father Talbot accused him of incompetence and even the gentle Father John LaFarge was led to compare the *Commonweal* editor to Nero, standing by neutral while the church was destroyed.

The same individuals and groups who had ignored the fate of the church in Mexico and were actively supporting the anti-Catholic forces in Spain appeared to Catholics to be the leading sympathizers with the persecuted German Jews. Even Father James M. Gillis of the *Catholic World,* among the most outspoken opponents of anti-Semitism, deplored the fact that Catholics under persecution did not receive the same under-

standing and support as their Jewish counterparts. At the other
end of the Catholic spectrum, the Brooklyn *Tablet* had long
decried the sympathy for the Jews among those who showed
little concern for Catholics. The Tablet became Coughlin's leading supporter in the East, resisting efforts to suppress anti-
Semitism and supporting the Christian Front which had been
organized under Coughlin's inspiration, though he evaded
responsibility for its actions.

In Brooklyn, anti-Semitism found a solid social foundation.
The Irish population, which had arrived in the city in the
mid-nineteenth century, had risen to the lower middle class, but
as Daniel Moynihan has pointed out, they were slow in ascen-
ding beyond this level of the social scale while their Jewish
neighbors, arriving later, rapidly attained comparable and even
higher status. The resulting tensions were felt for years and
came to the fore in the 1930s. Patrick Scanlan of the *Tablet*
gave expression to those feelings when he asked of the editors
of *The Voice,* the Catholic journal which combated anti-
Semitism: "Why do they not assail the discrimination against
the Germans, Italians, Irish and other races of New York who
are fast being reduced to the most inconspicuous places?" It
was in this context that the incendiary writings of Father
Coughlin were received and acted upon; though he might deny
being anti-Semitic, he was sure to be taken seriously in an area
predisposed to view the Jews with dislike and suspicion. The
priest himself was not reluctant to play upon Catholic frustra-
tions, urging "the spineless Christians of America to wake up
and demand that their coreligionists in other parts of the world
be offered the same protection, the same sympathy and the
same comfort which four million American Jews demand for
their co-nationals."[17]

Convinced that communism was a greater danger than
Fascism, Catholics were naturally suspicious of opposition to
Germany on the part of those who appeared to ignore the
totalitarianism and aggression of Soviet Russia. Resentful of the
indifference of their countrymen to the murder of priests and
nuns at the hands of the "Reds," a picture forcefully drawn by
their hierarchy and press, Catholics were not likely to be attracted to action against the Fascist states based upon their

persecution of the Jews or their infringement of civil liberties. At the same time that Catholics were becoming increasingly anti-Communist, however, their fellow Americans were awakening to the dangers of Nazism, a development that intensified the ever-present self-consciousness and sense of isolation of American Catholics. In this situation Father Coughlin's activity was particularly deplorable. His skillful argument fixing responsibility on the Jews for Catholic isolation and the drift toward war were sure to seem plausible to some Catholics. Those who resisted the anti-Semitic conclusions, on the other hand, were fearful of dividing the Catholic body in the face of war pressures on the part of individuals and groups who were thought to be anti-Catholic and pro-Communist.

Yet failure to condemn Father Coughlin exacerbated the very conditions which were thought to make unity essential. The honest fears of many Americans that the church was moving toward an accord with Fascism were given added weight by the refusal of his superiors to discipline Father Coughlin and the failure of much of the Catholic press unequivocally to disassociate itself from him. Archbishop Mooney may have feared another McGlynn scandal, a possibility that *Social Justice* had raised in 1937. Others, with far less grounds for inaction, were too preoccupied with their own fears of Communism and bigotry to recognize and repudiate the priest's propaganda. Whatever the motives involved, Coughlin's presence and his popularity in some heavily Catholic areas constituted a standing rebuke to the church in America.

The patterns established in the 1930s held firm in the postwar years. Catholics, arriving rapidly in the middle class, remained anxious to assert their full Americanism, and some did not disdain to express this in anti-Jewish terms. A new factor was added, however, when the cold war made the already deeply rooted Catholic anti-Communism thoroughly respectable. Catholics, even more than other Americans, were inclined to associate Jews with radicalism, for radical Jewish labor leaders had frequently clashed with their more conservative Catholic counterparts; few Catholics had joined the Communist party in the 1930s, but many Jews had. The most prominent victims of Senator McCarthy were, significantly, WASPs with impeccable native credentials, but Jews were not immune to the hysteria of witch hunting, indeed they were very vulnerable. So it was that the decline of the myth of Jewish economic power was compensated for by the myth of the Jewish intellectual as liberal dupe of the reds or even leaders of the subversive forces.

Another factor ensured that increasing entry of Catholics into the middle class would not lessen but even accentuate intergroup tensions. Middle-class parents are education conscious, they want good schools and the opportunity for a college education for their children. Middle-class Catholic parents shared these desires, but for the most part they also insisted on retention of the parochial school. More confident of their importance and their power than ever before, they provided strong support for the increasingly militant demands of their religious leaders for public aid to parochial schools, demands sure to bring them into conflict with the Jews, for whom strict separation of church and state was an article of faith. It was to this doctrine that American Jews attributed their success and their security, and they were the staunchest defenders of the public schools. Jews "because of their long experience in cultural pluralism have theologically, institutionally, and emotionally a much easier task than Christians in being absolutely consistent and unambiguous in their theoretical articulation and also in their practical implementation of the American principle of the separation of organized religion from the state." The school question, which had once found Catholics and Jews united, now became the greatest source of conflict between the two groups, bursting to the fore every time the question arose, punctuating public discussion with dogmatic affirmations of justice by the leaders of the two communities. "The public schools must continue to share responsibility for fostering a commitment to morality, ethics, and good citizenship without presenting or teaching any sectarian or theological sources or sanctions for values," a 1957 statement of a number of Jewish groups asserted. "The maintenance and furtherance of religion are the responsibilities of the synagogue, the church and the home, and not of the public school system; the utilization in any manner of the time, facilities, personnel, or funds of the public school system for purposes of religious instruction should not be permitted."

Thus as the self-confident Catholic community became more vociferous in its demands for aid they clashed repeatedly with Jewish organizations. On the question of aid to parochial schools, the Jewish community was at one with most Protestants, but in the 1960s a new shift appeared. The Supreme Court decision banning prayer and Bible reading in the schools caused many Protestants to re-examine the secular drift of public education and offered alert Catholic leaders a chance to forge new alliances, a possibility aided by inner city tensions and the ecumenical movement. In an apparently friendly warning, *America* magazine told "Our Jewish Friends" that they were in danger of painting themselves into a corner, isolated by their militant secularism from Christian Americans. Even as intelligent and humane a Catholic spokesman as Msgr. John Tracy Ellis warned a Jewish audience against "using the numerous high and influential posts to which their superb talents have brought them in American society, whether these be in the press, the fine arts, the drama, or the communications media, in a way that gives justified offense to their gentile neighbors, to say nothing of offering a handle to their enemies."[18] That way, Ellis spelled out, with obvious reference to the prayer decision, was "secularism," which because they had benefited from it, some Jews sought to impose as a national philosophy on America's pluralistic society. These signs of the times led Rabbi Arthur Gilbert to issue his own warning: "We tear away the defenses that our Christian neighbors have built up to handle their anxieties. Out spills the anger and fear that these defenses have held in check and the anger touches us. The Jews then are identified with those who are against these holy symbols. They are identified with the Communist and secularist, with persons blind to the real problems that confront the American community."

One way to envisage the contemporary situation of Catholics and Jews in the United States then is to see each as a distinct group placed upon parallel conveyer belts labeled assimilation. The destination of each is labeled "middle-class respectability," a state of being where ethnic self-consciousness is no longer present and is replaced simply by the phrase "Catholic" and "Jewish," both of which are fully American. The Catholics, led by the Irish, arrived in America in large numbers somewhat earlier than the Jews, and they attained lower-middle-class rank rather swiftly. But they tended to stop there and not until the great changes of World War II and the G.I. Bill of Rights did they move in large numbers into the professional and managerial elites. Jews on the other hand arrived later, but rose more swiftly, in large part because of their greater willingness to take advantage of the opportunities of public education. Thus by the 1930s and '40s they had attained positions of leadership in such areas as entertainment, the media and the learned professions, and they had shed ethnic consciousness for the more inclusive definition of themselves as Jewish. The present strains in American Catholicism are in some extent parallel to those which Jews experienced thirty years ago, before the German question and the formation of the state of Israel rallied a fragmenting Jewish community to a common cause.

The fact that many American Catholics are now securely middle-class should not be interpreted to mean that tensions are at an end. As Nathan Glazer and Daniel P. Moynihan discovered in their study of New York City, the gap between Irish Catholics and Jews is very great. They constitute, indeed, two distinct communities: "One is secular in its attitudes, liberal in its outlook on sexual life and divorce, positive about science and social sciences. The other is religious in its outlook, resists the growing liberalization in sexual mores and its reflection in cultural and family life, feels strongly the tension between moral values and modern science and technology. . . . Thus a Jewish ethos and a Catholic ethos emerge: they are more strongly affected by a specific religious doctrine in the Catholic case than in the Jewish, but neither is purely the expression of the spirit of a religion. Each is the result of the interplay of religion, ethnic groups, American setting and specific issues. The important fact is that the differences in values and attitudes between the two groups do not, in general, become smaller with time."[19] The end of the consciousness of being a minority subject to possible persecution or exclusion may well release

Catholics from the need to subordinate their prejudices for the sake of unity against the common Protestant-Yankee enemy. The fact that assimilation does not produce a common Americanism but Americanism via religion, emphasizes the common Christianity of Catholics and Protestants, and this is increased by their common middle-class experience. In addition to this release from minority consciousness, which held prejudice in check, the end of the transition from Protestant to post-Protestant pluralist America makes way for legitimate institutional conflicts. The Catholic church can now contend strongly for aid to parochial schools because it does not have to fear an anti-Catholic reaction, while Jews can oppose such aid because they do not have to fear an anti-Semitic response. Institutional differences and conflict are normal in a pluralistic society and should become more open and honest, if no less bitter, in a society that has moved from the immigrant to the pluralistic stage. One cultural feature of the general Christian community is that it shares a common anti-Jewish bias. More important, while the proportion of Catholics who hold religiously negative views of the Jews are less than those among Protestants, they still constitute a significant proportion of the population.[20]

While it is important to realize that the rhetoric of good will and togetherness can be misleading, Catholic attitudes surely have improved. Most Catholic papers today lack that sharp sense of group solidarity, ghetto-mindedness and readiness to interpret all issues in terms of their effect on the institutional interests of the Catholic church. Instead there is a healthy and even radical temper of self-criticism, one aspect of which is awareness of the tendency of all Catholics and Christians to affirm anti-Jewish views. The honest assessment of the issues raised by Hochhuth's *The Deputy*, the insistence upon a clear-cut repudiation of anti-Semitism at the Vatican Council, the widespread criticism of the equivocations of the council's final position, all stand in sharp contrast to the hypocrisy of thirty years ago. But *Commonweal*, the *National Catholic Reporter* and *America* are not American Catholicism, and sharp changes among the intelligentsia have not always filtered down. Most Catholics are new to the middle class, and they will remain susceptible for many years to the pressures of status and the fears of change common to the middle class.

More and more Catholics and Jews alike are concluding that the surest roads to better understanding lie in internal renewal and reform and common programs of social action. In addition a degree of historical consciousness, with particular reference to the inter-relationship of religious faith and social location, might assist in promoting the humility necessary for dialogue while providing the knowledge needed to overcome the insecurity and fear that are the roots of prejudice.

Similar preoccupations might have general applicability to inter-group relations. Christian ecumenism, for example, greatly enlivened by the council, has stalled over such questions as inter-communion, although institutional cooperation continues at all levels. Increasingly aware of common problems, church professionals feel an ever greater kinship with one another. School aid and abortion remain thorny issues but rarely are the echoes of the old polemics heard from the churches or their presses.

Yet, in a real sense, the ecumenical movement has reached a dead end. Most young Christians have little concern with ecumenism considered as inter-Christian dialogue and movements toward church unity. While they may follow developments in this field with varying degrees of interest, their most pressing concerns lie elsewhere. For one thing their emotional investment in denominational institutions is slight. Participation in parish or specifically denominational organizations is minimal. Lacking, for better or worse, deep personal commitment to formal church structures, they tend to minimize doctrinal differences among Christians, a tendency reinforced for Catholics by a breakdown of old certitudes and the resurgence of an equally venerable stress on love and community, vague terms less susceptible to self-righteous partisanship than the virgin birth or papal infallibility.

The challenge of Catholics to the church of their fathers is a highly personal one, originating in the consciousness of conflict between strictly held personal values of love and honesty and the realities of power, deception and compromise that too often characterize the institutional church. They insist on freedom of the individual conscience and locate responsibility for Christian commitment and loving service in the individual. Glorying in their supposed emancipation from the dead hand of the ecclesiastical paternalism, dogmatic and moral rigidity and liturgical conformity, they seek personal satisfaction and fulfillment through liturgical experimentation and social service. This last point is the second reason for lack of concern with ecumenism. The same personalism and dedication characterize the profound commitment of younger Catholics to social action. People who are Christian enough to be horrified by the glaring absurdities of today's world can hardly regard church unity as anything but a secondary objective. While it is good for Popes and Patriarchs to meet and it is a good thing Protestants, Catholics and Jews are not at each other's throats any more, these things are hardly worthy of notice while an entire people are being obliterated on the other side of the world, cities go up in smoke and people are starving to death. Even if such meetings result in pronouncements about the need for charity and social justice they can seem positively sinful if the churches these leaders represent do not fully manifest such commitments in their own lives.

Religious self-centeredness and personal indignation with social injustice combine to minimize ecumenical concern. Yet upon reflection it is clear that meaningful religious life and effective social action necessitate immediate and profound commitment to the goal of Christian unity. The central committee of the World Council of Churches in the minutes of its meeting of 1951 wrote, "It is important to insist that this word, ecumenical, which comes from the Greek word for the whole inhabited earth, is properly used to describe everything that relates to the whole task of the whole church to bring the gospel to the world. It therefore covers equally the missionary movement and the movement toward unity and must not be used to describe the latter in counter-distinction to the former. Every attempt to separate these two tasks violates the wholeness of Christ's ministry to the world." Considered in these terms ecumenism means the entire movement Christians accept to unite themselves to one another and to Christ and to serve their fellow man. Recognizing this, more and more Protestants and Catholics are looking beyond discussions of theology and of church structure to joint attempts at social service. Catholics and Protestants in the United States for example are more frequently joining together in a common front in opposition to the war in Viet Nam or in demands for massive programs to change the way of life of American cities. Robert MacAfee Brown, one of the most prominent American Protestants associated with the ecumenical movement, has drawn attention to the fact that the Protestant movements toward church unity early recognized the fact that unity presupposed actions for the alleviation of social injustice under the slogan "Doctrine divides, service unites."[21]

There are then two dimensions to the ecumenical movement: organized efforts to attain church unity and the similar efforts to bring Christians together to act upon common social concerns. These two things are not separable but are intricately involved with one another. The quest for a meaningful liturgy leads to realization of the necessity for community. Liturgy cannot create real Christian community, it can only express it and deepen it. To have Christian communities, men must be open to their fellow men whomever they may be. If such openness is to mean anything, it has to mean that men are open to particular people and certainly it means they must be open to their fellow men who also profess their acceptance of Christ. How can Christians truly testify to faith in Christ while accepting the disunity of his people? How can they profess their desire for union with one another, deepened and strengthened around the altar table, when they allow to pass unnoticed the first opportunity in 400 years to restore the unity of the people of God. If the failure of today's parishes is that they bring men of vastly different backgrounds, interests and taste together in a highly impersonal liturgical setting, the failure of much of Protestantism was that while it was able to create real communities it could not reach beyond those communities. Perhaps by coming together with their Protestant brethren Catholics can find a road to meaningful worship and meaningful structures which will allow the personal fulfillment of participation in meaningful community while at the same time retaining a concern for and actual contact with others beyond denominational or sectarian boundaries.

Something of the same thing is true of the second major concern today, social action and social justice. In today's world simple expressions of charity are not enough; dedication to Christian service means something more, must mean something more, than visiting the sick and the aged or cleaning up the house of a crowded family. It must mean political action, attempts to organize the poor themselves and those who are concerned about the poor in order to obtain influence and power. The problems of American society are fundamentally structural problems and not problems of personal greed and selfishness. Problems of poverty, discrimination, poor housing and the aged are problems that must be dealt with first of all on a public level; they necessitate a fundamental reordering of the distribution of power in society. All those who feel a fundamental responsibility for their fellow man, and particularly for the oppressed and the poverty stricken, must join together. Again Protestants can supply a necessary corrective to the intense personalism of Catholic social action. For years Protestants attempted to awaken the conscience of their congregations so that individuals would act in a benevolent manner in society. Many Protestant leaders today recognize the inadequacy of that approach and might be able to assist in finding ways to make Christian social and political involvement realistic, meaningful and effective.

The suggestion which emerges from consideration of American pluralism is that, while conflicts between Catholics, Protestants and Jews remain natural and unavoidable, they pale into insignificance before the massive problems of war, racism, poverty and pollution that confront the world today. In the light of these issues, an undue preoccupation with group concerns and interests, particularly when the group is a Christian church, seems positively obscene. Far better for the several churches to recognize the limitations their own histories place on their ability to overcome religious differences and instead accept their common Christian and American responsibilities. The common dedication of Christians is not to their church or their nation but to that Kingdom which is to come. The building of the Kingdom of God, both by unifying those conscious of their commitment to Jesus and by attempting to make the structures of society realize the justice and love Christian commitment must mean, this is a task which emerges from their history as one to which Catholics can dedicate themselves in the future.

6
THE CLIMAX
OF CATHOLIC AMERICANISM

Developments in postwar America strengthened the unity and self-consciousness of the Catholic community and temporarily pushed into the background the internal dissent and the concern with social and political issues that had been growing in the 1930s. Yet, as the school controversy indicated, considerable diversity of opinion did exist, and differences would re-emerge in the 1950s to a point where they would make possible the true revolution which accompanied and followed the Vatican Council. These differences were no longer basically ethnic, nor were they yet doctrinal or ecclesiastical. Rather they had to do with the substance and the style of the Catholic presence in the United States. Beginning with the school question and with controversies over public policy during the McCarthy era, the growing ferment was accelerated by a critical re-examination of the intellectual and cultural life of the American church, it spilled over into discussion of the liturgy and culminated in searching criticism of the role of the laity in Catholic life. By the time John F. Kennedy became President of the United States and Pope John XXIII summoned an ecumenical council, the groundwork had been laid for an American *aggiornamento*.

In a very real sense the period which extended from 1950 to the middle of the next decade marked the climax of American Catholic history. The Catholic people of the United States had long pursued two major historical goals: growth in numbers, influence and prestige and acceptance as a valued part of American society. It seems clear that this period marked the fulfillment of these goals. We have already seen the manner in which the Americanist impulse emerged victorious as the council ratified much of the liberal program, and, even more important, the presidency of John F. Kennedy demonstrated the respectability, the arrival of Catholics as Americans. Kennedy's campaign was "a tremendous experience for American Catholics," Thomas T. McAvoy has written. "The American Catholic way of living had been exposed to unrelenting criticism and defended by Protestants and Jewish friends as well as by Catholics. The great achievement of the election of Kennedy was that the barriers against a Catholic being president had been erased and the American Catholic was by just that much elevated socially and politically. Tension between Catholics and non-Catholics was by no means ended by the election but the happy regime of John F. Kennedy as president helped lessen the tension and his death at the hands of an assasin in 1963 sealed with glory the first Catholic presidency."[1] However troubling such words may be, there can be little doubt that the experience of the Kennedy years did much to destroy the age-old minority consciousness of the Catholic population.

Father McAvoy had always believed that the economic deficiencies of the Catholic community explained its cultural weaknesses and that it could expect influence and recognition as its resources increased. The postwar progress of the Catholic people, then, laid the groundwork for the culmination Kennedy represented, and the church as an institution shared fully in that progress. During the 1950s the Catholic population grew by 44%, the number of students in Catholic high schools by 60% and in elementary schools by 66%. There were 43,000 priests in the country in 1950, 54,000 a decade later. The number of seminaries grew from 388 to 525 and their students from 26,000 to almost 40,000. Overall the growth of the church in the 1950s was unprecedented.[2]

Yet never was the ambiguity of success more evident than in the agonies of mind and spirit that beset American Catholicism in the years that followed. No one could deny that the church had attained its historical objectives, yet, at the very moment of its greatest achievement, its own members and many of its most revered leaders at home and abroad began raising in terribly sharp form disturbing questions about the validity of those very objectives. In Rome the Council Fathers taught that size, power and wealth, schools, churches and ceremonies were quite inadequate yardsticks for measuring Christian progress. Was the American church a credible sign of Christ's presence in the world? Did it honestly and effectively proclaim the Gospel? Was it a community of love, fellowship, trust and freedom? Did it take seriously its tasks of diaconea, serving all men, rich and poor, black and white, Catholic and non-Catholic? At home, events were raising equally brutal questions. While growing and winning respect what had the church done to heal the nation's racial divisions, to humanize its economic system, to moderate its messianic ambitions?; all questions put sharply to men's consciences by the brutal events of the decade. Had the American church, in its single-minded devotion to its own survival and growth, neglected important elements of the Gospel message? Had it done what it had always warned its people against, gained the world and lost its soul?

During the 1960s many charged that all these things had happened, while many others denied the charges with equal passion. But the very fact that such questions were being asked meant that the church's unity was shattered, its ability to influence the nation was gravely impaired and its collective identity and self-confidence was put to a test few institutions could survive. In reflecting on how this all came about, however, it is crucially important to bear in mind that these profound questions were not simply matters of reformed Christians confronting a corrupt church, or of a divine institution confronting sinful men, as most of the participants seemed to believe. Rather, at their most fundamental, they were challenges both to persons and their institutions, the perennial questions that always challenge men in history, and their impact could be felt both by the church and in the depths of the conscience of very many of its members.

Few would have realized a decade before how serious were the forces which were at work around them. None would have believed that by 1970 news of priests leaving their rectories for married life would be commonplace, that a self-proclaimed Catholic resistance movement would be engaged in a nonviolent war with American government, that monasteries would sponsor conferences on women's liberation and that the leader of an important lay organization would use obscenity in a discussion with bishops. More important, few indeed would have anticipated the changes, the confusion and the anguish the years would bring to their own faith.

Indeed, the most clearly apparent feature of pre-conciliar controversies, from the perspective afforded by the experience of another decade, was the relative absence of any serious debate about fundamental elements of Catholic life. There was little questioning in those days of such potentially debatable doctrines as papal infallibility, the real presence of Christ in the Eucharist, the indissolubility of marriage, the evil of artificial contraception or the various Marian formulas. Nor was there any significant assault on the historical institutions of American Catholicism: the parish, the school or the many social and charitable agencies. Few doubted the viability of the territorial parish, though many questioned its administration and the spirit of its community life. While some worried about the ability of the church to maintain its schools and many criticized the quality of what was taught in them, few questioned the value of a separate Catholic education. Dissent was limited and confined, and had to do with two basic issues: the image of the church in the eyes of non-Catholic Americans and the inner spirit and atmosphere of the church, which seemed impervious to serious dialogue with American culture. The one complaint motivated and shaped debate with those outside the church, the other dominated intra-mural discussions.

John Courtney Murray, John Cogley and other pioneers of Catholic ecumenism sought during the 1950s to demonstrate in word and deed that the Catholic church contained a wide variety of attitudes and ideas, particularly on social and political issues, for McCarthyism had rekindled the specter of a monolithic Catholic bloc. Moreover these men tried to offer reasonable arguments for the Catholic position on such outstanding issues as birth control and aid to parochial schools, however irrational or unseemly the partisanship and polemics of other Catholics might be. The ecumenical leaders of the decade labored courageously to moderate the church's image without abandoning any point of doctrine or any major institutional interest.

These same men also fought hard within the church to

uphold the major tenets of American democracy, and for the same reasons. They were convinced that Catholics did not take seriously enough the principles of individual liberty and democratic participation that they considered the fundamental maxims of American society, and that this failure accounted for much of the suspicion and hostility with which many non-Catholics regarded the church. An anti-Catholic reflex was particularly common among liberal intellectuals, whose view of the church was a matter of great concern for educated, cultured Catholics. In the later part of the decade Cogley, a former editor of *Commonweal,* organized a symposium of American religious leaders on the subject of "Religion and the Free Society." The papers presented at these meetings showed quite clearly that the major outstanding issue in inter-church relations was the old one of the compatability of Catholic teachings and American democracy, a question which involved in the 1950s, as it always had, both the image of the church held by outsiders and the sincerity of its members' own commitment to liberal democracy. The focal point of those discussions was the school question, which brought out the near obsessive preoccupation of non-Catholics with national unity and their fear of the church and its schools as a divisive force in American society. Reinhold Niebuhr, for example, regretted the fact that the separation of church and state required the secularization of education so deplored by Catholics. Nevertheless, he argued, "however steep the price, such a separation of religion and education represents a gain for our public life, since organized religion is bound to be divisive, and it is a divisiveness we simply cannot afford. . . . The nation can afford some slight deviation from the principle of the common school; it cannot afford the total loss" which Niebuhr believed would result if public aid was made available for private education.[3]

To meet these fears it was necessary both to correct the image of the church held by non-Catholics and to promote American values among Catholics themselves. "We were trying in a sense to secularize the American Catholic community," Cogley recalled years later. "At least we were trying to take those values which are American values—e.g. civil liberties, the Bill of Rights, the separation of church and state—and to offer a rationale for them which would be conformable to Catholic doctrine."[4] In this effort Murray's *We Hold These Truths* was the most notable, successful and influential document. In discussions with men inside and outside the church, Murray and other liberals were engaged in the same task that preoccupied their nineteenth-century precursors, "working out the conformity between Catholicism as a religious philosophy and what might be called in a good sense 'Americanism' as a political commitment."[5]

Men who had undertaken this task had long recognized the fact that the low state of Catholic intellectual effort constituted a serious obstacle to their success. The liberals of the 1890s had hoped that the new Catholic University of America could help overcome the cultural handicap. George Shuster, a pioneer in the twentieth-century effort to reconcile Catholic and American principles, was also an ardent critic of American Catholic culture. *Commonweal,* which both Shuster and Cogley served as editors, devoted much of its attention to raising Catholic cultural standards, hoping that this would improve the church's image and generate a sincere and effective rationale for Catholic Americanism. It was appropriate then that in 1954, when John Tracy Ellis described and analyzed the low state of Catholic intellectual life, his paper would become the subject of lively comment and debate. The paper itself clearly demonstrated a concern both with the image and the substance of the church's relation to American culture, and the controversy that followed often centered around the need for men steeped in the Catholic cultural tradition to creatively confront the quite different realities of American society and culture.[6] Some were satisfied to try simply to awaken their fellow Catholics to the richness of their own, European cultural heritage, while others were more preoccupied with shaping a style of controversy and behavior they believed suited the American situation. In neither case were the leaders happy with the progress of the decade, for, while there was an obvious improvement in the quality and visibility of Catholic thought, many Catholics seemed indifferent if not downright hostile to the entire effort, so that some feared that the church and serious thought were on quite different paths. "The real problem of American Catholicism,"

Cogley wrote as late as 1960, was the growing alienation from the church "of those who are trying to relate Catholicism to existing culture."[7]

Of course Cogley, like Orestes Brownson and John Ireland earlier, often confused "existing culture" and "Americanism" with the attitudes and views of a selected group of Americans, usually secular and liberal Protestant intellectuals. Because they defined the problems of the church's image in terms of the Catholic-American dichotomy held by their "significant others," they tended to regard Americanization and the intellectual effort to relate Catholicism to "existing culture" as more or less synonymous. Thus very frequently they identified anti-intellectualism with the immigrant heritage and the so-called "ghetto mentality." Yet, as Gary Wills has pointed out, the liberals often had to turn to France for their models, hoping that Jacques Maritain and the worker-priests would show them how to Americanize their church.

The truth was, in the 1950s as in the 1890s, the conflict was not one of Americanization versus the preservation of "foreignness" but between differing interpretations of the situation and differing styles of response. Just as historians have shown that the melting pot did not work as expected and that ethnicity was as much a mode of adjustment to America as a reactionary effort to resist the new society, so it is clear that however hard the liberals of the pre-conciliar years fought for the Americanization of the church, they were really trying to reform to their model of an American church men and institutions already quite at home in the United States. It may not be too much to say with Garry Wills that the "Catholic liberal . . . opposed the American church because it was too American. Its bishops had been shaped more by the ethos of the local Chamber of Commerce than by the American Academy in Rome. The pastor was obnoxious, not for his theology and transnational ties, but for his lack of theology and parochialism. He was Babbitt in a biretta—as conversely Billy Graham was Fulton Sheen in a business suit."[8]

Yet, that may be going too far. While the liberal intellectuals to whom Catholic reformers hoped the church could relate were indeed a minority, they were rapidly becoming the arbiters of

American culture. Broadened college education, transformation of Catholic schools by the growth of lay faculty trained in secular universities, exposure to the highly centralized mass media, easing of ethnic and ideological conflicts, all helped homogenize national culture and leave the liberal style, secular and Protestant, in the ascendancy. As a result, Cogley's fears were more than justified. A whole generation was maturing in the 1950s for whom the old polemics had become sterile. The continued implication that there was some great chasm between Catholics and adherents of other religions that justified exclusive education and social life did seem to stifle Catholic culture and give Catholics a stigma of inferiority in the eyes of their non-Catholic fellow citizens, a feeling particularly acute among Catholic intellectuals and men newly arrived to middle-class status.

The difficulties facing those concerned with cultural quality were confounded by a repressive internal atmosphere that deprived Catholics of their freedom to creatively relate their religious and their secular life and deprived the church of the enormous benefits that could spring from a free and honest confrontation with American society. Walter Ong, S. J. was merely the most articulate of a number of Catholics who believed that American society presented in microcosm the problems of contemporary Christianity generally. "Because the culture of the United States has so many of its roots outside the United States, this country often serves as a kind of proving ground or point of focus for certain problems, including those particular problems faced by present day Christians," Ong wrote. If American Catholicism would shuck off its historical consciousness of being a minority at home and its feeling of inferiority to European Catholicism in matters of the mind and spirit, Ong believed that it could make a crucial contribution to the future of Christianity in a post-Christian world.[9]

What was needed, it seemed to these men, was primarily a new sense of freedom in the church, a willingness to allow, even encourage, experimentation, speculation and dialogue. "In this country the Catholic community was so tightly disciplined in order to insure freedom *for* the church," Cogley wrote in 1963, "that until recently precious little attention was given to insure

freedom *within* the church."[10] This issue was intimately related
to the sense of subordination felt by many laymen, a theme
heard with increasing frequency in the pre-conciliar years. In
social action Donald Thorman and Ed Marciniak urged that
laymen be free to relate to secular society in a mature fashion,
free of clerical control. Thomas O'Dea, like other participants in
the intellectual life debate, called for greater openness to non-
Catholic currents of thought and an end to the repression of
theological speculation of which Murray had been a recent
victim. The whole matter was summed up by Daniel Callahan in
The Mind of the Catholic Layman. The suppression of lay
responsibility that had emerged from the trusteeship controversy of the previous decade had to end, Callahan argued. The
mature, Americanized layman no longer could honestly uphold
democratic values in his public life while remaining docile and
silent in church. In addition, Callahan made it explicit that the
key problem of Catholic progress was the creation of an image
of the church that was thoroughly American, a task that obviously required emancipation of lay energies and assumption
by the layman of new responsibilities. While using his freedom
to witness in society to his dedication to human values, the
layman was also bound to "give witness within the church by
showing those who have authority within it that freedom and
self-direction are not incompatible with the maintenance of
legitimate authority."[11] A better image for the church, a more
serious consideration of American society, a more vigorous
intellectual and cultural life, greater freedom and responsibility
for laymen, such was the program of liberal Catholics as the
American church entered the conciliar era.

Pope John XXIII's major encyclicals and his call for an
ecumenical council gave respectability and authority to all these
arguments, but it was the 1963 lecture tour of theologian Hans
Kung which climaxed the controversy and made the work of
the council relevant to the American situation. Probably never
before had a touring professional theologian met with such
large, informed and enthusiastic audiences. In city after city the
Swiss theologian delivered the same message. There was repression and authoritarianism in the church, and it was a scandalous
contradiction of the gospel's proclamation of love and brother-

hood. The continuation of outmoded policies would destroy the intention of the council to make the church a more credible sign of God's will for modern man. Finally, Kung maintained, it was each Christian's responsibility to defend freedom and assist the development of an informed public opinion in the church. Kung's words coincided exactly with the frustration and the hopes of many American Catholics. When James Cardinal Mc Intyre of Los Angeles prevented Kung from speaking within his jurisdiction, there was an immediate outcry of protest. From that point on, every overt manifestation of repression in the church was alertly seized upon by the media and made a matter of public debate. As the new quest for freedom spread to clergy and religious, conflicts with authority became more frequent, but now they invariably entered the public arena. The days of quiet suppression of dissent were over, and, at the end of the decade, it was clear that only establishment of new procedures of due process could restore an authority in the American church that would be generally recognized as legitimate.[12]

For Cogley, Callahan, Ong and others, establishment of freedom in the church was necessary in itself, but their sense of urgency about the issue derived from their conviction that once achieved it would open the door to a real, honest confrontation of the church and American society, vitalizing the church and providing a model for Christians everywhere of the creative reconciliation of faith and the world. The council and its surrounding events seemed to do just that. "There is occurring around us today one of the most unique events in the history of human society and in the history of that very special kind of human society (which we Catholics believe is more than human) called the Catholic church," young sociologist Andrew Greeley wrote in 1962. "Catholicism is confronting American civilization."[13] Observers of the third session of the council felt, as did Philip Sharper, that it marked the emergence of American Catholicism on the world scene, as the American bishops brought to Rome the willingness to experiment and the concern with practical consequences that were the major characteristics of the American temperament. "One can now speak, not of Catholicism in America, but of a developing American Catholicism," Sharper wrote in 1965. "If it is true to its genius, it can contribute to the church universal the hard won fruits of the American experience: that freedom is not to be feared but fostered, that risk cannot be divorced from decision, that one can safely gamble on the virtue, intelligence, and honor of the average man, and, finally, that the past, no matter how splendid, is forever but prelude."[14]

This optimism, which seems so misplaced only a few years later, was one of the most striking features of commentary on the council. Michael Novak's excellent book on the council was filled with acute analysis of the strengths and weaknesses of the American church and its bishops, but he too was convinced that American Catholicism could and would produce the leaders required by the modern church. "The basic modern experience of non-ideological democracy, pluralism, advanced and widespread education, the wealth and homogenization produced by technology have been felt in the United States almost a generation before they are being felt in other lands," Novak wrote. "Often, in spite of themselves, non-Americans look to the United States for leadership; when the United States does not provide leadership, a vacuum is often created."[15] Novak recognized that the American bishops were unprepared by training or experience to exert such leadership, though they did demonstrate a humility and willingness to learn that augured well for the future. It was laymen like Callahan and Cogley who were articulating the American experience and, according to Novak, they won a wide audience. Theirs was a unique opportunity. That generation of American Catholics who matured in the late 1950s and the years of the council—"The generation of the third eye" they called themselves—were, it seemed "the natural leaders of the Catholics of the world in the struggle between the forces of man and the forces of technique. The time in which we live is germinative," Novak concluded in words typical of the enthusiastic anticipation of the day and reminiscent of those John Ireland addressed to the world over a half century earlier: "it is the beginning of an era; small efforts now will have effects for many generations."[16]

As late as 1965, the year American bombers began their destruction of North Viet Nam and hundreds of thousands of American troops poured into the south of that doomed land, the confident Americanism of Catholic liberals remained unimpaired. "The American society has formed a dynamic balance and tension of disparate elements permitting and facilitating the simultaneous advancement of the individual citizen and the community. When one gets more in this land of expanding horizons, it means there is more for the other," Gary MacEoin wrote the year that Lyndon Johnson launched the war on poverty and terrible riots hit American cities. MacEoin typically urged the completion of the Americanizing program so that Catholics could bring to America "the spiritual leavening of their participation in national, state, city and village affairs." [17] From the liberal perspective the future seemed bright because the immediate past had seen incredible progress. "The distance between 1962 and 1965 is little short of amazing," Michael Novak wrote in the latter year. But, he was careful to add, "the distance covered is only, let us say, from 1789 to 1945." To get from 1945 to the present it would be necessary to complete the agenda laid out earlier, to recognize that the old order of traditional parish life was "bankrupt" and to go on to make of "the whole church, every day and everywhere, . . . one large community: full of free speech, argument, dissent, respect for diversity, and the slow search for consensus."[18]

Greeley, Novak, Callahan, "the new breed," had a firm grasp of the theology of the council and the yearnings of thousands of young, educated laymen and priests. Their sense of the tremendous potential of the situation and their feeling that both church and country could derive enormous benefits from the revolution going on in the church, expressed and gave direction to the feelings of many of their fellow Catholics. Older men who had deplored the cultural level of the Catholic people a few years earlier were amazed at the new excitement, interest and intelligence. People were reading and discussing conciliar documents and works of serious theology, they were joining new style organizations, like the militant National Association of Laymen, and offering their energies and services to the parishes and to vigorous new experimental congregations. They were supporting the revitalized Catholic press, protesting archaic suppressions of scholars and social activists and taking great satisfaction in the widespread and sincere interest of non-Catholics in the proceedings of the council. These were surely years of promise and of hope.

Yet there were great dangers in the situation, dangers that were hard to discern in those days but were implicit even in the most popular ideas. No idea had wider currency in the mid 1960s than the thesis of German theologian Kark Rahner that the church in the modern era was living in a "diaspora situation."[19] The present writer's first published article, which appeared in 1966, argued to his own satisfaction at the time that the church in the United States indeed lived in a diaspora more clearly defined than elsewhere in the world.[20] Few recognized the full import of Rahner's vision or the price that acceptance of the diaspora would exert on traditional and still cherished notions of church and country. The essential points of Rahner's thesis were a statement of fact: Christians are a minority in the modern world, and a theological insight: there is no reason to believe that they can be or should be a majority. The idea that the church is not necessarily destined to embrace all men, that membership is no criteria of health and that the church must redefine its mission in terms of its minority status, purging itself of all triumphalism, became the central theme of controversy about the church. The effects of this "diaspora consciousness" were profound. While Catholics in America had always been a minority, they had never been comfortable with that position, for it contradicted many things they were taught. Plagued by enemies without and dissension within, the modern church had nevertheless shaped its policies by the demands of universality. Dogma and moral prescriptions were true for all men; other churches, doomed by heresy and contradiction, would sooner or later fall by the wayside. Only the Catholic church would endure; in the end it would emerge triumphantly vindicated.

Given such thoughts about the church, its leaders were pulled in two directions. On the one hand they were required to preserve unity and discipline to ensure the preservation of truth and of the sacred ecclesiastical institutions. On the other hand they were called to mission: to proclaim Christ's message and win men to the church. These responsibilities were often in conflict. Isaac Hecker and John Ireland believed that if the church could be made a credible sign of God's presence, if it could throw off its association with foreign, un-American symbols and prove its value to American society, the nation would soon be ripe for conversion. Their opponents feared that a policy designed to implement such a mission would risk the destruction of the institution whose very existence was crucial to the work of Christ in the world. Thus the more conservative leaders were satisfied to preserve the faith of those already in the church and to channel their missionary impulses into overseas mission work.

As a result the opponents of Americanism built a church whose unity and identity depended largely upon an external enemy. Just as many immigrants came to recognize their ethnic distinctiveness out of conflict with native Americans and other immigrants, so the church came to define its distinctiveness in contrast to its non-Catholic opponents. In practice, the identifying features of American Catholicism were not belief in the divinity of Christ or in the sacraments of baptism and the Eucharist, doctrines held and practiced by many non-Catholics, but those beliefs and practices which set Catholics apart: certain Marian doctrines, papal infallibility, confession, special feasts and rituals, prohibition of birth control, Friday abstinence. These, together with distinctive social and political attitudes and practices, were the rough points of inter-group controversy and thus the sources of Catholic self-consciousness. As columnist John Leo put it, "the community has stayed together through history by developing its own culture, and by sustaining the energy of that culture *in some sense* in isolation from the world—a common enemy marked out the boundaries of the ghetto and helped provide the dynamics within."[21]

As Leo and others learned, the diaspora, with all it implied in terms of the nature and mission of the church, at once removed the enemy and brought him within the gates. Those outside the church were no longer to be regarded as antagonists against whom the citadel must be defended, but as men and women, persons, called to life in God's kingdom. They were not to be fought or proselytized, but served. A diaspora church, according to Rahner, was a church for others, called to be a minority in the service of the majority. When Pope John XXIII visited prisoners and bearhugged communists, he was personifying the idea that no one, even adherents of the "red menace," could be regarded simply as enemies, but only as men, in need of love, understanding, compassion, to be engaged in dialogue but never assaulted in the name of righteousness.

Not only were enemies removed, but the things they had represented appeared within the church itself. If the church was destined to be a minority, with no control over civic and cultural life, and if this fact was both recognized by its members and regarded by them as legitimate, then church affiliation was indeed a voluntary thing and Christian commitment a matter of personal decision. When the decree on Religious Liberty was adopted by the Vatican Council, historian H. Stuart Hughes noted that freedom of conscience, now legitimatized for non-Catholics, could not long be denied to Catholics themselves. They would necessarily begin to pick and choose among long-accepted church teachings, ignore long-followed prohibitions, form new communities for which they would claim the name "Catholic."[22]

The council's other actions almost ensured the result Hughes predicted. The ecumenical example of pope and council helped lay the axe to the external props of Catholic identity. By restating the doctrine of the church in biblical imagery, the council relativized the canonical hierarchy of authority long regarded as sacrosanct. Emphasis on episcopal collegiality weakened papal centralization, while a similar stress on the fraternal relations of bishops and priests dispersed this new spirit throughout the church. Finally, the stress on common Christian vocation exalted the dignity of the laity, asserted its responsibility for ecclesiastical decisions and left the priest's role uncertain. Such aggiornamento, conservatives had always warned, would bring not reform but revolution; once begun the process of change could not easily be halted and might well threaten the whole structure of the historical church. It turned out that such fears were quite justified. "Now that we are back in the diaspora (alas, without a major enemy) and now that the pendelum has swung toward freedom of conscience," John Leo wrote in the wake of the council, "it is at least debatable whether the long feared fragmentation of the church is about to take place."[23]

Perhaps nothing better symbolized the depth of this change than a 1966 *Ave Maria* editorial eulogizing Margaret Sanger, pioneer advocate of birth control and planned parenthood. No one had been vilified with greater unanimity by Catholic priests, journalists, bishops and lay people than Mrs. Sanger. Indeed Kenneth Underwood had written a monumental book on Catholic efforts to prevent the hated Mrs. Sanger from speaking in Holyoke, Massachusetts, a study that laid bare the bitter divisions Mrs. Sanger symbolized. Yet, at her death editor John Reedy wrote that Margaret Sanger was "not only an altruist, but a practicing altruist, and our respect is compelled by the courage of her convictions, her willingness to put herself on the firing line, her fidelity to her vision and to her cause."[24] Such understanding and charity were like a breath of spring air in the household of American Catholicism. But they were also portent of the dangers that always accompany rapid changes in values.

It would of course be easy to exaggerate the effects of the new "diaspora consciousness." A growing non-involvement in the church on the part of the young, a steep decline of religious vocations, the financial crises in Catholic schools, the breakup of religious communities and establishment of underground churches all manifested its effects, but it would be a mistake to underestimate the tenaciousness of ingrained religious habits and the powerful hold the parish, the parochial school and the church generally have on the loyalty of millions of Americans. Regular church attendance and reception of the sacraments remain features of the lives of most American Catholics. Large numbers still think of the church and its mission in traditional terms, as the Gallup polls continually demonstrate, and, if many ignore the church's teachings on birth control, few generalize from that rejection to a re-evaluation of religious authority as a whole.

Still the impact of these changes upon church professionals, on priests, nuns and those intellectuals who consciously approach such matters as Christians, has been immense and ultimately far-reaching in its effects. Already there have been serious conflicts between segments of the divided laity and the church professionals over liturgical experimentation, finances, parish councils and catechetics. Moreover, as the 1961 study of

Boston area priests by Sr. M. Augusta Neale showed, there are serious divisions between clergy in administrative posts in diocesan and extra-parochial agencies on the one hand and pastors on the other so that "the diocese can at the same time be articulate in its value commitment to change and resistent in its day to day program in the routine of the parish."[25] The description obviously has application beyond the diocesan level. In short the "diaspora situation," the ecumenical spirit and the new sense of freedom and responsibility in the church did not swing Catholicism in united way to a new stance toward itself and the world, but occasioned deep and serious divisions, which are bound to grow in the years ahead.

The conflicts occasioned by the events of the 1960s had ramifications far beyond the difficulties they posed for the institutional church. Martin Marty wrote in the midst of the increasingly bitter exchanges between Catholics bent on further reform and ecclesiastical leaders determined to go slow that a two-party system, which had long existed within Protestant communions, now was emerging into public view in the Catholic church. For all the publicity given to church reform in the 1960s, the victory of the liberals had not gone unchallenged. Many still held fast to the old ideals and devotions and deplored the changes taking place around them. At the same time the political views of many Catholics had long been at odds with those of the liberals. In the 1950s William F. Buckley's *National Review* had given conservatives an organ as popular and influential as *Commonweal*. Buckley and *Commonweal* editor William Clancy engaged in a number of highly publicized debates over the relationship between Catholicism and social and political policy, an argument that was raised to new heights of intensity by the liberal stance of Pope John and President Kennedy. Indeed when *National Review* seemed to dismiss one of the Pope's encyclical with the words "*Mater* si *Magistra* no," a heated debate spread throughout the Catholic press and caused one observer to speak of a "running Cold War now splitting American Catholics."[26] It was a rather strange war that found liberal Catholics calling upon their opponents to give due weight to papal teachings and Garry Wills, then a *National*

Review contributor, defending "Catholic freedom" against such liberal reliance on authority, positions later sharply reversed. [27]

As the council proceeded to endorse religious liberty, a vernacular liturgy and positive social action, conservatives became increasingly disturbed. In 1965 they presented a book of *National Review* essays under the title "What in the Name of God is Going on in the Catholic Church?"[28] In part this expressed shock at the speed with which long-held positions seemed to be reversed. As "new men" like Callahan, Novak and the pseudonymous Xavier Rynne were taken up by the secular media as spokesmen for the American church, conservatives began "lashing out at the new liberalism which had swept them from the influence they enjoyed in the immigrant church and its Americanized successor."[29] Some felt as did the non-Catholic Will Herberg that the council was destroying the church as an effective opponent of what Herberg had called "the idolatrous new religion of Americanism." Indeed few comments showed such extreme hostility as Herberg's remark that "what the church needs today is not incitement to aggiornamento but—I dare say it—another, hopefully more adequate, more intelligent and discriminating Syllabus of Errors for our time."[30]

For a time the sentiments of such conservatives expressed in *National Review, Triumph,* a new monthly published by L. Brent Bozell, Buckley's brother-in-law, and a few diocesan papers, seemed the isolated complaints of a defeated minority. But, as events at home and abroad and the logic of renewal itself brought an escalation of demands for freedom and for change, the ranks of conservatives were gradually strengthened. Bishop John Wright, for example, was regarded in the early 1960s as "the shining light of the American hierarchy" but had become by the end of the decade a symbol of institutional intransigence and ecclesiastical authoritarianism.[31] Defenders of papal authority, opponents of further liturgical revision, the theologically orthodox and the politically moderate all found reasons to question the pace of change and reach out for some solid, familiar anchor to hold them firm. Masses of lay people shaken by the transformation of their church, the weakening of their schools and a hundred personal and political pressures provided further recruits for a movement to call a halt to renewal and reform.

Andrew Greeley, for example, was in the early 1960s a leading liberal in Catholic circles. As a social scientist, Greeley punctured many of the myths and pretensions of church authority; as an intellectual he called loudly for academic and intellectual freedom in the church; as an enthuiastic Americanist he believed firmly that the age of American leadership had arrived. Without abandoning his liberal principles, Greeley gradually began to look upon those he considered radicals as greater enemies to the realization of the promise of the 1960s than were the men who wielded power in the church. His tough-minded sociological outlook made him highly critical of the more extreme demands of reformers. He was equally offended by what he considered the disloyalty of many who continued to attack the church after it had demonstrated its ability to change. The celibacy debate also offended him, and he was appalled by the political radicalism of the Catholic resistance. Like others who had fought for reform in the 1950s and early 1960s he was acutely conscious of how much had already been accomplished and feared that radical thought and action would polarize the church, thus preventing the balanced implementation of the conciliar reforms. "When Pope John spoke of the prophets of doom he presumably meant the conservative forces in the church who wanted no part of the modern world," Greeley wrote. "But there are new prophets of doom who in their morbid fascination with the weaknesses and failures of the church refuse to recognize the sweeping progress of the recent past; any church short of a perfect one (and by their standards of perfection at that) is a church which moves them to gloom and despair. These are the prophets of doom of the left who would have us believe that the church is quite irrelevant at the very time when it is becoming more relevant than it has been in half a millennium."[32]

In this atmosphere of deepening polarization between those who demanded that the church immediately undertake a new mission in an age when critical issues threatened human values and even human survival and those who felt that only balanced, reasonable reform could realize the hopes stirred by the council, men at all points of the spectrum began to speak of a crisis. "Obviously the Catholic Church finds herself today in the midst of the gravest crisis she has experienced since the Protestant Revolt, and the American branch of the Church Universal is no exception," wrote the scholarly and judicious John Tracy Ellis in 1967.[33] A rash of post-conciliar books reflected a similar conviction that at a time when basic decisions had to be made on a host of issues, radical impatience and conservative blindness prevented an honest facing and resolution of outstanding issues.

One sign of the times was that many took less and less interest in church affairs. While Michael Novak retained a keen interest in theological issues, he was even more strongly drawn to the political and cultural upheavals which wracked the nation. Daniel Callahan wrote in 1969: "In my more honest moments, which come and go like the seasons, I'm sometimes tempted to admit to myself that I'm just tired of religion: its theologies, its institutions, its worries and its problems."[34] He could not entirely break off from the ongoing Catholic debate but devoted most of his time to a monumental analysis of the problem of abortion. Other men similarly found it more and more difficult to justify the energies invested in intra-church debates and struggles in the face of such problems as racism, violence, uncontrolled technology and the alienation of youth. Even Father Greeley, who would contribute his share to every discussion, said in exasperation after a long session on "issues that divide the church": "Most of the controversy in the American Church is little more than verbal. To engage in such play in a time of grave crisis is childish and irresponsible."[35]

But some of the older liberals kept up the fight. Donald Thorman, whose *Emerging Layman* had been an important contribution to the liberal movement of the early 1960s was, at the end of the decade, publisher of the *National Catholic Reporter*. While recognizing that a crisis existed, Thorman remained convinced that "for every danger facing us there are at least twice as many opportunities for beneficial development and change now present within the church." He was optimistic because he sensed a "new mood developing today among significant numbers of Catholic laymen," a mood of "self-confidence as a functioning citizen and a successful and increasingly affluent member of American society." By 1968 Thorman believed that laymen had emerged and begun "applying new criteria to the church and its leadership based on their own experience in our modern society." In such movements as the death of God, the new morality and the quest for secular sanctity Thorman saw plenty of evidence of a maturing Christian consciousness. Whereas in the pre-conciliar years Catholics had tried to reverse the thrust of industry and technology, they had in the 1960s "stopped fighting modern civilization." Instead, Thorman believed, "the new generation of American Catholics are set for the task of confronting American society as it really exists."[36]

As far as the layman was concerned, the liberal program had apparently succeeded. But there was danger, Thorman felt, in that the bishops had failed to keep pace. "The failure of our bishops, as a group, to provide dynamic, loving leadership is the most important single reason for the continuing crisis in the American church today and for the widespread failure of renewal and reform in American Catholicism," Thorman wrote. [37] Ellis and Andrew Greeley made the same charge, in even stronger terms. For Thorman the solution was to "Christianize the Church," but what he meant was the introduction into official church practice of intellectual freedom, popular participation and due process of law. The Americanist framework held firm.

Douglas Roche, a Canadian, had a somewhat different view of the nature of the crisis. "The new age is one of transition from the stereotype of the past to a free floating style, from convention to conviction, from certainties to inquiries." "Most of all there is a new sense of discovery in the Catholic Church, which for ages thought she knew everything. . . . Catholics have discovered that they are on a pilgrimage through history in constant search of truth." It constituted a real revolution, and like all revolutions it brought great suffering and ambiguous results. "The price of the Catholic revolution is fewer numbers in the church, shortages of priests and sisters, harder times, confusion and even despair." Many opposed further change;

many would regard balanced progress as inadequate, so Roche foresaw "a mammoth crisis of conscience on the horizon."[38]

The crisis of the church was then also a crisis of conscience, not only for the intellectuals who had difficulty relating their churchly concerns to their more pressing secular interests, but for priests and lay people in churches around the country beset by the conflicts that stirred every institution in America in the later years of the decade. Rahner's words at the beginning of the decade seemed almost prophetic. In the diaspora, Rahner had written, the Christian's faith is "constantly threatened from without," faith becomes a matter "of personal achievement constantly renewed amid perilous surroundings."[39] By the end of the decade the surroundings had become perilous indeed, and many men in many ways were seeking to renew their faith. It had become a time of doubt, of malaise, but also a time of honesty and warmth. Catholicism had surely become American, and like America, it was stirred to the depth of its soul.

The Catholic press provides one illustration of the depths of the changes that have occurred in recent years and of the growing chasm that separates younger Catholics not only from conservatives but even from the liberals of the early reform movement.

No one familiar with the tone of Catholic writing in the pre-council years could be anything but shocked by the new style and content of Catholic publications. The *Brooklyn Tablet* was a somewhat extreme example of the Catholic press, but its editor long carried a sense of the purpose and function of the press that reflected the ghetto orientation of most church publications in the pre-conciliar years. "The *Tablet* today is fighting the battle of every Catholic man, woman and child," the paper editorialized in its 25th anniversary edition of 1933." It strives to spread Catholicity to the four corners of the earth, to encourage Catholic education and support Catholic charity; it makes known Catholic history; spreads broadcast deeds of Catholic achievement . . . and chronicles the story of the trials and tribulations, victories and defeats of the church in every land; it champions Catholic principles, protects Catholic rights, preserves Catholic teaching, arouses Catholic thought and stimulates Catholic enterprise."[40] Such words make credible the probably fictional story of the Catholic newspaper headline "Plane Crash in Kansas; No Catholics Killed." Yet it had not always been so, for in the nineteenth century there had been several intelligent, well-edited Catholic publications. However the events of the turn of the century left the Catholic press "subdued and reserved, if not completely docile." No wonder that one Catholic editor, commenting on the rash of new publications of the post World War II years concluded that "there is nothing wrong with the Catholic press in America that an acute paper shortage wouldn't cure."[41]

Few would make such a comment at the end of the decade. *Commonweal, America* and a few diocesan publications had long set high standards and during the council many other publications began to introduce national and international issues, serious theology and often superb reporting of church events. The Davenport *Messenger,* the Boston *Pilot,* the *Delmarva Dialogue* and several other diocesan papers achieved real excellence while such weeklies and monthlies as *Ave Maria* and *The Catholic World* broadened their interests and revised their editorial policy to give strong backing to the reform movement. Most important was the *National Catholic Reporter,* founded in 1964 to provide a forum for national Catholic news and opinion. Within a few years its circulation approached 100,000, hardly indicative of its enormous impact on public opinion, particularly on younger clergy, religious and laymen. While its reporting varied enormously in quality, the *National Catholic Reporter* was an indispensible element in the process of aggiornamento in the American church of the 1960s.

There were severe tensions in the changes that beset the Catholic press. Good editors were fired by diocesan officers themselves under pressure from a divided people, and some good magazines fell with many bad ones. Even internally, generational and ideological conflicts were often present. *Commonweal,* long the leader of Catholic liberalism and the voice of educated, articulate Americanized laymen, seemed to one of its old editors to have fallen on bad days. "A certain juvenile snideness and rudeness have appeared in recent years that somehow seem a mild betrayal of the tradition that gave the magazine its special character in the past," John Cogley wrote in 1969. It was unfortunate that *Commonweal* had not resisted these trends, so widespread in American society, and "waited out a bad period in American life." The *National Catholic Reporter* had similar faults, Cogley believed, regretting its "constant story of Catholic unravelling," yet he admitted that the *Reporter,* unlike *Commonweal,* had "no tradition to betray" because "there never was a decent Catholic newspaper before."[42]

The reply to Cogley issued by *Commonweal* editor Peter Steinfels manifested in dramatic terms the chasm that by the end of the decade separated younger men not only from the bishops, who seemed to live on another planet from the church's own new left, but even from the liberal Catholics who had given shape and form to the consciousness of the able and articulate laity for generations.

Commonweal of the 1950s, Cogley's *Commonweal,* had been regarded at the time, and regarded accurately, as a truly radical voice within the church, yet it seemed to Steinfels to have "meshed nicely with the mood of conservatism which swept American intellectual life" in the decade of Eisenhower. Despite its dissent on some issues, Steinfels wrote, the magazine had "expressed a profound agreement with the major trends of American and church policy." Solidly behind the over-all goals and strategy of American foreign policy, convinced that the church was "the Rock of Ages in whose bosom were kept the absolutes which safeguarded human rights—and without which the world would collapse," apparently unaware of the Church's complicity in modern war and oppression, *Commonweal* had indeed represented a civil and urbane tradition. Speaking for his own generation, Steinfels caught clearly the root of the crisis in Catholic liberalism, the collapse of America itself as the solid anchor and norm for reform in church and world. "How much easier it is to be urbane and civil when one believes that things are fundamentally right with America," Steinfels wrote. "It is more difficult (and sometimes simply inappropriate) when one believes that America is waging a criminal war, immorally murdering people day after day, and about to destroy herself at home."[43] Feelings like these would lead men to exile and prison and would call into question all those things that men had taken for granted just a few years before. In the heat of this new American revolution, the future of American Catholicism would be decided.

7
CATHOLICS AND POLITICS

The Church is a political institution beset by the same issues of authority and legitimacy, rights and obligations that haunt the broader public life and the church experiences the same processes of pressure, struggle, negotiation and compromise that blur the distinction between ideal and reality in the governance of all organizations, including the state. Perhaps this political character of the church finds its corollary in the religious dimensions of political life, as men supposedly involved in the mundane affairs of democratic government find in their nation the symbolic manifestation of their deepest hopes and fears and honor political leaders who endow public actions with religious significance. As Christians move into the ambiguous future they do so with a growing consciousness of the intimacy and interaction, for better or worse, of religion and politics.

Although there are times when articulate, active Catholics seem to feel that they are the first of their faith to have discovered politics, the fact is that politics, both secular and ecclesiastical, has been both a vocation and an avocation in their community. Indeed, for many years secular politics shared with the church and the athletic arena the distinction of generating the symbolic heroes of the American Catholic community. The Catholic church always presented each age and each culture with its own saint, a person who embodied all those qualities valued by the church and its members. Sometimes these were national heroes like Joan of Arc, sometimes functional heroes like Thomas Aquinas for the intellectuals or Dismas, the supposedly repentent thief, for prisoners; often they were saints for an age, like Vincent de Paul or the uncanonized Newman. Americans have had few such saints, the immigrant Francis Cabrini, and the convert Elizabeth Seton, but they have had some heroes who served in their stead, Bishop Carroll, Father Finn or Joe Dimaggio. Each highlighted some feature of Ameri-

can life and Catholic faith, which teachers sought to instill in
the young; each lived for a time in the minds of his people as a
true hero, confronting in real or symbolic terms the hostility of
non-Catholic America while remaining true to his church and
loyal to his nation. To take only a very recent period, that of
World War II, Francis Cardinal Spellman's friendship with the
president, his service to American troops and his vigorous struggle for Catholic schools and against communism all manifested
the heroic style of leadership. The Sullivan brothers, Bing Cros-
by, Father Keller and others have done the same on other levels.
Nevertheless, in the new age inaugurated by Catholic ascent into
the middle class and the changes emanating from the reign of
John XXIII and Vatican II, these old heroes seemed less useful,
less attractive, even gross, unsophisticated and disrespectable. A
new saint, a new model, was needed.

Andrew Greeley, the University of Chicago sociologist whose
work has contributed so much to the increased self-awareness of
the last decade, has been one of the few to see this need and to
try to meet it. In his book, *The Catholic Experience*, he entitles
one chapter "John F. Kennedy, Doctor of the Church." The
title is an apt one and Greeley makes a serious and convincing
case for regarding Kennedy as the most complete expression of
all that is best in American Catholicism. The book is a history
of the American church and in it Greeley presents the great
figures of the nineteenth century: Carroll, England, Hughes,
Gibbons and Ireland as personifying a tradition of adaptation to
the demands of the American situation. With the exception of
the combative Hughes all the great prelates sought to assimilate
the immigrant Catholic to the new society, to promote better
relations with non-Catholics and to encourage the participation
of laymen in social, political and intellectual life. Implicitly, and
sometimes explicitly, they recognized that in America the
church's claims to dominate all phases of social life would have
to be restricted, that the demands of religious freedom necessitated the preservation of an area of secularity that could only
be made moral and just by the work of Catholic laymen. As a
result, they opposed any attempt to shut the church and its
members up within a ghetto, cut off from creative contact with
the powerful secular movements of their day, but urged Catho-

lics to actively encounter these forces in the life of society, confident that they could be guided and shaped in a Christian direction.

Leo XIII's condemnation of "Americanism," in Greeley's view, abruptly ended this creative dialogue between Christianity and America. The church withdrew from the field, removed itself from contact with outsiders, and became more defensive, more preoccupied with slights and rebukes from non-Catholics than ever before. While the laity shared this attitude, Greeley argues that the exigencies of the situation—the need to learn English, the desire for success—led them to ever greater involvement in the secular activities of American society. The climax of this diverging movement of the church into isolation and Catholics into full participation came with the election of John F. Kennedy. The latter was the very exemplar of all the qualities valued by the early Americanists: quiet and unobtrusive loyalty to the faith, acceptance of America in all its secularity, exclusive concern as a politician and leader with the temporal welfare of the nation. In his Americanism he stood in judgment on his church, which had little to say to him beyond carping criticism of his opposition to federal aid to parochial schools. The contrast between Kennedy's dedication to the public interest and the continuing preoccupation of many church leaders with narrow group interests mirrored the profound dislocation between church policies and the realities of the American experience. Not Spellman but John Fitzgerald Kennedy was the American Catholic for the new age, and only if the church was able to follow him, perhaps to develop its own Kennedy as a bishop, could it fully enter into the life of the nation and catch up with the problems and possibilities of its own members.[1]

Certainly Greeley is not alone in his admiration of Kennedy, for many commentators of varying persuasions have seen him as the epitome of a new America. Young people in particular responded to him, both before and after his tragic death, as a model for themselves. His intelligence, his cool and unruffled style, his easy appreciation of the modern, his confidence in the ability of Americans to face and to resolve the great questions of the age, had an attraction beyond anything offered by any other American leader of the postwar years with the possible exception of Martin Luther King. Catholics shared in this fascination, and even older laymen schooled in the harsh anti-liberal polemics of traditional Catholic political commentary found in his success vindication for the slights and discrimination they and their fathers had suffered. Whatever doubts the older generation had about his foreign policy or his modernity, they were bound to be pleased by his success.

Yet as a saint for the new age, much less as a "doctor of the church," Kennedy as man or as myth had certain limitations. He was quite clearly a man of his times, an assimilated Irish-Catholic educated at Choate and Harvard and schooled in the politics of postwar America. He fit few of the old categories, for he contained and transcended the Irishness of his father, the machine politics of his grandfather, the liberalism of his teachers and the conservatism of his class. Yet his contact with Catholicism was ephemeral at best and could provide little basis for attraction for committed Catholics of right or left. For the conservatives, as Greeley clearly saw, he was a questionable hero. For them the test of Catholicity was and remained loyalty to the institutional church and identification with those Americans who defined themselves as Catholics. For the dogmas of such men on matters of parochial schools and the cold war Kennedy had little use. His speech to the Houston ministers during the 1960 campaign, in which he affirmed his freedom from the hierarchy and his reliance on conscience, marked his break with the demands of the old church. His was a secular point of view and as such necessarily anthema to the old Catholicism. Indeed the qualities the young liked about Kennedy, his modernity, his pragmatic realism, his humanitarian idealism, were the very things the church's leaders had been decrying for half a century.

On the other hand "new breed" Catholics, so enamored with Kennedy in 1960, moved during the ensuing decade to positions from which Kennedy's attraction needed to be questioned. Their enthusiastic endorsement of neo-Americanism in the 1950s gradually gave way before the breakdown of the America of their imagination. The America Daniel Callahan had described in 1961 as characterized by freedom, openness and democracy was replaced by an image of America as militarist, racist and oppresive. Even the most casual observer could not help but notice the rapid change which occurred in the 1960s, from the enthusiasm of new opportunity and reform of 1960 to the near despair of 1967 and 1968. The America of John Tracy Ellis and John Cogley, much less that of Ireland and Hecker, disintegrated in the reign of Lyndon Johnson. At the very moment when America gave its complete acceptance to Catholicism as a part of the natural order of the nation, the nation appeared no longer a safe haven for the Christian conscience. By 1967 younger Catholic commentators and activists were discussing public issues in moralistic terms that John Kennedy had acknowledged were foreign to his nature. Not technique but principle, not reform but revolution, had become the slogans of the middle 1960s. In retrospect the Kennedy years were the years of the Bay of Pigs and of a deepening involvement in Viet Nam; Kennedy's Americanism, his greatest virtue in the eyes of Andrew Greeley, seemed now to have been his vice, his fatal flaw. With Kennedy as a model, the new breed American Catholic was supposed to take his Catholicism and his Americanism for granted; now many could not in conscience do so.

Were there other, alternative heroes, candidates for the role of models for the new age. For conservative Catholics a prospect could be found in William F. Buckley, a rich Irish-Catholic, writer, lecturer and editor, whose magazine, *National Review,* had spearheaded the conservative revival of the 1950s. In 1966, when Buckley ran as Conservative Party candidate for mayor of New York, he gained a public exposure which brought him national fame. Buckley possesses all the flair, sophistication and coolness of John Kennedy. He is a very modern man, at home with the mass media, a full participant in the cultural life of New York City, a casual and relaxed exponent of tried and true American values. He offers all the appeal of modernity while remaining loyal to the most basic dogmas of the old America and the old church. He is a conventionally loyal Catholic, prepared to defend the church and its interests, dismayed by the pace of change within its ranks. Together with his brother-in-law, Brent Bozell, editor of the conservative Catholic monthly *Triumph,* he speaks for the dismay and the confusion besetting many Catholics. At the same time he offers a political and social philosophy directly linked to that they learned in their youth. America is the nation that offered and gave them success; its system of free enterprise and limited government had given them their newly achieved status. Communism remained the most severe threat to the nation, and the church remained the surest defender against its spread. Buckley's brother James was elected to the Senate from New York in 1970 with considerable support from Catholics, both working-class Catholics dismayed by urban and campus unrest and by the failure of liberal political leaders to consider their problems with respect and young Catholic professionals and businessmen. Yet James Buckley is a far less charismatic and colorful man than his brother and offers little hope of becoming a symbolic culture hero.

William Buckley has been such a hero. Yet Buckley is a contradictory figure, and the contradictions of his ideas limit his acceptability as a new model for the conservative Catholic. Against secularism he is a completely secular person; against mass democracy he is a product of the mass media; against government control and regulation, he speaks to an audience whose education and standard of living are dependent upon government spending. To an audience who yearn for the stabilization of the status quo he offers a philosophy that would turn back the clock. A professed exponent of libertarian individualism, he propounds a foreign policy that necessitates militarism and the draft. To an audience who desire peace and prosperity he urges policies that would keep the world an armed camp, with the cities in turmoil, and that would probably destroy the delicate mechanism of postwar prosperity. Like Barry Goldwater, he serves as a useful vehicle for discontent and uneasiness, but even many of his greatest admirers realize that when the chips are down he offers little beyond ideology and myth.

In any event, Buckley could never serve as a model for liberal and radical Catholics, any more than his followers could look upon the heroes at the other end of the spectrum, Daniel and Philip Berrigan and Dorothy Day, as their saints for the new age. If a new leader was to be found who could symbolize the community, he would have to be closer to the religious and political center. In 1968 many thought they had found such a man in one of the two contenders for the Democratic presidential nomination, Robert Kennedy and Eugene McCarthy, men who embodied the divergent options in American Catholic politics.

"Be more Irish than Harvard," poet Robert Frost had told John Kennedy on inauguration day, 1961. That advice sprang from the poet's insight into the blend of political pragmatism and liberal idealism that shaped the personality of the new president. Even more it pointed up the significance of an important segment of the American population who achieved political maturity with the election of John F. Kennedy. Irish Americans had long found in political action a vehicle for the achievement of power and respectability but their attempts to move onto the national stage had been checked by the 1928 election and its supposed lesson that no Catholic could ever win the presidency. Kennedy changed all that, winning for his fellow Catholics release from the feeling of exclusion and second-class citizenship. Fearful that the president and others like him would find in their new respectability reasons for forgetting the heritage that had shaped them, Robert Frost warned against a headlong abandonment of Irish ways in favor of the more fashionable manners of Harvard style liberalism. Robert Kennedy and Eugene McCarthy represented different streams of that Irish-Catholic heritage, just as they excited the emotions of different sectors of the American reform movement. Had it not been for the tragic events of that terrible spring and summer, the clash might well have determined the shape of American politics for a generation.

One must go back a century, to Jacksonian New York in the 1830s, to set the background for this struggle. The flood of Irish immigrants was still a trickle compared to what would come in the famine years, but the Irish had already chosen the path of their future politics: an association with the Democratic party so close that, as many have noted, Irish, Catholic and Democrat become interchangeable terms. The newcomers found in that party a warm reception, which contrasted with the hostile anti-Catholicism of the elitist Whigs. The Democrats, on the other hand, found in the Irish remarkably loyal and skillful allies in the struggle for power. Slowly the Irish rose to positions of leadership and power in the party by virtue of hard work, unquestioning loyalty and respect for the primacy of the organization over individual interests and values. Tammany Hall became an Irish closed corporation that served their interests, bringing the intangible benefits of status and the more meaningful benefits of power. Enthusiastic young men who found "No Irish Need Apply" signs in the hallways of business found in politics (and the church) an arena for the ascent from poverty to affluence, from impotence to power, which was the object of the success mythology. Ideology was irrelevant: the machine was neither liberal nor conservative. It served its constituents and its members in clear, bread and butter ways, while affording them the heady experience of exercising power over their more respectable Protestant neighbors.

Yet the motives that led the Irish into politics and the skills by which they excelled at it had little to do with theory or purpose. "The very parochialism and bureaucracy that enabled them to succeed in politics prevented them from doing much with government," Daniel P. Moynihan writes. "They never thought of politics as an instrument of social change."[2] From the start machine politicians were brokers of power, doing the business of politics and government. They had little sympathy with reform movements, which often had a strong anti-Catholic or anti-immigrant orientation and were led by men of the upper classes who were their natural enemies. The hostility was reciprocated.

The machine served Irish interests and sensitivities well, but it horrified native Protestants, who believed that government, not politics, was the thing that mattered. Government, enshrined by law, stood above the petty interests, protecting the public and providing a means for the realization of moral principles. Honesty, integrity, civic mindedness, so important for the native, seemed cold, distant and hostile to lower-class immigrants in need of jobs, aid, power. But not all were immune. Many Irish Americans, as they moved out of the working class, yearned for acceptance by the native majority, adopted its values and turned on the machine the continued existence of which was a constant reminder to their Protestant neighbors of their origin and identity. Thus it was an Irish lawyer, Charles O'Connor, who led the fight against the Tweed ring and most anti-Tammany reform movements found many respectable Irish Americans in their ranks.

The politics of Catholic bishops were often ambivalent even contradictory. On the one hand, like many other Americans the bishops never fully accepted the validity of the political party. The Founding Fathers, while they constructed a political system that made parties inevitable, deplored them when they appeared. Parties were "factions," divisive, self-interested, prepared to subordinate national principle and national interest to the particular goals of their members. Partisan politics was an arena of "strife," which spread "a pestilential atmosphere" that endangered "honor, virtue, patriotism and religion," according to Bishop John England. "You are accountable not only to society but to God for the honest, independent and fearless exercise of your franchise," England warned his flock. "It is a trust confided to you not for your private gain but for the public good." England made an exception when Catholics were singled out "for insult and for abuse," but in his over-all view of the political process he was at one with his successors among the best leaders of the hierarchy in calling for independent, non-partisan voting that took the public interest as its criterion.[3]

Church leaders, secure in their own status and distressed by the lack of political leverage caused by over-identification with one party, often lashed out angrily at the group-conscious partisanship of their flocks. Just as non-Catholics feared that the church divided the nation, so Catholic leaders hoped to overcome the evidence of partisanship that seemed to confirm such fears. A century later, alarmed at the "spread of subversive teaching," the bishops inaugurated a "Catholic crusade for Christian Democracy" aimed at achieving a solid identification of Catholics with the national interest. Catholics were to be "held in the conviction that love of country is a virtue and disloyalty a sin," the bishops wrote.[4] National loyalty and Catholic unity were crucially important to church leaders, who, as experience demonstrated, could easily blend together a self-righteous aloofness from the political process and a deep involvement in elections, legislation and governmental administration.

Such considerations occasionally led a bishop to mobilize an organized group of Catholic independents to support church objectives in the secular realm. Archbishop John Hughes, a close friend of such Whig and later Republican leaders as William Henry Seward and Thurlow Weed, tried hard to break the hold of the Democratic party on the Catholic vote. In this effort, which he hoped would make the government more responsive to Catholic interests, he had the backing of many native-born, respectable Catholics.

One of the younger political historians, Lee Benson, has become convinced that "at least since the 1820s when universal manhood suffrage became widespread, ethnic and religious differences have tended to be *relatively* the most important sources of political differences."[5] In New York, in the 1840s, Benson discovered that immigrants of British stock, predominantly Protestant, were the strongest supporters of the Whig party while non-British newcomers, mostly Catholic, were the Democratic party's most loyal adherents. Yet not all Catholics were Democrats, for one Whig newspaper noted that 80% of native-born Catholics were Whigs, while church leaders labored vigorously to break the bonds between Catholics and the Democratic party. "The politicians must leave us alone;" the New York diocesan paper editorialized. "They must not profane our religion by mixing it up with their intemperate and often unprincipled strife, nor must they drag it and us, singled out from the nation, into the arena to become targets for mob fury." While Archbishop John Hughes and his successors did not always hold to the line of political independence, there was a clear and constant tension between the bishops' perspective on political life and the political behavior of their Catholic flocks.

This division persisted, as did the split between the group-conscious polities of the machine and the liberal attitudes of Americanized Catholics. In the 1890s the liberal John Ireland identified with and actively promoted the Republican party, leading to open conflict with New York Catholic leaders. Rochester Bishop Bernard McQuaid publicly attacked Ireland's political activities from his Cathedral pulpit. Later, Boston's colorful James Michael Curley had an implacable enemy in the aristocratic William Cardinal O'Connell. Although the work of such leaders and the concern of successful Catholics to overcome the social stigma of their origins led many to support movements aimed at destroying the political machine and its operators, most Catholics continued to identify with the Democratic party. Only in the 1950s did any serious break come about when many Catholics abandoned the party of their fathers to vote for Dwight Eisenhower, but it is clear in retrospect that the break was not profound or permanent.

Yet the old division continued to exist, transformed by the political changes of the twentieth century. Earlier reform movements had been markedly anti-Catholic, inhibiting Catholic participation, or they had been associated with the Republican party, thus challenging local and personal loyalties. In the 1930s, reform found a new home in the Democratic party of Franklin D. Roosevelt, and ambitious Catholic politicians and politically concerned Catholic intellectuals found themselves in the midst of significant intra-party struggles. In the course of time there was a growing divergence between the liberalism of those Catholic intellectuals who identified closely with the party intelligentsia and the more pragmatic, bread and butter politics of Catholic leaders of urban machine and trade unions.

John F. Kennedy was a peculiar mixture of these two streams. His father had communicated to his children an ambition that derived from his own sense of deprivation, for despite his wealth and influence he never overcame identification as an Irish Catholic. His son's education at Harvard and London introduced him into the world of liberal reform but never erased the Irish legacy. He maintained the two in uneasy balance, sustaining a liberal voting record and eloquently articulating the symbols of reform, while at the same time refusing to challenge the horribly archaic machine politics of his home state and maintaining close alliances with bosses of old and new vintage. Although liberals like Arthur Schlesinger, Jr., eventually found a home in John Kennedy's camp, the latter confessed his discomfort when placed among "ADA types." He remained until the end more Irish than Harvard, more at ease with problems of technique than with problems of principle, more successful manipulating power than embarking on crusades. If to many Catholics his sophistication and style seemed alien, part of that upper-class Protestant world they both envied and despised, his tough-minded realism was abhorrent to just as many old-line liberals. It was almost ironic that Protestant theologian Reinhold Niebuhr, long a passionate exponent of just such realism, thought that Kennedy carried things too far. "I write to you to make a confession," Niebuhr told Felix Frankfurter after the 1960 Democratic convention. "One who had preached a lifetime to Protestant purists that they must come to terms with the moral ambiguity of the political process found it very difficult to swallow Kennedy."[6]

Niebuhr's dislike did not last. The Kennedy presidency witnessed the marriage, after an often stormy courtship, of reform and the machine, of Harvard and the Irish. All the changes had not been on the Irish or Catholic side. Twentieth-century liberalism had itself been gradually transformed not only by events like the depression, the war and its aftermath, but by the political force of urban organizations, which began to exert significant leverage in national politics during the New Deal years. Following the war liberal leaders, chastened by experience, once and for all abandoned the moralism and utopianism that had long characterized their approach to government. Instead, the liberal establishment committed itself to nationalist, bi-partisan foreign policy aimed at the defeat of communism. In domestic affairs they adjusted to the demands of the existing deadlock between themselves and the conservative coalition in Congress and took what pleasure they could from the liberal phrases of Democratic platforms and Truman-Kennedy state of the union messages. Adlai Stevenson rekindled their idealism, and John Kennedy seemed for a time to have restored idealism to power. But it turned out that Kennedy's rhetoric and sophisticated pragmatism brought no basic shift in outlook. The political machine's preoccupation with getting and holding power while pacifying discontent through ad hoc measures seemed solidly entrenched in the federal government with a president who talked like Schlesinger but welcomed power and could exercise it ruthlessly.

Yet the Kennedy policy and style, with its inner tensions and moral ambiguity, was perfectly in accord with the stance of liberal Catholics early in the decade. Men were aware of the difficulties of liberal politics, as the frequent debates over morality and foreign policy and the lively public interest in Pope John XXIII's encyclicals indicated, but they could imagine no real alternative. Writing several months after the Cuban missile crisis of 1962, John Cogley told of meeting with government officials involved in the decisions of that fateful time when the world had gone to the brink. "I am unequivocally for the men who have to make the decisions that so far have spelled the difference between life and death," Cogley wrote. "I am for them by inclination, by temperament, and by conviction." In language typical of the time Cogley condemned critics of the administration for their "purism," "feigned innocence" and "self-righteousness." For realists like Cogley only the nuclear balance preserved the peace, and all mankind must be grateful for the cautious, calculated response the American government had made to the Russian challenge. In any other direction, be it the militance of the right or the left, lay disaster for the United States and all mankind.

Yet Cogley was an intelligent, sensitive and good man, and the necessity for such realism obviously disturbed him. He recognized the horror that stood beyond the brink, and after making clear that he was on the side of the administration rather than with its moralistic critics, he went on to call for a "new politics" that would place human survival above power, ideology or national interest. These considerations nevertheless seemed built into the human situation, inescapable and relentless, forever displacing consideration or the human community. So, even while recognizing what the arms race was doing to the planet and its people, Cogley could find no answer but the oldest and most utopian. "Is it really too much . . . to hope that the politics of humanity will triumph over the politics of power?," Cogley asked. He could only respond "Perhaps. But if there is no such hope, what is there to pray for?"[7] The politics of the end of ideology, at the very peak of its ascendancy, drew its leading Catholic advocate to lay hold of the power of prayer.

In retrospect it is clear that the liberal stance could not last, and in those very days the grave of such politics was being dug in Indochina. Kennedy's brutal assassination, the Viet Nam war, the ghetto riots, irrational violence at home and abroad, shattered the complacency of establishment liberalism. The merger of Irish realism and Harvard sophistication turned out to have marked not a new beginning but the bankruptcy of old ideas, even if held by new men. Bowles, Bundy, Rostow, McNamara, Rusk, the agents of the new frontier, stood in Viet Nam at the hither edge of the American empire mouthing the same tired cliches that had so irritated them in the 1950s when they came from the lips of Eisenhower and John Foster Dulles. From the campuses and the ghettos came protest, stated in terms so extreme as to seem unpatriotic. Men who had learned in the dramatic events of the 1930s that all great dreams end in destruction—Madrid, Stalingrad, Hiroshima—could not but regard the moral protest of a new day as romantic, unhistorical, utopian. Having lost sight of the end themselves, they could no longer bear to be reminded of it. They had made war to end war, crushed people to protect democracy, allowed their country to decay while pursuing the ghost of security. Realists all, as they saw themselves, even the fires of their cities could not bring them to see the reality of failure and the need for a new vision and new ideas. But the facts would not go away and gradually more and more of them came over to the opposition camp, determined to restore sanity if they could, but retaining their hostility to moralism, to any serious questioning of the ends which their techniques were supposed to serve. They found in Robert Kennedy a standard bearer around whom they could rally, whose rhetoric and style appealed to the young, to the moralistic, to men tired of old ways and old problems. But while a man of compassion and intelligence, Robert Kennedy presented no great challenge: political and economic rather than military containment of the communist challenge, sharper clarification of the national interest, restoration of American prestige, encouragement of private investment in the ghetto. Nevertheless, liberals who could not stomach Lyndon Johnson's style and old-guard politicians who could not accept his rigidity flocked to the Kennedy standard. Robert Kennedy thus offered the Democratic party the promise of remarriage of old allies, a new coalition marked by flexibility, sophistication and results.

The problem was that the old politics, even with a new style, could not solve the nation's problems, for America was enmeshed in a series of dilemmas that could only be resolved by resolution. The secure consensus on the value of political democracy, personal liberty and free enterprise, which lay behind the supposedly tough-minded realism of machine politicians and post World War II liberals, had come very close to vanishing under the impact of racism and militarism. As Gerry Wills wrote recently of Richard Nixon: "It is only a calm realization that our main myths are dead or dying that can make us, as a nation, live on. We are shaped by those beliefs, but we are something more than they ever were, we can outlive them . . . it is comforting—needed comfort—to reflect that this is so, that we can survive our own creed dissolution; for Nixon, by embodying that creed, by trying to bring it back to life, has at last reduced it to absurdity."[8]

In their effort to deal with the crisis of the 1960s, the liberals of the Democratic party have been only a mirror image of the Richard Nixons. Like him they are unable to deal with the fact that Americans are face to face with what their traditional politics have never been able to handle: moral questions that challenge their most cherished myths, their most sacred customs and institutions. If Americans wanted to know how to gain, hold and use power to implement their decision, the Irish tradition could help. If they wanted a program to translate moral commitment into concrete reality, Harvard could help. But if they want to know to what they should commit themselves, if they felt the need for goals and values which could transcend the apparent necessities of modern America, neither has much to offer. For both Irish politics and Harvard liberalism have been, at least since the 1930s, concerned with technique, efficiency and quantity, and have regarded the "big questions" either as settled or unanswerable.

There were moments when Robert Kennedy seemed to understand these things, when he spoke genuinely and eloquently to the nation's longing for faith and values. Like his brother he

held in creative tension the latent conflict between political
realism and pragmatic idealism, with perhaps a greater emphasis
on the former. But he demonstrated as well a remarkable
capacity for growth and a quality of humaneness that expressed
itself in moments of real vision. His shocking murder did terrible damage to the national spirit, damage which is impossible
to estimate but equally impossible to exaggerate.

Kennedy's main opponent, Senator Eugene McCarthy, was a
quite different man. Nurtured in the West, educated in Catholic
schools, working as a teacher in a Benedictine college, McCarthy
became for a short period of time the embodiment of national
outrage and repentence. Unlike the Kennedys, McCarthy was
very clearly a Catholic, a man whose public stance reflected an
inner commitment and temperament characteristic of Christian
Democracy, hardly a native American movement. Accordingly
his closest counterpart was not the American Catholic Kennedy
but a French Canadian who, at almost the same time, emerged
to take control of the government of Canada.

The choice in 1968 of Pierre Elliot Trudeau as leader of the
Liberal Party and Prime Minister of Canada was a sign of the
emergence in North America of a new political liberalism.
Paradoxical as it may seem in our supposedly post-Christian era,
Trudeau and McCarthy both personify the major concerns and
attitudes long associated with European Christian Democracy.
Certainly mass political parties like those of Adenauer and de
Gasparri have no place in contemporary North America, but
Christian Democracy was never merely a movement of partisan
political action. It was more importantly a body of ideas and
values that represented a distinctive approach to the individual,
society and the state. This school of thought, the best-known
representatives of which are Jacques Maritain and Pope John
XXIII, has always sought to reconcile strongly held convictions
concerning the dignity of the individual with equally firm
commitments to the attainment of social justice. When the
"mystique" of Christian democracy was translated after World
War II into the "politique" of organized mass action, it almost
inevitably ended up offering conservative support of the status
quo against the church's age-old bogy of socialism. Nevertheless
the failures of Christian Democratic parties need not detract

from the importance and the relevance of the insights that the intellectual tradition, which transcended them, can bring to bear on the problems of modern society.

That tradition was very much a part of the atmosphere of the Quebec left of the 1950s in which Trudeau matured politically. It was an even more explicit element in the thought of the professor of political science from a small Catholic college in Minnesota. Both these new men brought to the political stage a point of view markedly different from the quantitative pragmatic liberalism that has dominated the recent past. The central themes of their political message: concern for individual liberty, strict limitations on delegated power, administrative decentralization and social justice, confused American observers long accustomed to associate liberty and justice with a strong central government. Eugene McCarthy thus sounded at some points like Franklin Roosevelt and at other times like Barry Goldwater, yet his blend of what were contradictory categories in American politics seemed for a time to be just what the situation required.

The popularity of Trudeau and McCarthy can be traced to the failure of traditional liberalism to confront the most pressing problems of contemporary North American society. In the Untied States the Negro revolution and Viet Nam raised fundamental moral and political questions that directly challenged pragmatic politics. Doubts had been raised earlier by the cultural criticism of the 1950s and the hesitant realism of President Kennedy, but it was the riots and the war that brought home to many Americans the failure of New Deal liberalism. In a situation that demanded immediate commitment and decisive action most liberals drifted with events. In a real sense Viet Nam was their war; they were compromised by it and shared responsibility for it, and yet few were willing to admit their errors and publicly enlist in the opposition. Eugene McCarthy, however, placed his career on the line because he believed that his country had passed moral limits no man or nation can transgress.

This sense of moral restraint had been clearly expressed in McCarthy's book *The Limits of Power*. In addition, McCarthy had as congressman and senator devoted his energies to limiting the excesses of government and politicians, first by combating the anti-communist hysteria of the 1950s and later by seeking to impose congressional control over the CIA. Like his hero, Adlai Stevenson, he tried to speak the truth about power, while relying on the decency and common sense of the people. Faith in the value of democracy and in the ability of rational men to order their affairs justly, while at the same time checking the power of government by means of law and ensured rights, had been at the heart of McCarthy's career and exemplified the influence of Maritain, who always stressed the need for moral consensus, embodied in law, for limited government, and for rational discussion of political alternatives.

What Viet Nam was for McCarthy, the Canadian constitutional crisis was for Trudeau: an issue focusing on the problem of power and its limitation, which had been his central concern and which became the major issue of his nation. Federalism of the Trudeau variety, with clear and explicit delegation of powers, is designed to limit power and to protect the individual. A Bill of Rights similarly safeguards the individual against the encroachment of private and public bureaucracies and makes the constitution truly a "shield." Trudeau's hatred of nationalism is related to his deeply rooted fear of the impact of emotional discussion of public issues, inhibiting rational solutions and opening the door to demagogues whose use of government power may end in repression and tyranny. Canada stands in need of moderation of its internal controversies, while it simultaneously develops strong national economic policies. For Trudeau the solution remains federalist: the division and delegation of necessary powers so that individuals and groups may develop freely toward whatever goals they set for themselves, consistent with the rights of others to similar autonomy.

Trudeau's pressing concern for individual liberty leads many to regard him as conservative, just as many so regard McCarthy. This is an understandable reaction in light of the traditional framework of political rhetoric in North America with its sharp division between conservatives dependent on individualist traditions and liberals appealing to state responsibility. Yet Trudeau, in the manner of John XXIII, insists upon both liberty and social justice as components of the "just society." Like the spokesmen for Christian Democracy he warns proponents of a more equitable distribution of wealth of the danger of depending on big government and its potential to threaten civil liberties that events in the United States have made clear. The alternative is greater reliance upon institutions of popular democracy, and it is interesting that both Trudeau and McCarthy were associated in their early careers with a reforming labor movement, although both have since lost interest as the unions' reforming zeal has waned. It might be expected that what Pope John called "socialization," the proliferation of private agencies of effective social action, will become a central feature of the new liberalism in the years to come. A trend in this direction is already apparent in the United States in the community action program of the war on poverty, in the neighborhood development work of the Students for a Democratic Society in its early years and in the program of the Saul Alinsky's Industrial Areas Foundation.

What all this means is that the basic approach of Christian Democracy was well known to McCarthy and Trudeau fifteen or twenty years ago. Both men were academics, concerned with political philosophy and aware of the work of the Catholic left in Europe. Both matured in political struggles against powerful reactionary movements closely associated with the Church, McCarthyism in the States and Duplessissism in Quebec. They developed in those years a set of attitudes and values that centered on the problem of uniting personal liberty and social justice, an issue that has now become central to the entire left in North America. Both Canada and the United States require centralized planning linked to clear national priorities if they are to deal with the pressing internal problems of urban decay, regional disparities and, in Canada, foreign ownership. At the same time students and disaffected adults are insisting on a more direct participation in the decisions that effect their lives. The conflicting demands for central planning and individual participation can only be reconciled by a federal system that demands national unity on goals and maximum utilization of rational social planning, but imposes strict limitations on bureaucratic power and encourages the fullest possible participation by citizens in the institutions, new and old, that influence their individual and collective destinies. Traditional pragmatism, with its willingness to experiment with new solutions, remains necessary, but alone it cannot supply the moral sensitivity needed to ensure the protection of individual liberty and to motivate the cooperation necessary for effective local institutions. Neither Trudeau nor McCarthy had all the answers, but because they risked an appeal to the people based on concern with ends, not means, they reawakened the political vitality of a continent. Without such political excitement and political participation, no solutions can be found. The future may seem even more secular than the past, but if it is a secularity permeated with dedication to individual liberty and social justice, and relying on reason and politics to dynamically relate the two, then Christian Democracy may have obtained its goals in North America far more than it ever did in Europe.

While the general approach of a Trudeau or a McCarthy has real relevance to contemporary America, there are obvious weaknesses in Christian Democracy, weaknesses partly evident in the post-1968 careers of these two men. McCarthy's enigmatic withdrawal from a seat of power and Trudeau's overreaction to Quebec terrorism point up some of the ambiguities of their school of thought, particularly its failure to deal with the problems of power and of consensus. Equally important, in the United States there is no viable political basis for Christian Democracy that by transcending traditional American categories, divorces itself from the historical experience that generated those divisions. For Catholics, long hopeful of discovering a consistent synthesis of Catholic and American political ideals and practices, Christian Democracy could possess greater attraction, but even for them it does not provide sufficient grounds for a new politics.

Despite the hopes of many neither McCarthy nor the followers of Robert Kennedy have been able to create a new politics. While the 1968 elections demonstrated the continued allegiance of many Catholics to the Democratic party, numerous local and state contests were marked by sharp conflict between more or less conservative Catholics disturbed by crime, drugs and racial unrest and liberal Catholics hopeful of finding rational and humane solutions to public issues. In addition a significant movement of Catholic radicalism further confuses and fragments the political life of the Catholic community. Thus in New York, machine Democrat Mario Proccacino and insurgent Conservative James Buckley both commanded wide Catholic support, while many of the city's Catholic intellectuals gave their backing to liberals like John Lindsay, Charles Goodell and Richard Ottinger. Clearly the conflicting historical models of the group-oriented politics of the machine and the reform politics of the Americanized middle class continue to dominate Catholic political participation. While adherents of various positions often seek to bolster their position by reference to religious principles or ecclesiastiastical interests, they seldom recognize how much they rely upon particular interpretations of American political experience.

Perhaps one reason for the failure to develop a distinctive American Catholic politics lies in the continued identification of the American side of the equation with the values and traditions of east coast politicians. Highly educated liberals and shrewd machine politicians have not been the only bearers of the American "creed." There is another tradition, a radical tradition, that found little favor in the eastern citadels of liberal thought or the clubrooms of city politicians. It is the tradition of Jefferson, of the Populists and the IWW, of Eugene Debs, Norman Thomas, and A. J. Muste, a tradition every bit as American as that of Woodrow Wilson and Franklin Roosevelt, of Herbert Hoover and Richard Nixon.

That tradition, in its early development, has been ably described by new left historian Staughton Lynd.[9] In the days of America's first revolution, American radicals created a revolutionary ideology. "They addressed to the opinion of mankind the dramatic proposition that all men are created equal with natural liberties which, if taken away at all, cannot be justly taken without consent." While the ideology of the American Revolution was drawn from John Locke, the radicals succeeded in infiltrating Lockean rhetoric with their own subtle modifications. That truths were "self-evident" meant a reversion from Locke's sensationalism to an earlier radical Protestant stress on intuition, the ability of all men to grasp fundamental truths. That rights were inalienable meant, for the radicals at least, that they remained so and could not be surrendered, even in the social contract. Freedom as a condition of the spirit, suspicion of government and concern for individual liberty—the tenets of Jeffersonianism—followed upon these modifications and provided the basis for the real and very important controversies of the 1780s and 1790s.

For Lynd early radicalism went much further than the Bill of Rights. As early as the 1780s Jefferson, Richard Price, Tom Paine and others questioned the need for government, the right of private property and restriction on individual action. The abolitionists of a later generation were led by the force of events to develop the half-hidden radicalism of their predecessors. For Thomas Skidmore the Jeffersonian idea that "the earth belongs to the living" became the basis for a radical attack on property, while for William Lloyd Garrison it provided another argument against slavery and the wage system. The right of revolution against kings was transformed into the semi-anarchism of Thoreau by the example of the Quakers and the evangelical insistence on unity of conviction and action. The cosmopolitanism of Franklin became the universal reform and citizenship of the world of Garrison by the development of notions of conscience and the inner light. *Civil Disobedience* was the manifesto, the goal and the tactic of abolitionists, whose preoccupation with slavery opened the door to unforeseen ideas of communal property, individual freedom and integrity and local community few had foreseen when they started.

The development of American radicalism assumed a dialectic form. The revolutionary coalition failed to clarify whether inalienable "rights" were retained undiminished in society. When the coalition divided into the sectional components, northern radicals described more explicitly the contradictions between the rights of man and slavery and, because of southern strength in the federal system, they were led to a theory of civil disobedience. While unprepared to pursue their nascent critique of property, the pre-war radicals were able to energize a broad-based, anti-slavery consensus. In postwar years the victorious forces again divided, providing the setting for "a third revolutionary movement" that assaulted unrestricted private property.

Historians of the twentieth century usually implied that

radical dissent was un-American, but New Left scholars like Lynd are effectively demonstrating that radical idealism and constant tension are not only part of the American tradition but the source of much that is inspiring and important in the American experience. The contention that American society must always render dissent and protest irrelevant, that all problems can be solved by accommodation and compromise, the arguments of modern liberalism, represent a relatively recent departure—under the impact of the corporate society—from the traditional idealism of the American left. The progressive generation began the process of emasculating the radical tradition by utilizing a pragmatic methodolgy which gradually lost contact with the framework of democratic commitment that originally inspired the effort. The result was the disillusionment of the 1920s, illustrated in Carl Becker's conclusion in *The Declaration of Independence* that the faith of the Founding Fathers in the inalienable rights of man "could not survive the harsh realities of the modern world." Becker's odyssey led him beyond such pessimism to the eventual reassertion of the democratic faith, and when he republished the book in 1941 he wrote:

> The incredible cynicism and brutality of Adolf Hitler's ambitions . . . have forced men everywhere to re-appraise the validity of half-forgotten ideas, and enabled them once more to entertain convictions as to the substance of things not evident to the senses. One of these convictions is that "liberty, equality and fraternity" and "the inalienable rights of men" are phrases, glittering or not, that denote realities—the fundamental realities that men will always fight for rather than surrender.

Becker made this restatement of faith while accepting the burdens of history and throwing off the romantic nostalgia for lost innocence so characteristic of American social thought. His affirmation of American ideals and acceptance of the realities of history remains the necessary combination for a morally acceptable radicalism in our times.

American Catholic political thought and action was a struggle between old world categories and new world assumptions, between group-interest organization and national-interest ideology. In seeking to bridge this gap men like the Kennedys sought to embrace both the machine and reform. Catholics ignored this native radical tradition, save for an occasional denunciation when, in the guise of socialism, it sought a foothold among Catholic workers. That tradition had much to offer the Catholic people and much to contribute to Catholic thought. It was appropriate that the first modern American Catholic radical, Dorothy Day, was a convert whose early life was spent in the struggles of Wobblies, socialists and suffragettes. Unfortunately she stands almost alone as an authentic exponent of that tradition in the Catholic community. Yet it may well be that native American radicalism alone can provide a bridge between the America of the past and the new America decent men must build in the future.

Of course there are other options available and many regard Lynd and his version of the New Left as utopian and visionary. Within the left it is Eugene Genovese who has subjected the modern exponents of that tradition to its most scathing critique.[10] For Genovese moral judgments are products of specific historical circumstances and are intimately related to the material conditions in which men live. Thus slavery, for example, was wrong insofar as it hampered historical development, but slaveowners were not evil, for they operated within a cultural context that was coherent, consistent and true to the social and economic needs of the anti-bellum south. Moral opposition to slavery, on the other hand, "did not harden until the material antagonism between North and South had matured."

Accordingly Genovese belittles Lynd's demand for the assertion of freedom and responsibility. Marxist analysis establishes, to Genovese's satisfaction at least, that the power of American liberal capitalism is at present secure, and that it possesses the ability, and potentially the will, to absorb or to crush dissent and movements for change. In this situation the strategy of black and white radicals alike must be geared to the long run, preserving those areas of freedom available to them, educating potentially revolutionary groups to the contradictions of American society, ensuring that when revolutionary change does become possible, they will be ready with a program and a vehicle for action. The strategy is necessarily defensive for the time being, and tactics must be adjusted to this relatively defeatist view of the situation. Radicals must align with liberals to preserve freedom for dissent. Confrontation, which arouses the fascist potential so alarmingly real in America, must be avoided at all costs, and destruction of those who advocate it must be a goal of all radicals who desire to act effectively. On this basis most New Left student and religious protest can be seen as visionary, romantic or nihilist. Lacking a sophisticated understanding of the dynamics of industrial society the young strike out blindly in the name of non-historical abstractions, without regard for the consequences of their actions. Intolerant of detachment, objectivity and scholarship, profoundly anti-intellectual, they threaten the freedom and independence of the liberal university, the only place where development of a real radical critique is possible.

There are many difficulties with these arguments, and most of them have been pointed out before. If revolution means a radical redistribution of power in American society brought about solely by the mobilization of groups of the materially deprived, then Genovese is probably right in denying its possibility. If it means a drastic reordering of the nation's priorities arising from renewed consciousness of the gap between promise and practice, or if post-industrial society reorients the nature of social change, then Genovese may be wrong. If morality is simply a matter of conforming behavior to the demands of history, then Genovese is right to reject an abstract morality based on the feeling that some things are just plain wrong. If morality is a more complex problem, if Genovese's polarization of personal conscience and social effectiveness creates a phony issue, then his argument is weakened considerably.

In addition, the belief that the possibilities for social change are severely limited in America today is one shared by most responsible commentators. Even Staughton Lynd hardly runs around proclaiming the advent of utopia, as Genovese seems to suggest. Rather, what Lynd demands and what Genovese rejects is adherence to principle. If one believes that war and racism are wrong, one must oppose these things. Surely the ability of student militants to win widespread support on so many campuses is not due simply to the supposed alienation and destructiveness of their generation but to their ability to dramatize issues in such a way as to make demands on the consciences of their fellow students. Of course strategy and tactics are important; of course men must find effective means to realize the goals to which they are committed. But the use of some means can corrupt the end, as historians surely should recognize, and there must be some limits to the distance men can travel in adapting to the possibilities of the situation. For Genovese history provides the sole standard of morality: "the moral case against modern slavery must rest on its being an historical anachronism." An American left that adopted such a point of view would hardly be new and would be even more open to becoming totalitarian than a left that sought to balance the demands of morality and political effectiveness. Genovese accuses Lynd and by implication most younger radicals of escaping this dilemma by adhering to one of its horns, "moral absolutism." It is much more clear that Genovese has resolved it by adherence to the other horn, historical absolutism.

Most important, Genovese's case can only seem hypocritical to those he criticizes. Like them he obviously feels there are many things about American society today that are intolerable, if not "wrong." Indeed, he goes further than many, arguing, for example, that most of the "stern, repressive and totalitarian measures" adopted in socialist countries, including Stalin's Russia, resulted from a Western imperialist conspiracy. Yet he judges the pre-eminent need of the moment to be the destruction of those members of the left who, for all their aberrations, have provided the most dynamic leadership in combating war and racism in recent years. Just as fair-minded men could not tolerate communist attacks on Norman Thomas in the 1930s, so they must deplore Genovese's attack on Staughton Lynd today. If the power of the ruling class is as secure and repressive as Genovese claims, surely one must question the wisdom and even the honesty of treating Lynd, and presumably everyone else from Senator Fulbright to Dave Dellinger, as men with whose ideas "socialists have no more essentially in common that they do with those of the ruling class." If anything would convict American liberals of hypocrisy it would be alliance with Genovese. Yet some may choose to accept such an alliance, for his position, with its moral ambiguity and its dependence upon "objective" historical analysis, is very close to the position of some of the worst elements of American liberalism.

Indeed the historical question is crucial. Both Lynd and Genovese belong to a group of younger American historians seeking, in Genovese's words, "to establish the ideological foundations for their political movement." Lynd, however, is read out of the movement by Genovese because he allows his moral views to influence his history; he supposedly abstracts ideas from their context and shapes his judgment not by the situation alone but by principle. Where Lynd insists upon condemning the founding fathers for failing to resolve the contradiction between their liberation pronouncements and their ownership of slaves, Genovese exempts them from harsh criticism because, in his opinion, historical conditions for abolishing slavery did not then exist. The implications are clear. For Lynd, history provides a basis for insisting upon the responsibility of all men to act honestly and courageously in accord with their principles. History vindicates human freedom and thus personal responsibility and it educates men to the possibility of change here and now. The object of historical study is the making of history. "The past is ransacked," Lynd writes, "not for its own sake, but as a source of alternative models of what the future might become."

For Genovese history's lessons are more clear. The scholar must separate historical and political judgments. He need not ask whether slavery could have been abolished in 1789; only why it was not. While men can act, their basic responsibility is to judge historical possibilities and act accordingly. The past can be known with certainty if the historian only frees himself from abstractions. It is Genovese, then, and not Lynd, who is part of the intellectual tradition against which radical historians are rebelling. The specific historical dimensions of that tradition have been aptly described by Hayden V. White.[11] Emphasizing detachment and objectivity, in imitation of nineteenth-century positivism, the professional historian effects the reconciliation of theory and practice and thus eases conscience and inhibits action. History as understood and communicated provides explanations of the present, it legitimates the "burden of history" that men experience. History, writes White, "is not only a substantive burden imposed upon the present by the past in the forms their specious authority."[11] Genovese, at first glance a *way of looking at the world* which gives to these outmoded forms their specious authority." Genovese, at first · glance a radical scholar, is not far removed from the establishment historiography diagnosed by White. Like his moderate colleagues in the profession he would teach the conservative that change is inevitable while warning the radical that drastic change is illusory. A sane and reasonable stance it surely is, but hardly satisfying to a Nietzsche, who sensed the irrationality of modern life, or to a young American, who is tired of a realism, liberal or Marxist, that he knows leads both to the physical destruction of men and the corruption of their souls.

The Lynd-Genovese controversy, with its implications for students and radicals, parallels debates in other areas, notably in ethics. These disputes are raised beyond the academic by the insistent question posed by Christopher Lasch "What must a moral man do?" To accept Genovese's response to the question will enmesh us once again in the failures of the old liberalism and Marxism: the confusion of means and ends, the postponement of the moral life until material conditions allow, the adaptation to possibilities defined by "history," as Genovese would have it, more likely by power possessed and exercised by real men here and now. Undoubtedly there are risks in asserting that each man must create new possibilities, must make history rather than adapt to it. The danger of fanaticism is real, as Genovese points out, but many men have already experienced fanaticism cloaked in the shroud of realism and the horrors unleashed by those who believed they had discerned the course of history. At the very least Genovese's own writings, with their self-righteousness and dogmatism and their demand for "radical surgery" to destroy deviationists like Lynd, manifest a fanaticism as virulent as anything likely to come from his opponents. Given a choice between Genovese's brand of ideology and scholarship and that of Staughton Lynd, the rest of us must stand with Lynd, who wrote in the book which Genovese so cruelly attacked: "One cannot entrust men with a collective right of revolution unless one is prepared for them to revolutionize their lives from day to day; one should not invoke the ultimate act of revolution without willingness to see new institutions perpetually improvised from below; the withering away of the state must begin in the process of changing the state; freedom must mean freedom now."[12]

For the Christian the choice is clear. If Lynd and Genovese represent the available options, then Christians must join with Lynd. The new theology of liberation and of revolution eminating from European Christian-Marxist dialogue and from the Third World, particularly from Latin America, points toward an emerging Christian social thought that rejects any closed future and any determinist present. Instead the open horizon of the future and the necessity for free political responsibility provide the primary points of reference for the new theology. The former requires constant criticism of all human ideologies that would subordinate men to the supposed demands of history, while the latter summons men to accept the responsibilities of their humanity, to free themselves and others for the necessary work of liberation from the toils of necessity. As Richard Shaull writes of the Brazilian educator Paulo Friere: "he operates on one basic assumption: that man's ontological vocation (as he calls it) is to be a Subject who acts upon and transforms his world, and in so doing moves towards ever new possibilities of fuller and richer life individually and collectively. This world to which he related is not a static and closed order, a given reality which man must accept and to which he must adjust; rather, it is a problem to be worked on and solved. It is the material used by man to create history, a task which he performs as he overcomes that which is dehumanizing at any particular time and place and dares to create the qualitatively new."[13] If the position represented by Friere, Jurgen Moltmann and Johannes Metz is indeed a valid Christian option, then it requires those who accept it to reject the dogmatism of a Genovese in favor of the personalism of Lynd. It means sympathetic engagement with the New Left, particularly with that branch of the New Left that shares with the early Students for a Democratic Society the conviction that the future is man's responsibility.

Peter Steinfels, commenting on the decline of European Christian Democracy, accurately described the conflicting atti-

tudes toward politics that agitated the Catholic community
during the last decade, a division that Christian Democracy had
for a time succeeded in straddling. On the one hand there was a
liberal approach that set the church at a certain distance from
the political order pronouncing "general principles" and leaving
"specific applications to the individual judgement of Christians,
who, inspired by these principles and formed by the imperatives
of their religious lives in general, enter politics as individuals, as
citizens, who may differ and dispute with one another." On the
other hand a growing number felt that this position, while
respectful of the pluralism and complexity of modern political
life, restricted the church to vague generalities and a kind of
neutrality that could result in "failure to address the most
obvious and *simple* of evils." Equally important, if the church
as church kept out of the nitty gritty of political analysis and
action, out of "the twentieth century arena of seeking justice
and making peace and feeding the hungry," how could it be "a
genuine community living out the Gospels." Men recognized the
basic dangers of "neutrality" and a "new clericalism," and they
realized "there would always be tension" between the two
positions.[14] Poised at a time when the "half-way house" of
Christian Democracy was collapsing in Europe, when the solid
ethnic communities that had so forcefully influenced the behavior of earlier generations were gradually losing their hold on
the loyalty of church leaders and articulate, educated Catholics
and when, finally, the assumptions of liberal politics were being
challenged by events, American Catholics were politically on
their own, perhaps for the first time.

So American Catholics have not found their new saint for the
new age. The brutal deaths of the Kennedys and the self-
inflicted demise of Eugene McCarthy have left Catholics with
alternative models, the Buckleys and the Berrigans, but with no
leader who can draw them together by articulating their basic
yearning for a fully integrated American and Catholic political
style. Perhaps that is as it should be, for perhaps the age of such
heroes is past. The kind of secular unity John Kennedy symbolized has been eroded by changes so fundamental that it will
probably never return. Unable to rely any longer on symbolic
figures who can fulfill their hopes but also vicariously fulfill

responsibilities that are theirs alone, American Catholics are left solely with themselves. If they don't do what they say should be done, then the flame of human liberty and the hope of human destiny may well flicker and die. The task is theirs, and they must get up the courage to meet it.

8
CATHOLIC RADICALISM

In an age that has called into question the most cherished myths and most basic assumptions of Christian faith and American democracy, the American Catholic community has produced men of courage, vision and hope: the Kennedys and Eugene McCarthy, the late Bishop Hallinan of Atlanta and Monsignor George Higgins, Caesar Chavez and James Groppi, Tom Cornell of the Catholic Peace Fellowship and the almost legendary Dorothy Day, a host of young Catholic conscientious objectors and draft resisters and hundreds of inspired young priests, nuns and students. Of them all it is Daniel and Philip Berrigan, activists, scholars, men of faith and courage, who, by their words and their lives, personified the new vision of Christian responsibility that generated the upsurge of Catholic radicalism in the 1960s. While they hardly provided all the answers to the problems agitating the church and the nation, the Berrigans nevertheless moved the consciences of other Americans by their willingness to live as they believed men should, in risk, danger and jeopardy. As Chavez wrote of the Berrigans at the moment of their greatest need: "in the manner after Jesus they have cast their lot with the poor and the oppressed. In giving their lives, they find life. In serving others they lose the fear which cripples freedom. In reaching for the best in every person, they make each of us more human. In respecting the life of every man and woman they make life more precious for us all."[1]

Daniel Berrigan, S. J., and Philip Berrigan, S. S. J., were convicted of violation of federal statutes for their participation in the destruction of Selective Service records on May 17, 1968. Although the Berrigans pleaded innocent at their trial, they freely admitted that they had committed the acts in question. They are criminals, of that there can be no doubt; "criminals for peace," as they see it, decent and sincere men who broke the law, as the trial judge saw it. At first they had expected and welcomed the prospect of jail. "We stayed and were taken," Daniel Berrigan wrote, "because we believe our society and our church have no need of a romantic hit-and-run underground. The need is for at least a few who will act on behalf of public decency and pay up, as I believe Christian and Gandhian ethics demand."[2] Later, arguing that "the courts have become more and more the instruments of the war makers," they concluded that the entire judicial system lacked moral and legal justification.[3] They therefore evaded arrest and were jailed only after pursuit by federal authorities.

The Berrigans see themselves, and are seen by their admirers, as prisoners for conscience, men jailed for exercising their basic right to follow their convictions. For others, Daniel Berrigan is, like his brother and friends, "a moral zealot," even "a self-righteous fanatic."[4] The emotions revealed in this controversy reached new heights in early 1971 when the Justice Department charged Philip Berrigan with masterminding a plot to blow up Washington steam tunnels and kidnap White House aide Henry Kissinger; Daniel Berrigan was named a co-conspirator although his name was later dropped. These new charges brought the Berrigans and their ideas to the attention of a far greater segment of the American public than they had been able to reach themselves and generated new debate about these radical priests and the war they have sworn to resist. In this respect at least the Catonsville draft board raiders accomplished their purpose, for, as Thomas Melville put it at the trial, the defendents asked "only that America consider seriously the points we have tried to raise."[5]

The Viet Nam war is not the first event in American history to occasion such protests, and the Berrigans are not the first Americans to find dramatic methods of confronting the government and awakening the conscience of their fellow-citizens. Colonial patriots, opponents of slavery, labor organizers, suffragettes, radicals and pacifists, all broke American laws and appealed to a "higher law" for justification, which meant in effect appeal to the conscience of the people. Deliberate lawbreaking is not foreign to Christian history either, for laymen and clergy in most Western nations at some time in their history have felt compelled by circumstances or conviction to oppose the state, to suffer imprisonment or to become fugitives. Judgment of these earlier rebels is relatively easy, for it is believed that they resisted in circumstances much different from our own (for example Nazi Germany). Many rebels who suffered for a cause, which later proved victorious in the struggle of history, were later enshrined as national or religious heroes. In addition, people usually envision yesterday's rebels as resisters of active, repressive power. Even those who do not practice pacifism and civil disobedience, can and do respect its adherents: a Thoreau, a Dorothy Day or a Martin Luther King. At one time the Berrigans fit this mold. When Daniel Berrigan was sent out of the country in 1965 in an apparent effort to stifle his antiwar activity, or when his brother Philip was transferred from Newburg, New York to appease right-wing Catholics, they enjoyed widespread sympathy and considerable support. But their actions in 1968 shattered that support, for then they moved beyond a simple pacifism to active, militant resistance. Earlier they had insisted on the obligation of Christians to work against war and racism, a call sufficiently familiar to raise no great commotion: the church and the nation had always had their share of such idealists. After Catonsville the challenge of the Berrigans went much deeper, their demands became much greater and their enemies became much more powerful, determined and ruthless.

At the time of the Catonsville draft board raid the Berrigans were near a turning point in their lives. Previously they had labored to expose the evils of American society, particularly its oppression of black people at home and its immoral conduct of war in Southeast Asia. Like so many others they believed that once the American people saw such obvious wrongs, they would move to correct them. Gradually, however, their confidence in the ability of American institutions to respond to demands to end the war and begin the necessary reform at home had declined. Philip Berrigan and several companions signalized this frustration in the first major draft board raid at Baltimore and several months later Daniel joined his brother at Catonsville. When friends questioned these actions, Daniel Berrigan responded that liberal political work was not achieving significant results and the situation demanded more drastic commitment of those who truly believed in the sacredness of life. "We find that those who hope to change things massively often miss the first meaning of human change, which is to submit oneself to change," Daniel Berrigan wrote. The man who would change, who would undergo conversion, would have a profound effect on the processes of society: "a man dies, to his ego, his ideological paralysis, his culture-enslaved religion, to his freedom and good name even. And new forces are released: good men move in new directions, neutral men become thoughtful."[6] The demands the Berrigans made on those who understood the brutality of the war, its genocidal destruction of a people and their culture, were now escalated beyond any simple resolution, for they went to the heart of each person's life. Every American was an accomplice to this criminal war, and every American had to face that fact and change his life accordingly.

After their dramatic trial and conviction, the Berrigans and several others decided not to voluntarily surrender to the authorities. This decision was yet another step on the road from liberal protest to revolutionary resistance. By then it had become clear to the Berrigans that American society was sick, maybe even dying, at its very roots. "The crisis is of such enormous extent and depth, that all solutions based on the sanity and health and recoverability of current structures are quickly proven wrong, untimely, unmanageable, bureaucratically infected: the same old kettle of fish, stinking worse than ever in the boiling juices of change," a fugitive Daniel Berrigan wrote in 1970. To "open the eyes of more and more of our friends," to bring a larger "community of resistance" into being at a time when America was "going, downhill and pell-mell, into a dark age, a progress led by neanderthals armed to the teeth," the Berrigans chose to say no, to make, and to lead others to make, "the saving act of resistance."[7]

It is altogether too easy to underestimate how serious is the challenge these men present. Of course the symbolism of the actions they took was to contrast the destruction of property in draft files with the burning of children in Viet Nam, but it is not enough to recognize the message and respect the messengers—to do so, and not to change dramatically the style and direction of life is to evade or reject the whole intent of their sacrifice. Nor is it enough to call them "prophets," for while the term when properly understood has some relevance to the Berrigans, it frequently encourages an evasion of personal responsibility, for most people feel that the prophet belongs to a special class of men chosen by God for an unusual mission. The prophet should be listened to with great seriousness, but not necessarily heeded, much less imitated. Others emphasize that the Berrigans are priests, exercising a "new ministry" somehow emanating from the ecclesiastical changes of the Second Vatican Council. In this view their clerical vocation is a special one, which requires them to teach in a dramatic and personally hazardous fashion. But the laymen, or the parish priest for that matter, has other responsibilities to take account of. Called to a different vocation, he must take the Catonsville action with the same seriousness he gives to the pastoral advice of his bishop or the sermon of a visiting priest noted for his holiness and dedication. These images do less than justice to the claims Daniel and Philip Berrigan have made. Those very workaday responsibilities of job and family that compel a moderate response to the radical evil of our times are for the Berrigans the very heart of the problem, for these commitments to comfort, security and success cut men off from the poor, the oppressed and the innocent victims of American military power. In the vision of the new Catholic radicals, it is involvement in private affairs that prevents the living of the Christian life for others and allows those who possess the reins of power to systematically destroy people in every nation who struggle for freedom, dignity and justice.

In short, the Berrigans summon their fellow Americans to what *Commonweal* describes as "a moral revolution, a regeneration that is based on the personal conversion of individuals through acts which break them off from established powers of the world and which link them, through suffering and the fate of being outcast, with the poor and the oppressed."[8] All of America, its governments and courts, its businesses and unions, its churches and its schools are implicated in the evils of war and oppression. All Americans are implicated, not simply to the degree that they refuse to act publicly to correct these things, but to the degree that they refuse to cut themselves off from the jobs, associations, good and services they enjoy in this country, and to the degree that they do not aid, abet or imitate the actions of the Berrigans and their colleagues in the resistance.

How are Christians to formulate a responsible position in the face of the terribly crucial questions the Berrigans raise? Part of the answer must lie within each person, in the inner depths of conscience where men make those fundamental decisions that determine the character of their lives. There are those who regard this as the only relevant arena of decision: what really matters is the inner commitment to love, to a life for others, to the suffering people of the world. Few indeed are those who have made such a commitment, and the need for decision, for choice, for acceptance of responsibility is of central importance. Yet those who present this argument sometimes convey a rejection of intellect and contempt for reasonable analysis of consequences that could easily lead to fanaticism. While the inner commitment to peace and love, to a life for others, is crucial, what it means in action will depend upon hard, often difficult and ambiguous judgments about the sources and nature of social and political change. A decision to disrupt a draft board or bomb a building or quit a job might help end the war and save thousands of Vietnamese lives. It might just as easily deepen national divisions, harden the hearts of many in and out of government, prolong the war, and occasion new wars at home and abroad. Free, responsible and, therefore, morally significant decisions require careful analysis and judgment. This in turn requires close attention to the social and political implications of Christian faith, matters on which the churches are severely divided.

There is a third stage in formulating a response to "the burden of the Berrigans," the stage of analysis of American society. Out of their deep involvement with the people and the culture of this country, the Berrigans have forged a radical perspective on Christian responsibility today. It is a distinctively American perspective, generated out of their assessment of America as it is and their beliefs about American values and traditions. In the last ten years Daniel and Philip Berrigan have experienced little if any change in their central beliefs about their faith or in the basic direction of their lives. What has changed is their view of America, the gradual transformation of the almost naive faith in the goodness of America and the ability of its people to live up to its ideals to a shocked awareness of the scandalous failure of the nation to resolve its moral, and its economic, contradictions.

The Berrigans, according to Daniel, never had any great interest in "the internal questions of the Catholic community," "retarded questions" about parochial schools and ecclesiastical government that were truly scandalous "in the face of the terrible, terrible issues which face this planet's two billion people." The church in America in their view had always been "narrowly preoccupied with its own power." Now, thoroughly a part of the American scene, Catholics have a responsibility to reach out across the barriers separating them from others, particularly the poor and the oppressed. Daniel and Philip Berrigan had believed this even in the days of utopian optimism of the early 1960s, when Philip Berrigan was personally confronting American racism and Daniel's imagination was probing the shallowness of American culture. At the end of the decade their feelings regarding the church had not changed: they believed "that there's an important chapter of history to be written in our time ... which, we hope, will see the center of the church's concerns located at the edge of society—where human lives are involved in a really tragic struggle for survival and human dignity."[9] The Berrigans have lived and worked at the "edge," and events have sharpened and deepened their sense of what that "edge" is like, but the central Christian vocation that took them there in the first place has never changed.

This preoccupation with the "others," with its explicit rejection of churchly matters and its determination to face with Christian hope the central issues of the age, constitutes a creative and important response to one of the central issues of Catholic life today. Many observers felt that this call to service by Christians and by the church to the real needs of contemporary man was the central motif of Pope John XXIII's pontificate. Certainly there is a great deal of truth in Daniel Berrigan's contention that the church has long been sinfully concerned with its own power and influence. As William Bosworth has pointed out, "Catholic social action organizations date for the most part from the era when church and state were in active conflict. Their primary goal was to support the interests of the Church in what seemed like a life and death struggle."[10] Having already defined the nature and mission of the church in a way that emphasized its crucial importance to human salvation and identified its growth and power with the progress of the Kingdom of God, Catholic church leaders tended to measure and judge social and political action in terms of the welfare of the institutional church. The pioneers of Christian democracy from Felicite de Lamennais to Dom Luigi Sturzo could testify to the church's willingness to use or discard their efforts in accord with prevailing political sentiment. In particular the Roman leaders of the church and many bishops were vigilant against all movements for change that operated outside the control of church officials. Even the relatively liberal Pope Leo XIII, in discussing the efforts for social reform that had received his encouragement in the encyclical *Rerum Novarum,* warned against their involvement in politics and held that even non-political "Christian action in behalf of the people" in "whatever projects individuals or associations form . . . should be formed under episcopal authority." "Let your solicitude watch and let your authority be effective in controlling, compelling, and also in preventing, lest any under the pretext of good should cause the vigor of sacred discipline to be relaxed or the order which Christ has established in His Church to be disturbed," Leo instructed the bishops of the world.[11] Such control easily led to manipulation, as Pius XI's dealings with Catholic Action or Pius XII's suppression of the French worker-priests made clear. Always genuine concern for the poor and oppressed was subordinate to the presumed welfare and influence of the church, not for its own sake but for the good of all men who, whether they knew it or not, needed the church. The overwhelming sentiment of church leaders was that true social harmony and welfare was identical with Catholic influence and power. "Let it become more and more evident," Pope Leo wrote, "that the tranquility of order and the true prosperity flourish especially among those people whom the church controls and influences."[12]

In practice control over Catholic social action was used with close attention to concrete ecclesiastical interests and little regard for abstract principles or for the needs of those outside the church. "In any crucial situation the behavior of the Catholic church may be more reliably predicted by reference to its concrete interests as a political organization than by reference to its timeless dogmas," philosopher Sidney Hook once wrote.[13] Reinhold Niebuhr, while recognizing that the church had a good record in dealing with many questions of industrial life, nevertheless agreed with Hook. "I think that the Catholic Church tends to identify the historic church with the Kingdom of God," Niebuhr wrote in 1954, "and too often its final criterion is what a political movement promises or does not promise to the historic church."[14] A similar theme emerges from Guenter Lewy's study of the church in Nazi Germany, in which the author concludes that "the Church's opposition" to Nazi tyranny "was carefully circumscribed. It was rooted in her concern for her institutional interests rather than in a belief in freedom and justice for all men."[15]

The reasons for such attitudes and policies are varied and complex and moral judgments about men in situations other than our own are seldom easy or even worthwhile. But the central indictment of the church has a great deal of evidence to support it. As Catholics have realized this, out of their own sensitivity to the horrors of recent history and to the suffering of the poor, the oppressed and the outcast, they have been led beyond defining the "proper role" of the church, to confront deeper issues, including the meaning of Christian faith itself in a world yearning for liberation.

The 1960s have been a time when many Americans have been forced to confront themselves and their world in new and radical ways. Daniel and Philip Berrigan, through their passionate involvement in the world, have followed that path. For them and many like them it became less and less a matter of persuading the church to condemn the war or pressuring Congress to end it, but of defining amid the stark revelation of American hypocrisy and injustice the meaning of their own humanity. As Philip Berrigan explained when he was sentenced for the first draft board raid: "The point at issue with us was . . . not being a danger to the community or a benefit to it.

The issue was simply what it means to be a democratic man and a Christian man."[16]

Yet the Berrigans were not left with a blank slate, they were not and could not be stripped of their own past or of the heritage that shaped them. They are, and wish to remain, Catholic priests, a fact that has its own significance. They symbolize by their retention of that identity their fidelity to past as well as to future, their openness to that future within, and not just beyond, human history. The radical and the prophet both know the need to take this world, history in process, with the utmost seriousness, while at the same time summoning it to conversion and regeneration. Daniel Berrigan's sense of urgency, his almost apocalyptic consciousness of crisis, never causes him to break with that Christian tradition that is the cradle in which his very ability to judge the historical situation was nurtured. While underground, in flight from the federal authorities, Daniel Berrigan affirmed that his situation was "primarily an experience in and of the spirit," as, at the moment of greatest jeopardy, he seemed to many the most free of men. That it could be so, he admitted, was attributable to the living tradition in which he had been immersed for a lifetime and which bathed his soul at every juncture. "I claim for myself the dignity of a Christian and a man, present to his tradition (as chief strength), often faithless to that tradition (as large weakness)," he wrote. "But in any case within it: for good or ill, but unrecognizable to myself apart from it. To be drawn on here and now, quickly, because the times are rude and descend like a guillotine."[17]

For the Berrigans and thousands like them the times have surely been rude, for they have witnessed the collapse of the America of their hopes and dreams, an America that had formed the context of early life decisions. One sensitive observer of the Catonsville trial, noting the life history described by each of the accused, concluded "that the defendants might have just as readily led the lives they had selected and for which they had been trained—nurse, teacher, priest, missionary, even the life of the struggling artist—if it were not for the times we live in." All at Catonsville had, like the Berrigans, dedicated their lives to active service to others, to ending racial and

economic injustice and building a new church to aid mankind in
its quest for freedom, dignity and justice. All were led by the
events of the 1960s to drastically alter their assessment of the
American context of this commitment and this work. "It is not
a time for building justice," Philip Berrigan said, "it is a time for
confronting injustice."[18] By 1968 they had concluded that
Americans who truly believed in the nation's ideals could only
act on their beliefs by resisting the nation's institutions, by
being willing "to be accounted a felon," by making the central
commitment to "Say NO!"

In a sense, then, the problem posed by the Berrigans is less
one of Christian than of American responsibility. It was not the
message of Pope John XXIII or the Vatican Council that turned
liberal Catholic idealists into militant advocates of revolution
and evangelical preachers of judgment and regeneration. The
personal history of Catholic radicals has been made tortuous
not by any uncertainty about their own values or faith but by
doubt about their country. Marjorie Melville, former missionary
sister and later a convict, put the matter clearly: "I'm looking
for ways to make my country a land of brotherhood, to help it
contribute to world peace." Deeply, even desperately, the Berrigans want the American people and the American government
to live up their professed ideals. "Lead us!," Philip Berrigan
cried out to the nation's leaders. "Lead us by giving people
justice and there will be no need to break the law." If "the
system" is reformable, he continued, "Reform it and we will
help with all our conviction and energy in jail or out."[19]

For the members of the resistance, it is America, not Christianity which they have tried and found wanting.

In the 1960s young Catholics, their desire for service fired by
the black revolution and the models offered by men like John
F. Kennedy, no longer experienced the economic and social
pressures that had always forced minority groups to accomodate to American realities. In this situation there was an obvious
need for alternatives to the older forms of Christian identification and the older outlets for service to others. In the Kennedy
years the option was often the nation itself. How better could
one fulfill the functions of the older parish: contact with
community and service to others, than through active involve-

ment in programs for social betterment? John Kennedy set the tone in his appeal for public service embodied most significantly in the Peace Corps, while the civil rights movement provided innumerable opportunities for meaningful work for others. In the mid 1960s the war on poverty opened up thousands of jobs in education and community action, offering outlets for the talent, enthusiasm and idealism of the young.

It didn't work, at least not as expected. Part of the reason lay in the inherent weaknesses of the programs themselves, part in the incredible bureaucratic mazes that confounded workers in the field. Most important, events called into question the seriousness of national commitments. Locally entrenched powers fought against real change, while nationally funds dried up and moral leadership evaporated. On top of it all came the war, which sharply challenged the integrated Christian Americanism that had been completed in the years since World War II. The war made a mockery of a Christian identity forged around service to fellow man through American institutions. Indeed, the Viet Nam war and the events accompanying it destroyed for many the moral authority and credibility of almost every institution that could provide a context for finding meaning, identity and useful work. The government, once the apparent agent of democratic progress, now seems the purveyor of massive oppression, which in the form of the draft immediately impinges on the young. The churches seem so compromised by their respectability or so internally divided that they can provide no locus of meaningful commitment. The university's service to the nation has made of it an agent of the government's no longer beneficent purposes. Even social service agencies that work for the poor seem simply to put Band-Aids on the cancers of American society. Where is one to turn in this situation, to find community, to serve one's fellow men, to worship God with others?

It is just this vacuum in the lives of people, real, warm human beings, that the Berrigans and others like them are trying to fill. "I sense . . . a personal and public malaise, running deep and hard," Daniel Berrigan writes. "More people than we readily imagine have reached a stalemate of such proportions as chill the joy and assail the integrity of marriage, work, religion, education of children, the direction and meaning of life itself."[20] For the Berrigans, theirs can no longer be simply a personal witness against injustice. When all that was needed was the personal sacrifice of a few to arouse public opinion, the Berrigans were confident, sure of themselves, transparently courageous. But if that has failed, if they no longer can hope for quick and decisive public action, then their task has become immeasurably more difficult. Then, they must build a movement, communities of men and women finding together not only ways to work to end the war but ways to preserve their sanity and find some joy, some fellowship, some communion with others. From converting the church they must turn to rebuilding it amid its ashes; from saving America they must turn to making it over; from offering themselves as witnesses against evil, they must offer themselves as agents of rebuilding. Daniel and Philip Berrigan have thus become crucially important to the nonviolent antiwar movement, many of whose members, without their support and example, might, in one way or another, have destroyed themselves by despair and hatred. They are equally important for many troubled Americans in their surburban living rooms, anguished by the crisis of their nation and even of their family but unable or unwilling themselves to confront the state or to accept the terrible burden thrust upon decent men in an age of massive illegitimate, lawless power.

It is Daniel Berrigan, with his poetic insight and vision, who understands and articulates the subtle shifts in the needs of our people. "Even good people are quite generally resigned to endure a great worsening and rotting of the public fabric," he writes. "But what might it mean to weave a new fabric of life into a new garment, of such cunning and beauty that the wearer himself is transformed by putting it on; from beggar, outcast, bankrupt, alien, loser, prevaricator, imperialist, racist, exploiter—into a new man?" At one and the same time, he tells us, it is necessary "to pull the mask of legitimacy from the inhuman and blind face of power" and "to bring a larger community of resistance into being."[21]

The political implications of this position are far from clear or simple. The first requirement is that people "take control of their own lives," recognize their responsibilities and decide to act upon them. For some this may mean development of a new "life style of resistance" in new communities of committed men and women who try to find together ways of living authentically in everyday life the values they have long professed. Equally important, as Philip Berrigan has recognized, "taking control" of life requires a concrete political commitment whose center is the struggle of oppressed people for liberation from the control of illegitimate power. The experience of recent years has led men like Philip Berrigan to the conclusion that the struggle for liberation is going to be a long one, that it demands a more realistic strategy geared to both immediate needs and long range goals and that it requires as well work on two fronts: educational work to encourage people to take concrete steps to assume responsibility for their lives and their world and political work to effectively assist in ending the war, reversing national policy and supporting the programs of the poor and the oppressed. Gradually the Catholic resistance moves from the clear-cut tasks of denouncing evils and witnessing to the truth to the far more complex and ambiguous effort of bringing about fundamental changes in the structure and spirit of American life.

In this context, the actions of the Berrigans at Catonsville and in flight, their marvelous words in which they tell of the unfolding of their hearts, are signs of hope and not despair, of life and not of death, of reason and not fanaticism. If, as Philip Nobile wrote a few weeks before Daniel's capture, he seems less sure of himself, less certain that he has the answers, the reason may be that he has turned from resistance to revolution, from "saying no" to the evil of the present to saying yes to the promise of the future. In the difficult and ambiguous effort to build new communities and transform the heart and life of America the Berrigans have much to offer, a vision of better days, an appeal to our best values and traditions and a strategy that is principled and consistent. While others may differ with their assessment of American society and with the methods of political change they have chosen, none can avoid the challenge they pose and the responsibility for country and fellow man they thrust on our shoulders.

American radicals from Thomas Jefferson to Martin Luther

King stood against prevailing sentiment in the confident expectation that the American people, if they would but see the evil around them, would act to remove it and vindicate their professed ideals. Firmly within this radical tradition, the antiwar movement in its early stages, like the civil rights movement before it, took the basic decency of the nation and its people for granted. We have only to read the newspaper to know that the loss of that confidence has occasioned the most violent expressions of hatred and despair. Daniel and Philip Berrigan have gone to the edge of that abyss and peered in, in Daniel's words they have been "stripped naked." They have returned with their spirits intact and their hope unimpaired to summon their fellow Americans to be bold, confident and faithful.

Daniel and Philip Berrigan are the most prominent and most articulate exponents of a radicalism that exerts a great attraction for large numbers of Catholics in the United States. Their honesty, integrity and vision, and their willingness to place their lives in jeopardy, make them authentic spokesmen for a thoroughly Christian response to the contemporary crisis. Yet, however true their vision of the human situation in the America of the 1970s, and however correct their emphasis upon the need for personal decision regarding the character and direction of life, they leave many questions unanswered. In particular, although their political analysis has sharpened considerably in recent years, it is far more incisive in its critique of American government and policy than in its formulation of alternative structures and actions. Equally important they have yet to formulate a clear conception of social and political change and therefore to relate critique and positive response, goals and means at hand, ideology and action. Few things are more important both to the church and the country than the development of an intelligent Catholic radicalism; while appreciating the contribution of the Berrigans to that goal it remains necessary to relate their message to the historical situation of the broader community.

It should be clear by now that the 1960s were a decade of profound change in the Catholic church and nowhere has this been more true than in the United States. American Catholics, traditionally associated with immigrant working-class minorities, are now firmly integrated into the main currents of American life. The Vatican Council superimposed upon this dramatic social change a revolutionary challenge to traditional theological doctrines, ecclesiastical structures and devotional practices. The torrents of self-criticism unleashed by the council passed the bounds clearly present in the minds of the council fathers, creating a situation of doubt and uncertainty amid wholly new styles of religious thought and action. For many these developments took place within a context of growing concern with political and social problems in the nation at large, joining to changing Catholic consciousness some fundamental questioning of American values and practices. Liberal Catholics, who had prepared the ground for the conciliar changes, have been incapable of mastering the events of the decade. Their historical motive force was the desire to Americanize the church, to make it resemble in its internal life the democratic style of their own secular experience. This Americanizing drive depended in turn upon a deep faith in the goodness and decency of the American people and in the progressive character of American institutions. Nothing better indicates how extreme have been the challenges to these assumptions in recent years than the fact that the notion of Americanizing the church now appears to many as unworthy, even immoral.

This situation has been one of great promise for those who hope to witness a reinvigoration of Christian commitment and a profound change in the quality of American life. American Catholics have traditionally been among the most uncritical champions of the status quo in America; their affirmation of American values was a crucial factor in the failure of American radicalism to gain a foothold in the working class. As they rose into the middle class in the years immediatly following World War II Catholics provided solid mass support for the shibboleths of the cold war and the congratulatory consensus of domestic politics. The present situation, while it indeed threatens the very existence of the American church, offers Catholics at the same time an opportunity for critical reflection and constructive action unmatched in their history in this country.

If the promise of the contemporary situation is to be realized, theological reflection and efforts at ecclesiastical reform must be related to social and political analysis. Not only are such considerations essential if church reform is to be realistic, but they should lead as well to the realization that a church reforming itself is a people reforming their world. Increasingly church leaders realize that reform in the church, and closer union with the other Christian denominations, must be intimately related to a deepening commitment to—and a bolder effort to realize in practice— the church's traditional function of diaconea, service to the world. From this perspective more and more theologians believe that it is redundant to speak of Christian social thought or "Catholic radicalism," for Christianity may be a social theory and Catholicism may be socially and politically radical of its very essence. The conviction is growing that to be a Christian may indeed mean to be at least a reformer, perhaps even a revolutionary.

For many this would be paradoxical in the extreme, given the disposition to regard the church as an integral part of the established order and its teachings as the opiate of the people. Yet only such an interpretation can meet the Marxist critique of religion in its relation to society, which went beyond merely attacking the social stance of the churches to claim that Christianity was in and of itself a retrogressive social force: "Religion is the sigh of the oppressed creature, the feelings of a heartless world, just as it is the spirit of unspiritual conditions. It is the opium of the people," Marx wrote. "The people cannot be really happy until it has been deprived of illusory happiness by the abolition of religion. The demand that the people should shake itself free of illusion is the demand that it should abandon a condition which needs illusion."[22] Christianity's response must go beyond revising the stance of the church vis-à-vis the social question, as with the hierarchy's powerful if belated attacks on segregation. It must examine the very heart of Christian teachings to see if any political and social message is contained therein.

Something of this sort is quite clearly taking place throughout the world, but particularly in Eastern Europe, where dialogue between Christians and Marxists is becoming commonplace, and in Latin America, where a Catholic left is playing a creative role in social action and in development of a theology of liberation. In the United States, while much has been said of Christianity and Marxism on the theoretical level, there has been very little work done on its concrete application to American conditions. This is a serious ommission because Christianity and Marxism alike are theories, doctrines and beliefs that demand embodiment in everyday existence.

On the other hand, there has been a growing convergence of Catholics and other radicals on political, economic and moral issues, particularly on questions of war and racism. Until the Viet Nam war a Catholic pacifist was a rarity indeed. The few pacifists in the Catholic Worker movement were generally regarded by other Catholics as misguided, unAmerican, even as heretical. But as opposition to the war increased Catholic pacifists earned more respect both within the church and in the antiwar movement. This new found relevance of Christian pacifism was related on the one hand to the development of a weapons technology that makes war ever more obviously immoral and on the other hand to the peculiar conditions of the Viet Nam war, which raises moral questions in sharp form.[23]

At the same time the experience of Catholic pacifists and their sympathizers has forced an awareness of new economic, political and even educational perspectives. Like their non-Catholic counterparts, Catholic opponents of the war were led by Martin Luther King to link the peace movement and the civil rights struggle, leading to an increasingly radical perspective on both. The war was no longer the sole problem but it was placed in the context of the suffering poor and oppressed at home and abroad. Deepening radicalism led to new modes of political action as the two-party system failed to respond to public revulsion. The events in Chicago in the summer of 1968 provided a dramatic challenge to the idealism of Christian activists, for the repression of those who bore witness against the war seemed to be simultaneous with a breakdown of the political system. The hope that if the people showed their hostility to the war the government would end it seemed less and less plausible.

Under these conditions the plight of farm workers in California, the collective bargaining confrontation at General Electric or the educational crisis in New York City ceased to be isolated problems that could be solved by simple piecemeal legislation. At one time it appeared that issues like war and racism were matters for Christian conscience only when simply and dramatically presented: witness the Christian response to the appearance of Bull Connor's police dogs on TV or the horror of the arms race that so appalls the pope. Yet recent experience suggests that war, racism and poverty only really become issues for Christian conscience when their economic and political implications are developed and analyzed. It would appear then that an effort to bring together in a theoretical discussion the relationship between Christian commitment and political and social action and the practical efforts of dedicated Christians to live out their faith amid the realities of contemporary society is necessary for an authentic self-understanding of the Catholic people and progressive action toward realizing the potential of the present crisis.

Little effort has been made in this direction in the English-speaking world. The dramatic changes in the church in the last decade in America have yet to produce a positive social impact, despite the publicity the sensation-seeking media gives to the actions of exponents of a radical stance. While the official agencies of the church provide some support to draft reform and to efforts to restrain American violence, they have done little themselves to alter American policies or institutions. In the liberal phase of secularization, most Catholic leaders argue that the church as such has nothing specific to say about the pressing issues of the day. While the United States Catholic Conference officially called for an end to the draft, for example, a high-ranking official admitted that the theory of the just war provided at best only a guide to the individual conscience. It would be too much to expect, he added, that the bishops of the country would apply that doctrine to an American war. [24] Although in 1971 the bishops began to speak more directly to the Viet Nam war, the American church for the most part confines itself to statements so vague and general that they have little impact on day to day events. Reformed Catholics do little better, directing their attention to furthering internal changes in the church or, increasingly, defending the changes initiated by John XXIII and the council against the counterattack of the ecclesiastical establishment. Save for the now defunct *Slant* group in England and the continuing, though quite different, work of the Catholic Worker movement and the efforts of the Catholic resistance, little has been done to develop the social and political dimensions of the present revolution in the church.

Part of the reason for this lies in the nature of the changes here. The arrival of Catholics into the middle class undermined the basis of the old separatism of the ghetto, which had as one of its more depressing features a remarkable facility for establishing separate Catholic organizations and movements. The basis of these was not functional but socio-religious. Catholic prohibitionists were not advocates of Catholic prohibition but Catholics who happened to favor an end to the whiskey trade. Catholic philosophical and historical societies were not restricted to people who studied or taught a distinctive Catholic philosophy or history but were meant for philosophers and historians who happened to be Catholic. The label "Catholic radicalism" recalls the stifling atmosphere of this Catholic separatism and thus excites a negative response among younger people. For better or worse the fear of secularism and the pride in identity as Catholic, the two fundamental underpinnings of older Catholic organizations and movements, have been severely shaken, and no alternative common consciousness has appeared to replace them.

The new theology, the ecumenical spirit and the reawakening of social concern on the part of the church have reinforced the erosion of old attitudes associated with the upward mobility of American Catholics. Still, the results of these developments are ambiguous. The interpenetration of faith and life evident in Pope John's encyclicals and the conciliar decrees surely represents an important advance beyond the earlier emphasis on the danger of secularization and the insistence on a sharp distinction between the material and the supernatural. In recognizing that Christianity is a call to make history, not to escape from it, the best leaders of the church have laid the foundation for a positive response to social change and for a social basis for personal responsibility—in other words for a radical Catholicism.

On the other hand, one wonders about the impact of these

developments on the majority of the Catholic middle class. After all, in their popularized form these teachings simply obscure the line between the church and the world, and they frequently amount to little more than an insistence that, as one retreat master kept putting it, "work in the world is good." Stated in the context of a self-satisfied sermon designed to convince the congregation that their fears for the church are unfounded, "plus ca change, plus ca la meme chose," such sentiments simply ratify existing secularization; they provide comfortable assurance that one's job, whatever its political context, is not a distraction from the "real" demands of faith but is "a form of prayer." The American Catholic, newly arrived at affluence and status, finds in this an acknowledgment that his faith in technology, in progress, in the beneficence and virtue of America are indeed supported by the new theology. The age-old quest for an integral American Catholicism is thus fulfilled by a religious progressivism that endorses technology, success, religious liberty and pluralism and a "realistic" liberal stance on the problems of war and economic development. Freed from the incubus of ghetto separatism, the Catholic can involve himself in his career, his professional association, his service club and his political party, convinced that all are sanctified by his faith.

Paradoxical as it may appear, the very theological revolution on which a new Catholic radicalism must be based is at the same time part of the ideological structure supporting the moderate and conservative stance of many Catholics. The explanation may be that, in the absence of social criticism, the new theology is simply a rationale for the world as it is. Taught and preached by men who do not understand this society, and who uncritically affirm its values and its practices, the ideology of Catholic reform offers little basis for criticism or judgment, little challenge to the dynamic forces of technology, the corporation and bureaucracy, little reason for Christians to feel alienated or uncomfortable. If the secular city willy nilly prefigures the Kingdom of God, well and good; it is the contemporary Christian's natural habitat. But if that city is less human and needs change, then the new theology needs a new social criticism to become a force for reform or revolution.

Of course, liberal Catholicism, with an uncritical Americanism, does not constitute the entirety of American response to
the revolution in the Church. It represents rather the bulk of
moderate, centrist opinion dominant in the hierarchy and the
pulpits. On either side are the extremes. To the right are the
beleaguered Catholic conservatives, pressured by changes in their
churches, in their neighborhoods, even in their families. Frightened by the chaos of their country, confused by the disruption
of their church, theirs is what John P. Sisk has called "the sweet
dream of harmony," the yearning for a return to an order, a
consensus, a peace they feel was theirs in the 1950s, the years
when they "arrived," built their churches and schools and
settled down to enjoy the rewards that everyone agreed America could and would bestow on its citizens.

On the left are the radicals led by the Berrigans. They reject
the simplistic identification of the church and the world and
protest the moral confusion implicit in an uncritical champion-
ing of secularity. Like the right, they insist on the need to judge
the present from a standpoint independent of it, and they try to
live out the requirements of that judgment. They hearken to an
old tradition of Catholic dissent, recalling the institutional
church to the memory of its true commitment, frequently
obscured by economic and organizational imperatives. Like
their counterparts in the nation at large, Catholic radicals are a
mixed bag, nearly impossible to categorize. That they are dissatisfied with their church and angry with their country is clear
enough; so is their preoccupation with national issues like race
and militarism and their declining interest in the internal reform
of the church. Most are personalists, determined to be true to
themselves, to express their commitment no matter the cost.
They often exude Sisk's other extreme, a "sweet dream of
liberation" from the bonds of institutional conformity and
organizational discipline.[25] Taking the values of Christianity
seriously, they are overwhelmed by the gap between theory and
practice that exists wherever they turn. In this situation, their
quest for honesty and authenticity leads to new styles of life,
new modes of worship, new forms of community.

Such personalist radicals have a solid tradition with which to
identify. The Catholic Worker movement, established by Peter

Maurin and Dorothy Day in 1933, has always placed loyalty to God and fellow man above the claims of class, nation, ethnic group or ecclesiastical organization. The founders were determined to heed the call of Christianty to personal acceptance of responsibility for others, to a radical dedication to selfless service by means of voluntary poverty and the practice of the works of mercy. They found their inspiration and their hope in their awareness of Christian love embodied in the life and person of the Dorothy Day. "Love in action is a harsh and dreadful thing compared with love in dreams," Miss Day often quotes Dostoevski. "Love in dreams is greedy for immediate action, rapidly performed and in sight of all. Men will even give their lives if only the ordeal does not last long but is soon over, with all looking and applauding as though on stage. But active love is labor and fortitude and for some people perhaps a complete science. But I predict that just when you see in horror that in spite of all your efforts you are getting further from your goal instead of nearer to it—at that very moment you will reach and behold clearly the miraculous power of the Lord who has been all the time loving and mysteriously guiding you." [26]

The faith and confidence of this view has been a powerful force for initiating and sustaining a drive to make history in its most profound sense on the part of hundreds of men and women. The Catholic Worker's style of radicalism is deeply religious, hardly attractive to today's more secular youth. Yet it has had a profound impact on Catholic Americans. Beginning in the late 1930s, through the depths of World War II and the cold war years, the Worker stood bravely for the complete and total rejection of violence. In the 1950s, when millions of their fellow Catholics joined the McCarthyite hysteria, the Workers demonstrated against nuclear testing. In the Kennedy years they led successful resistance to civil defense in New York City. With Viet Nam the Catholic Worker came into its own as its members and fellow travelers became leading spirits in the resistance to the war.

Domestically the Catholic Worker made another major contribution by its early and wholehearted commitment to racial justice. But their stress on the works of mercy and personal responsibility, together with a dose of agrarianism, limited their immediate impact on social and political issues. Thomas Merton put it well in a letter to Dorothy Day a few years before his death:

> We are not liberals. We are still, I suppose, religious anarchists, except that the term has no political relevance whatever. But the Christian anarchist remains, unlike the liberal, clearly non-identified with established disorder. Or at least he tries to. In so doing he may exasperate everyone, but perhaps, sometimes he may see an opening to peace and love even when the sulpher and brimstone are at their worst, and when others have given up trusting in anything except weapons.[27]

In our day resistance to and denial of the "established disorder," indeed of power itself, is a crucial prerequisite for effective action, so that the Catholic Worker's personalism remains indispensible, though it may only be the starting point for building a radical Christian social movement.

The strength of this Catholic radicalism derived in the past from its relatively traditional theological base. In 1962 Peter Riga, describing the "crisis in Catholic thought," distinguished between two sharply different approaches to the temporal order: the incarnational and the eschatological.[28] Proponents of the incarnational perspective stressed the all-encompassing nature of Christ's entry into human history to redeem man and all creation. The old chasm of the natural and the supernatural was bridged by Christ; thereafter man was able to join through his work in the divine activity of creation. From this angle of vision men were called, not to cut themselves off from the world but to enter into it actively and positively, seeking to redeem the structures of society, pointing them in the direction of human liberation and fulfillment. Involvement and creativity should characterize the Christian life in the secular world, the arena in which men and women worked out their salvation. It was this approach that led the council to abandon the nineteenth-century dichotomy of church and world in favor of an open, positive response to the very things earlier popes had condemned: progress, freedom and modern civilization. Forward-looking American Catholics, hopeful of destroying the ghetto-mindedness of the church and increasing the impact of Catholics on national life, were enthusiastic exponents of this approach.

In Riga's analysis the opposite, and for him the less attractive, approach was the eschatological, the adherents of which felt a strong sense of disjunction between the world and the church. In this view the Christian was one whose full commitment was to Christ and his Kingdom, to a heavenly city with a character and an ethic in sharp opposition to the world of daily experience. In some cases this stance led to churchly isolation, to a siege mentality that sought to defend doctrinal truth and ecclesiastical discipline against the onslaught of hostile, worldly forces. More authentically, the eschatological vision was manifested in self-sacrifice, meditation or perfectionism, all sharply opposed to worldly pleasures and worldly achievement. Adherence to Christ's Kingdom provided a firm foundation for criticism and judgment of secular standards and goals and called the Christian out of his routine existence to another and better life.

It was easy for Riga and other commentators, conscious of the facts of modern secularization and ecclesiastical triumphalism, to interpret the events of the 1960s in terms of a liberal, incarnational viewpoint displacing a conservative, eschatological stance. What was less recognized at the time was that Catholic radicalism also drew much of its strength from an eschatological theological perspective. Dorothy Day and Peter Maurin called upon their fellow Christians to live now the message of the Gospel. The Christian was to love, wholeheartedly, unequivocally, without reservation; if he would do so he could release "the dynamite of the Gospel" and transform the world. Liberal Catholics could work through governments and trade unions, with their moral ambiguity and countless compromises; they could distinguish between just and unjust wars; they could seek possible avenues of reform in politics and race relations. But the radical marched to a different drummer: his was the heavenly city, Christ was his only model and he must go all the way. Voluntary poverty and absolute nonviolence were his way; suffering, prison, even death might be the price, one he would gladly pay.

As events in the 1960s broadened criticism of the national

order, there was a profound theological basis for conflict between liberal and radical Catholics. The older radicalism had
depended upon fairly traditional and clearly defined doctrines,
and many of its adherents drew strength and inspiration from
those sacraments and devotions liberals hoped to eliminate or
change. For Dorothy Day or Gordon Zahn Christianity taught
some plain and simple truths: the dignity and worth of each
man made in God's image; the impossibility of using violence to
attain any end; the responsibility of each man to live now the
Sermon on the Mount. That spirit remained viable in the 1960s.
James Douglass, a Catholic Worker product and leader of a
program in nonviolence at the University of Notre Dame, articu-
lated this position most clearly: "The Resistance message like
that of Jesus and Gandhi is: Therefore choose life . . . the life of
all men, and if that means suffering and going to prison, then
prison becomes the price of life, a price worth paying for the
life of mankind. Resistance means life. And those who have
risked their future for life have found in the process faith, hope,
and an incredible community as well."[29]

Many, inspired by this vision, nevertheless desired a more
moderate, less utopian, vocation than that offered by Dorothy
Day or James Douglass. Desirous of a career of social service, in
the optimistic years of Pope John and President Kennedy, many
enlisted in government-sponsored programs of social reform or
served as missionaries in foreign lands. They and others saw
themselves as adherents not only of the radical Catholicism of
the Catholic Worker variety but of what John Cogley called a
"Radicalized Catholicism," which turned the critical temper
against the church itself. But Jack Cook of the *Catholic Worker*
argued that such concern with the stance of the church was not
characteristic of Catholic radicals, who "went ahead and did
their own thing" and did not "wait upon the ecclesiastical
establishment to catch up with them." Truly radical Christians,
Cook argued, belonged to the tradition of "enthusiastic Christianity which has ever lived face to face with the parousia and
consequently lived out its ethic here and now."[30] For those
who could accept the relative simplicity of faith, which characterized this view, the important thing was the personal decision
to live now as if the Kingdom had arrived, with little concern

over the immediate, visible, political and social effects of one's actions. But for Catholics attuned to an evolutionary historical consciousness, an incarnational theological perspective and an American preoccupation with results and who were deeply alienated from the institutional church, the liturgy and the sacraments, the task was far less clear. In practice they often appeared to be less specifically Christian radicals than American radicals in quest of a religious identity.

There was, for example, Rev. Nicholas Riddell, O.C.D., in 1960 a studious, devout monk spending four hours a day in the chapel and the rest of his time writing a masters thesis on "The Effect of the Holy Eurcharist in the Worthy Recipient." In 1969 he was Nick Riddell, convicted felon, fugitive from justice and militant advocate of revolution. Riddell, one of the numerous priests who participated in raids on draft boards throughout the country, was similar to many others in the Catholic Resistance. Like Arthur and Thomas Melville he had been a missionary in an underdeveloped land where he had learned of poverty, oppression and American complicity at first hand. Like Philip Berrigan he had been radicalized by participation in the civil rights movement, in Riddell's case through his friendship with Milwaukee's militant Rev. James Groppi. Unlike Dorothy Day and James Douglass, whose theology schooled them to frustration and disappointment, Nick Riddell and a thousand like him are concerned, deeply concerned, with results, with ending the war, eliminating racism and achieving dignity and freedom for the poor and oppressed of the world. If the war does not end, new tactics and strategies must be found; if people will not listen, it is necessary to speak louder.

The 1950s, according to Riddell, were years of "protest in which the appeal was to justice and love, but that failed." Then came the period of resistance, marked by disruptive actions like the draft board raids; next "a period of open revolution against the system."[31] As honest and courageous as Riddell is, his words convey a subtle but profound break with his radical predecessors. Christian pacifists like Dorothy Day made little dent on warmaking in World War II or the Korean War, but their fundamental stance never varied, for it was rooted in unchanging truths about God and man, truths that made all periods times for "appeal to justice and love." The newer radicals, while maintaining much of the personalism and moralism of their forebears, do not share completely their ethical absolutism or their relative indifference to measurable gains. Instead, as each stage fails to produce the desired changes, their vision becomes broader, the enemy more vast and implacable, the language more apocalyptic, creating an atmosphere of permanent crisis with its danger of fanaticism, despair and self-destruction. Yet, Riddell also illustrates the growth, which so many experienced in recent years, and a humble willingness to learn from events and to relate personal conviction to historical necessity.

Personalist radicalism has many aherents, often operating out of different perspectives but all seeking the proper balance between prayer and action, between fidelity to the demands of the Gospel and sensitivity to the signs of the times. One who never ceased exploring new frontiers of historical experience was Thomas Merton. A noted convert, poet and Trappist monk, Merton seemed to traverse every avenue of human growth in the 1960s until his untimely death, which came appropriately while he was traveling in the Far East, dialoguing with Eastern religion. While his vocation as a monk manifested his personal adherence to the eschatological framework of faith, his was no otherworldly asceticism. For Merton monastic existence was life expressive of Christ's Kingdom that provided a standing critique of the world. From his peculiar angle of vision Merton testified to the profoundly religious significance of the events occurring around him. The Negro revolution in particular seemed to Merton to be God's judgment on America. The standard liberal responses to black protest were inadequate, he believed, because they invariably ended by defining "problems" and proposing "solutions" in the external, public realm while ignoring the roots of the racist dilemma, which lay in the depths of each man's soul. Merton, for his part, sought to awaken the American conscience to the fact that the "Negro problem" was a white man's problem: "the cause of injustice and hate which is eating white society and is only partly manifested in racial segregation with all its consequences, *is rooted in the heart of the white man himself.*"[32] Once this was grasped, the only authentic response was personal change, conversion, dying to the past. If men would make such a decision, if they would see their own complicity and seek to regain their humanity, America might yet "grow into a new society."

Theologian Michael Novak was another who defined the issue in personal terms, although he was far more concerned than Merton to reconcile the need for conversion with the equally compelling necessity for collective political action. "The revolution is political," Novak wrote. "But it is, even more, a revolution in consciousness." Novak contrasted Christianity's "criteria of humanistic life . . . centered on the human person and the critical community" with the criteria common to Marxists and many liberals, criteria centered on "the impersonal processes of technical pragmatic life." As a result, Novak, like Merton and Daniel Berrigan, called for "a conversion to social and political responsibility" for "it is only when persons become awakened from their sleep and recognize that the assumptions of a technical, pragmatic society have blinded them to their inner possibilities that hopes for a political revolution can be generated."[33]

The beginnings of real social change, then, lie in the human heart and revolution begins with conversion. This position, common to most American Catholic radicals, has deep roots in what Jack Cook called the "enthusiastic tradition." In America this tradition was identified precisely with evangelical Protestants who preached a message of radical conversion the fruits of which would be beneficence and good works and which often entailed commitment to a utopian, perfectionist ethic. Thus the most powerful advocates of antislavery were preachers who sought to convict the nation of the sin of slavery, convince their hearers of their complicity in the sin and persuade them to "immediatism," that is, to complete and immediate emancipation of the slaves. By and large they refused to acknowledge the validity of pragmatic questions: How was emancipation to be achieved without destroying the Union or without the cost of bloody civil war? Was the slave to be given land confiscated from his former masters (thus undermining private property)? Was he to be encouraged to move north (thus exposing northern racism, endemic even among the abolitionists)? Or was "freedom" enough, leaving the former slave "free" to take care of himself in a competitive society that excluded him at every turn? The evangelical abolitionists, courageous as they were, could not or would not answer these questions and, as a result, they must share responsibility for the Civil War and its far from satisfactory aftermath.

The personal conversion approach to social change was hardly limited to antislavery zealots. Post-Civil War evangelicals continued to stress personal conversion, but increasingly in a context of national complacency and righteousness. Once a powerful force for change, such preaching became part of an ideology of opposition to demands for reforms aimed at checking the power of the nation's growing corporations and humanizing the environment of city and factory. The individualistic ethic penetrated every church, leading to attacks on reformers who believed that in industrial society social ills had to be dealt with by collective action, trade unions and social legislation. John A. Ryan, the leading Catholic advocate of social reform, believed that personal righteousness, conversion to a life of charity and love, was pretty nearly impossible for the mass of men forced to struggle each day for the necessities of life for themselves and their families. Instead, like other American progressives, Ryan advocated legislation and institutional changes that would protect men against sickness, accidents, old age and unemployment and give them some ability to control the material conditions under which they lived. Again and again his efforts to gain Catholic support for such programs were stymied by men who justified their indifference by the claim that reforms by the state or by narrow, self-interested trade unions contradicted the requirements of personal responsibility and mutual respect and love that should characterize the Christian social order. In their often lonely struggle to secure immediate concrete benefits for the workers and farmers of America, men like Ryan, Raymond McGowan, George Higgins and other leaders of the Catholic social action movement could only regard the call for personal conversion, whether uttered by dedicated radicals or hypocritical conservatives, as irrelevant and irresponsible. It is not surprising, therefore, that a modern social actionist like Ed Marciniak should refer to an overemphasis on personal responsibility as one of the major obstacles to effective social action or that many a lifelong advocate of social action in the Catholic community should feel deeply estranged from contemporary Catholic radicalism. "If we are ever able to attain an ideal social order, it will probably be by a step-by-step approach," John F. Cronin wrote in the standard handbook of Catholic social action. "Men rarely adopt total changes in their philosophy of life. They change gradually, even imperceptably. Some will not change. . . . But if the general tone of society can be improved, and many men made better, then unsocial men can be quarantined and kept down by the force of public opinion and by law. This is the ultimate aim of Catholic social action."[34] It is difficult to think of a reform position farther removed from that of the Catholic radicals of the 1960s.

In this and other respects it is indeed unfortunate that the upsurge in social concern among Catholics has come at a time of widespread breakdown of church-related agencies of social service and reform. If Catholic schools and parishes had effectively taught the social encyclicals, sought vigorously to implement their appeals for social justice and encouraged study of the thought and work of earlier Catholic social action leaders, modern day Catholics might have understood the important issues that divided the Catholic Worker movement, the Social Action Department of the National Catholic Welfare Conference and the editors of *National Review*. Amid the shocks of the 1960s they might then have built on these predecessors and on dialogue with other religious traditions and the secular left. Instead the entire heritage of American Catholic social action and of the Protestant Social Gospel often seems to have been forgotten. Consequently, amid the talk of new beginnings, one cannot help but hear the echoes of battles fought long ago.

Personalism of the Catholic Worker variety is essential to the development of radical consciousness. If that consciousness is to find coherent and constructive expression, however, a more sophisticated analysis of society and its structures is necessary. It is for this reason that Christian-Marxist dialogue becomes so important, for whatever its strengths and weaknesses, Marxism supplies a set of tools for analysis of the problems of society as a whole and becomes at least a necessary adjunct to a meaningful personalism. In England a group of Catholic intellectuals attempted for several years to develop the theoretical basis and practical application of the union of reform Christianity and Marxist politics. The Slant group, as they were called after the title of the magazine they published, had a clear comprehension of the relationship between Christian renewal and social change. Their position in the Catholic spectrum was revealed in the aftermath of the Charles Davis affair, for the Slant radicals, themselves vigorous opponents of the moderate reformist hierarchy in England, nevertheless were highly critical of Davis. As historian Raymond Williams, an interested observer of these events, noted, Davis was "setting up personal values against the church as an institution, rather than stressing with the Vatican Council the necessary social structure of Christian belief, through which it could offer effective social and political change."[35] Davis charged the church with dishonesty. The Slant group agreed, but they located the corruption more in the church's external relation to others than in its internal effect upon its members. Such a view ties in with the notion held by many observers that Pope John's intention in calling the council was to streamline the church as an agent of social change of the type outlined in his great encyclicals. The Slant radicals took this idea much further to a positive vision of a socialist Kingdom of God.

There are three major features of England's left Catholicism. One is the so-called culture and liturgy argument, which suggests that the church as outlined by the council and as presupposed by the liturgical changes is a fellowship of brothers, a people of God marked by a radical equality. The liturgy or public worship of the community should express its common life while at the same time remaining open to and seeking to embrace all men. But, the liturgy is not only supposed to express the common life of Christians; it is supposed to foster and develop the life of the community. Liturgical reformers had stressed the former, but quickly found that no true community existed. The church as it was easily assimilated liturgical changes without coming any closer to true community life. Moreover, if the liturgy is supposed to foster community rather than simply express it, then social and political demands are laid upon the members. Community formation and growth require understanding of the broader society of which the church and its members are but a part. Analysis and action have to be shaped by the radical egalitarianism and stress upon community life present in the new liturgy and ecclesiology, a stance the Slant group feels runs directly counter to the central features of contemporary urban industrial life in Western liberal democracies. In short, as Brian Wicker put it in commenting on the liturgical reformers: "They did not understand that it was impossible to renew the liturgy without a renewal of the society in which it was to take place."[36]

Related to this is a second major theme of the Slant group, that the Kingdom of God must necessarily be socialist. While their analysis is heavily Marxist, it should be noted that the Slant intellectuals give a very general definition of socialism: "Socialism means full democracy—the greatest degree of participation by everyone in social processes."[37] Not only does capitalism systematically deny such participation to most people, but it increasingly dehumanizes and alienates men from their work and from one another. The Gospel, with its demand for love, brotherhood and incarnational participation in the building of the Kingdom of God, seemed to suggest a socialist direction confirmed upon close examination of current problems.

In more philosophical terms Richard Hinners has argued that the Christian model for society parallels the Marxist model. For Hinners the Kingdom of God is always both an ideal and an embodied actuality. The Christian is always called upon to witness to the truth, to renew the face of the earth, yet he always knows that the Kingdom is yet to come. As a result, "The Christian is both called to build the Kingdom of God and to build it now, but at the same time he is to be critical of any existing social order as not yet the final and perfect community."[38] So the Christian is in the world and not of it; he is never fully at home in any age or country, yet he must take his age and his country seriously. So Christianity is a social position and a revolutionary one, for it demands a negative critique and action (such as embodied in the Catholic Worker's personalist witness) and at the same time it demands positive projecting and building anew (concrete political action to find and develop alternatives). "It is never possible simply to deduce from Christian principles any one single pattern of the world as it ought to be," theologian Karl Rahner writes. "It is possible to reject certain conditions, tendencies, endeavors and actions as contradicting the Christian law of faith and morality . . . . But it is never, in principle, possible to say in the name of these principles that the world is, or has got to be 'thus and so' . . . ." [39] For Rahner, the Christian in the diaspora, which is his modern milieu, must be himself, he must be actively involved in building a world more true to man's dignity and humanity, but he can never give his particular version of the new order the full weight of his religious faith. For Hinners and for the Slant group, an understanding of Marx provides the best means of grasping the inter-relation between the many evils of the day and the surest road to building a better and more egalitarian community.

The third major theme of the Slant radicals is their insistence on the moral demand for revolution. Like the personalist radicals, they reject liberalism and pragmatism, with their sense of moral neutrality and their stress on piecemeal reform without an over-all strategy. They insist that Christianity demands commitment to fellow man and that this in turn requires a strategy for building a new social order rather than an ad hoc response to particular problems, an approach they feel invariably ends by shoring up the existing order. "What is required," Brian Wicker writes, is "an art of the possible geared toward attempting the impossible. It will be revolutionary in the sense that it is radically dissatisfied with the present state of things: but it will be conservative in the sense of understanding that the roots of the revolution are buried in the present order and that this order inevitably must shape the growth of the revolution if it is to be fruitful." [40] As a result, far from the Marxism of the Slant radicals issuing a new dogmatism, it accepts the inevitability and the constructive role of conflict and rules out no possibility save that which would rule certain possibilities out. Capitalism, Stalinism, Fascism, indeed any stance that would prevent men from shaping their destiny, are obviously not the direction dictated by a view the emphasis of which is on participatory community.

This emphasis stands in marked contrast to most contemporary American Catholic thought. The liberal center has found in the new theology a basis for its own instinctive acceptance, even its idolization, of American life. The native radicals have found in their reading of Christianity a justification for rejection of many of the most important features of American society. But by heeding the call to make history in personal terms the radicals have missed some crucial factors. Like the *Catholic Worker* before them, they have failed to confront the collective dimensions of history making, they have overreacted against manifestations of personal repression and they have done so because they have neglected social theory and history.

It is time for radical Catholicism in America to critically re-examine its perfectionism and its personalism. Without doubt the recognition and acceptance of man's freedom and the commitment to history making will be personal matters, and efforts to awaken concern and dedication will be essential tasks for Catholic radicals. Agitation, propaganda, confrontation, even dramatic gestures of civil disobedience and nonviolent disruption will always remain key elements of radical tactics. But they must no longer be regarded as constituting in themselves the essential elements of Catholic radicalism, nor should they be regarded as sufficient substitutes for a program or a strategy.

While striving to dramatize the inherent conflict between Christian commitment and American society, Catholic radicals must simultaneously strive to change America and the world. In doing so they must recognize that appeal to conscience is a primary tactic for all radicals, but divorced from political and social ideology it can easily excite fanaticism and ultimately end in despair. The abolitionists who awakened America to the sin of slavery could not sustain a commitment to national reconstruction. Similar moral revulsion may end the war in Viet Nam and thus fulfill the major immediate task. But in the absence of a positive foreign policy alternatives will such a step bring world peace or international justice any closer? The radicals' task is to seek paths to the solution of human problems; they might begin by taking *Pacem in Terris* seriously, or by trying to find out what relevance, if any, the Christian-Marxist dialogue has to the immediate, concrete issues. They must admit as well that personal moral integrity is no substitute for knowledge. Many who reject the supposed objectivity of social sciences make the opposite error of regarding morality as an excuse for ignorance. Frequently an abstract pseudo-Marx or Marcuse is regarded as enough to satisfy the demands of the intellect; all events can then be interpreted as fulfilling or confirming the theory. Catholic radicals must recognize the need to study, to learn, to be competent, if they would achieve the goals they would set for themselves. If they would alleviate poverty, end unemployment and abolish racism at home, then they will have to begin designating routes to those goals and developing the skills necessary to accomplish them. Both theory and practice are necessary; it is not necessarily a compromise to study urban planning or international trade. Seeking to implement the freedom budget or to develop new styles of mass education is not "copping out."

Nor is personal virtue a substitute for politics. Of course there are situations in which demonstrations and symbolic gestures are important, even essential modes of political action: the years since 1965 may have been just such a time. But, again, such activity does not exhaust political possibilities and necessities. Organization, planning, recruitment, programs, coalitions, compromises, elections, officeholding, administration, all are part of politics, and necessary parts. Radical Catholics must be prepared to engage in these activities and to do so with ability, with competence. Perhaps this suggests a reversion to liberalism, but one hopes that the commitment to peace, to justice, to human freedom and dignity, to the making of history, does not necessarily eliminate the possibility of morally engaging in democratic politics. If it does then the radical can resign himself to isolation not only from the middle class, but from the poor, the oppressed, the powerless at home and abroad for whom a self-righteous aloofness from the political arena must seem a middle-class luxury indulged in at their expense.

The task of Catholic radicals then is to begin the effort to translate commitment into effective action for positive change. If they cry any longer for "revolution" they must accept the responsibility of demonstrating not only why radical change is necessary, but that it is possible, that there are things men can do to bring about a new society and a new world. This means spelling out alternatives, showing how the ideal of personal freedom can be attained without destroying the possibility of material decency for all, showing that the allocation of national resources for the good of all Americans and for the alleviation of underdevelopment abroad can be reconciled with the ideal of personal participation in decisions that affect peoples' lives. It means, as Brian Wicker puts it, recognizing that love of God and our neighbor necessarily "entails working out the precise meaning of charity in terms of the technological organization, the scientific knowledge, the economic structures, and the political facts." If no serious efforts are made to do this, if radical Catholicism can go no further than the denunciation of evil, then it will end in despair. For now more than ever the forces of history—in the form of technology and bureaucratic structures—are able to shape and mold events and men. Unless Christians are able, now, to begin constructing new institutions through which all men may be able to fulfill the divine mandate to make history, then preoccupation with personal integrity, calm insistence that conscience forbids contact with organization or power or even mundane knowledge, will deserve the condemnation awaiting those who hear the Word, but fail to act on it.

9
POWER AND RELIGION

As the foregoing discussions have illustrated, politics in its broadest definition may well provide the arena in which the future of American Catholicism will be decided. If Christianity is to survive as a viable moral and religious force in modern society the drift toward domestic chaos and international anarchy and annihilation and the countervailing tendency toward technocratic control and manipulation must be checked by decisive human action, which means necessarily action that will enable mankind to gain some control over its destiny. Religion and culture are so intimately entwined with one another that, in the long run, it is hard to see how Christianity could remain true to itself in a culture headed for physical or moral destruction. The Catholic radicals, led by the Berrigans, have made that point by dramatizing the conflict between humanity and the forces of modern technology controlled by the state. Yet to construct the institutions required to ensure the survival of humanity and the dignity of man remains a political task of immense magnitude, one which few in the Christian community have begun to confront.

One reason for this is the difficulty that religious men, indeed which all decent men, have when they assume the burdens of history. In particular when men assume responsibility for their own future and that of the human community they must grapple with the problem of power. No single word has caused more difficulty for Americans than the word "power." In contemporary political discourse the word seems to have two very different, even contradictory, meanings. On the one hand, when used to describe an existing establishment, as in the phrase "American power in the world" the term means the ability of men or institutions to control or influence people or things outside of themselves. When linked with a group defined as oppressed, on the other hand, the word means that group's (or individual's) freedom to act, to determine themselves, to be free from the repressive "power" of others. Thus the cries for "student power" or "black power" seldom imply a goal of controlling others but rather a dream of students and black people to control themselves, that is, to shape their goals and actions free from external constraint. Power over others, possessed by men and their established institutions, thus confronts the demands of those others for power over themselves, power as control meets power as freedom.

The debate over the word power goes to the heart of many of our problems. Look for example at some of the ideological controversies familiar to those involved in liberation struggles. Many who accept the goals associated with the phrase "power to the people" interpret this to mean that powerless, helpless people must organize together to achieve through collective action what they are unable to accomplish as individuals. The relevant historical model is supplied by the labor union, which, when finally organized, was able to serve as a vehicle for checking the arbitrary power of management to control the lives of employees. In doing so it expanded the available options for its members and their children, broadening their freedom and their ability to shape their own lives. The teamster of thirty years ago had little choice but to find a job and use his income to meet the immediate needs of his family. Now he has job security and a far higher income, which he can allocate to home, hobbies, recreation or dissipation as he sees fit.

The powerless group today might simply follow the path of the unions and probably most Blacks, Mexican-Americans and others of low income would be quite satisfied to do so. But many of their leaders, and many younger, middle-class radicals, are inhibited from accepting this path by two considerations. The content of the vision no longer seems worthy: the unionists' acceptance of consumer goods as their choice, with the life style it entails, seems culturally and aesthetically unattractive. More important, it seems immoral, for it necessitates a perpetuation of the unequal distribution of power at home and repression of people abroad. At home the achievement of freedom to allocate personal resources left the big decisions regarding allocation of social resources in the hands of the nation's strategic elites. Unbreathable air, uninhabitable cities, unworkable governments are the price paid for the achievement of merely personal freedom and consumer power. Thus the "people power" approach by which the newly organized work into the existing structure of pressure groups seems to many to lead to a very limited and ultimately self-defeating power for its members.

Equally important, the achievement of power of choice within the existing system seems to demand participation and complicity in the power that system wields, arbitrarily, over much of the rest of the world. Attainment of respectability by a hitherto unorganized group means participation in the very system that deprives unorganized and powerless people at home and abroad of their freedom to act, to grow, to develop as men. Industrial unions won the right to organize in the 1930s in part by accepting the exclusion of farm workers from the National Labor Relations Act. Women who won the right to vote during World War I did so in part by turning a deaf ear to the cries of working women for economic justice. Black people in the southern states achieved substantial gains in the 1950s and 1960s, but they might have achieved more if their cause had not become linked with that of black people in northern cities. Again, it appears that acquisition of personal freedom and economic opportuntiy—power of choice—carries a price of deepening responsibility for the exercise of coercive power over the still deprived and powerless peoples of the world.

As Gustave Weigel once pointed out, the relation between right and power has been a central problem of political theory. Given the conflicting claims of men in society, the need for some mechanism of adjudication has long been recognized as imperative. Once men depended on God to do the job, through his priests and prophets. At other times Reason had been seen as the foundation of right. Most frequently men have failed to agree on the criteria for determining right and have left power as the instrument of decision. In American society, the paradox was contained in the notion that while men were acknowledged to possess the inherent right to "pursue happiness," they were also told that the possession of power over other men, "created equal," was immoral, even un-American. If happiness meant, as it frequently did, the amassing of wealth and property, it often carried with it, necessarily, the ability, witting or not, to influence and even control the lives of other people. The promise of America, a promise of economic and social advancement, inevitably entailed the deprivation of others of their access to happiness and success. Thus Americans constantly faced the embarassing contradiction between the promise of freedom and self-determination for all and the reality of inequality of wealth and power. Most clear in the case of black slaves and freemen, the contradiction was also present for immigrants, industrial workers, farm and migrant labor, all of whom were excluded from contemporary affluence. The shocked recognition of contradiction generated wave after wave of reform movements and gave them their distinctive character. Henry George expressed the reform sentiment in words that many contemporary reformers and radicals merely paraphrase. Again and again the reformer describes his youthful adherence to the American dream, his sudden exposure to its dramatic failure and his subsequent effort through reform to revitalize the dream for the poor and the oppressed.

The usual resolution of George's conflict between progress and poverty was found in the notion of equality of opportunity. While economic inequality exists, the argument ran, it is the result of men's unequal efforts in the free market where economic virtue was rewarded and economic vices punished. Study, hard work, thrift, self-discipline bring success; their absence ensures failure. Only after considerable struggle was it determined that society as a whole had a responsibility to guarantee equality of opportunity through provision of education and other instruments of preparation. What has made this position viable for so long is "the economy of plenty," an ever expanding supply of goods and services the division of which is the result of the free interaction of the citizens. Thus in the 1960s the United States faced the problem of poverty by emphasizing the necessity for sustained economic growth, while seeking in the Economic Opportunity Act, to assist those who did not start equal to acquire the skills and attitudes prerequisite to engaging in the struggle to share in the growing economy.

What this has meant very frequently is that power in society is divorced from responsibility. Few Americans willingly admit that they possess power, fewer still that they covet it. Instead they attribute their position to their character and to impersonal market forces and emphasize the limits of their ability to act and the insecurity of their tenure. "The privilege of controlling the actions or of affecting the income and property of others is something that no one of us can profess to seek or admit to possessing," John Kenneth Galbraith has written. "No American ever runs for office because of an avowed desire to govern. He seeks to serve . . . . The same scrupulous avoidance of the terminology of power characterizes American business. The head of the company is no longer the boss—the term survives only as an amiable form of address—but the leader of the team. No union leader ever presents himself as anything but the spokesman for the boys."[1]

Refusing to admit that they possess power, men hardly recognize the social foundations of their power and never admit to any but the most general responsibility for its exercise. Again and again difficulties between leadership and participants in universities, corporations, unions and churches are discussed in terms of responsiveness rather than responsibility. Leaders must be more sensitive to those dependent upon them; communications must be improved; the appearance of arbitrariness must be offset by consultation and discussion. Rarely if ever will leaders acknowledge the need for institutional change that will make them responsible to those dependent upon them. To do so would be to admit possession of power and to deny that virtue, talent or wealth are sufficient grounds to make possession of such power legitimate in the eyes of those affected by it.

Only in political life have Americans ever faced this issue. The Revolution confronted the new nation with the fundamental problem of legitimacy. Having severed their ties to the Crown, Americans had to find an alternative basis for the necessary inequality of power implicit in the establishment of government. Their response was two-fold. On the one hand they expressed their suspicion of government and governors by assigning to the state only the most limited tasks, defining bills of rights that were exemptions from governmental authority and then hamstringing government by complicated mechanisms of checks and balances. On the other, to legitimate these limited, often feeble, governments and the constitutions under which they operated, they invoked the consent of the governed, exercised through popular conventions to frame state constitutions and ratify the federal document, and through frequent election of officers. Americans said, in effect, that power of one man over another is, at best, a necessary evil; therefore government must be denied any but the most limited and clearly defined power and that must be legitimated and guarded by the watchful consent of the citizens.

This resolution of the problem of power and right was the product not of enlightened rationalists but of hardheaded men of affairs who had learned the danger of power from their own experience. In his first inaugural address Thomas Jefferson, often portrayed as the personification of liberal naivete, presented a rationale for popular government that was the same as that of the cranky Calvinist farmers who framed the Massachusetts constitution of 1780. "Sometimes it is said that man cannot be trusted with the government of himself," Jefferson said. "Can he then be trusted with the government of others? Or have we found angels in the form of men to govern him?"[2] Lacking available angels, and recognizing that kings and magistrates were men, too, Americans saw nowhere to turn but to themselves.

The intervening two centuries have left the central argument of the Founding Fathers unimpaired, but have exposed several flaws in its practical fulfillment. Outside the sphere of government the early Americans saw few dangers to liberty that could not be resolved by the people themselves through voluntary associations. Open space, cheap land, freedom of movement and an expanding economy all seemed to confirm this view. A host of voluntary agencies arose to aid men accomplish their goals, while the frontier served as a "gate of escape" from the growing complexity of settled society. As time went on, and the reality of economic power could not be denied, the state was called upon to regulate large corporations, guarantee equal education and employment opportunities, protect freedom of association for labor unions and ensure the stable, expanding economy that supplied the resources to redeem democracy's promises. These developments left the real inequalities of power in society untouched, while they vastly extended the power of government, a development accelerated by the wars, hot and cold, of the twentieth century.

The state in the mid-twentieth century has power over the lives of its people far beyond anything Americans of 1787 conceived in their most fearful fantasies. While still relying on the consent of the governed for its legitimation, the government's power seems to bear little relation to the needs and desires of the people. As Jefferson made clear, American government was intended to be self-government, requiring civic virtue and active participation. Indeed only if it was government of and by the people could it be government for the people. Yet American society's goals and values, its ceaseless activity, its promise, its rewards, all distracted people from public concerns and eroded their vigilance. Their attention to public affairs fluctuated with their private interests—preoccupied with private goals and satisfactions, they had little time left for the business of the community. Democratic institutions presupposed a democratic people, but the people too often saw the meaning of democracy in their personal success or in the achievements of their families and ethnic associations. Occasionally stirred to action by flagrant contraditions between America as promise and reality, they were usually satisfied with symbolic solutions, which left key decisions in the hands of organized, self-interested groups able to influence the legislative and administrative processes of government. Thus, as Gabriel Kolko and the "new left" historians are showing, populist and progressive reform movements, however radical their analysis and however idealistic their goals, left little imprint on government and less on the distribution of power in society. As a result the organized bureaucracies erected by technological industry and the warfare state accumulated more and more power with little challenge from the public.

Of all the reform movements the most successful was the social justice movement, a coalition of humanitarian reformers, social gospel churches and the poor who fought for such measures as insurance for the aged and the unemployed, aid to the

sick, the disabled and dependent children, sanitation and housing regulation and other legislation designed to compensate for
the more obvious failures of the economic system. Such reforms, when health insurance and improved education are
added, still constitute the basic liberal agenda in the United
States. However important and necessary such reforms were and
remain, however, they do not seriously affect the problem of
power and its distribution. They measure the responsiveness of
government to its people, but not its responsibility. They may
enable some to survive in urban America, and perhaps they will
assist some to improve their situation, but they will not check
the rampant centralization of power in our society or overcome
the sense of powerlessness that grips most of our people.

It is this inequality of power with its conflict with democratic pretentions that is the fundamental issue at stake in
American society today. Most glaringly evident is the failure of
public pressure to end the Viet Nam war, it extends beyond
government to infect every significant institution in the land.
Cut off from meaningful decision making in political, economic
and cultural life, the citizens are unable to exercise responsibility. Many therefore become irresponsible, reinforcing in a
vicious circle the very centralization of power that creates the
situation.

Campus unrest illustrates the point clearly. For years in
American universities, students were expected to accept rules
laid down "on the basis of an age-is-wisdom theory, combined
with a we-know-more-about-the-university-than-you-do pro-
fessionalism," writes Edward N. Robinson, former student body
president at the University of Michigan. "If students accept this
kind of policy, what have they in fact done?," Robinson continues. "They have accepted the fact that what most men say is
the ideal is usually quite different from what they actually do,
for most of these elders would express a belief in democracy
and representative government. They have accepted the contention that they aren't capable of acting for themselves, of de-
ciding what rules they should be governed by. They have
accepted the role of unthinking followers in a society already
far too full of such people."[3]

Of course it is just such people who are required by the

institutions of this country. Throughout America there are
organizations that exist to provide goods and services to large
numbers of people. All of them have developed bureaucratic
structures, that divide labor and diffuse responsibility and in the
process create forces that shape their lives toward institutional
advancement and preservation rather than maximization of
services or adaptation to the needs of the people being served.
Below are those persons dependent upon these organizations
but unable to influence their goals or direction. They take what
the system offers—or they rebel; they cannot really affect the
organization's behavior in any significant way. The federal government, the church, the university, all witness the gap between
the institution and those it is supposed to serve; all stand badly
in need of reforms that will allow substantive participation by
those at the bottom in decision making at every level. All resist
these changes as challenges to their efficient operation or to the
authority of those who are in control. In the battle the facts of
power at the top and powerlessness at the bottom become clear.
For those at the bottom the response is anger, frustration and
ultimately despair at the realization that they must adapt or
drop out. Change increasingly seems illusory, perhaps impossible.

Is the existence and exercise of such power as is commanded
by the leaders of our institutional life inevitable; one of those
realities given by history with which mature men must come to
terms? Perhaps not. Perhaps there is truth in that feeling Americans have always had that power, if it means the arbitrary and
relatively unchecked exercise of influence or control over another man and his environment, is indeed wrong. Men are in
fact equal as moral agents, and each has the right to determine
his own destiny, to make his own history. At best coercive
power is a necessary evil, to be regarded with suspicion, to be
hemmed in and checked wherever possible. When it must exist,
it must be legitimate, which means that it must be exercised
with the consent of those subject to it. These are the central
propositions of the American creed, which, at its best, teaches
that men have the right and indeed the responsibility to make
their own history and to rebel against unjust and illegitimate
authority. "One cannot entrust men with a collective right of

revolution unless one is prepared for them to revolutionize their lives from day to day," historian Staughton Lynd writes. "One should not invoke the ultimate act of revolution without willingness to see new institutions perpetually improvised from below . . . . Freedom must mean freedom now."[4] To affirm the truths of the Declaration of Independence and to deny their practical realization is hypocrisy. And surely the principles of self-determination and consent of the governed have validity not only in regard to political institutions but in any institution that is not purely voluntary but requires men's participation for their personal satisfaction and achievement.

The demand for student power, for freedom from arbitrary control and for freedom to determine the quality of their own lives is, then, a sign of the adherence of young people to America's most cherished pretensions and their rejection of its practice, which seems to deny to them and to many others that very self-determination that constitutes its moral foundation. If their demands often seem strident and unreasonable, perhaps it is because they sense the depths of America's betrayal of its own ideals and the threat that betrayal poses for their future. In its militarism, its worship of success, its bureaucratic centralization, its frequent and profound inhumanity, their society seems to be the very antithesis of the world envisioned by Thomas Jefferson, a world in which each man would be free to pursue happiness as he defined and envisioned it. If Americans insist on repression, they will confirm the fears of the young rather than strengthen their hopes; they will be told in effect that they cannot make history. Perhaps that is the truth, and men must accept the loss of power and freedom that it implies. If that is the new American faith, men should recognize its implications, cease claiming to believe in the central tenets of American democracy and admit that they are the prisoners of their technology and their social and economic system. If they do believe in America, how can they expect young people to become responsible participants in the necessary reconstruction that must take place in this country in the next fifty years if they do not do all in our power to encourage them to take control of and responsibility for their own lives? If Americans dare to hope that their country will witness the birth of the radically new institutions that must be built if men are to shape the burgeoning technology to distinctly human ends, then surely they must be prepared to abandon their power over the young and begin an effort to maximize each man's power to determine his own future. Of course there are risks in placing faith in the decency and honesty of students, but clearly the risks are no greater than those entailed in holding fast to the remnants of a bygone era.

The problems of education and of universities are not in another realm from those of war, poverty and racism. All are intimately related; a student power movement that simply seeks a more intimate integration into the university as it is is hardly worthy of attention. Fortunately many students see that the power they claim to control their own lives is a power denied most people in this country and abroad. The goal of student power must be not only the freedom of students but the transformation of the university into an agency of freedom clear in its commitment to the liberation of men from the bonds of ignorance and tyranny and in its deliberate dedication to providing people of all races and classes with the understanding and technical expertise to make real the dream of liberty and self-government that alone give meaning to this nation's existence. Of course this is politicization of the university, but not a commitment to the politics of a party or to the ideology of a particular sect. Rather it is a commitment to the ideals that alone give the intellectual life meaning and that, in a democratic society, necessitate a political stance. Freedom and reason are not political commitments of the order of the Republican party or socialism; they are political commitments in the sense that they imply a constant battle against those forces and powers that impede their realization for all men. Until the university and the men in it are willing to recognize and accept the responsibilities that their claims to intelligence and education imply, they will be plagued, and they ought to be, by disruption and opposition.

If these commitments were clear, scholars might not be so worried at the prospect of assuming an increasingly critical stance in regard to the other institutions of our society. The university, which, in William Arrowsmith's words, helped to create "a distinctive modern chaos" in which the quality of society as a whole is nobody's business, must now take the lead in restoring concern for the good of our society—and of mankind. "Where once family and church and school spoke for the public interest," Arrowsmith writes with some exaggeration, "there is only a silence broken now and then by angry students, gurus, madmen, and enthusiasts."[5] Somewhere such voices must be heard, and force be given to the concerns of the public; somewhere drift must give way to mastery. In the past colleges and universities have done many things for Americans; teaching the young of all races and classes; researching solutions to problems that mattered to people; offering a wide range of needed services to groups and individuals. In the future they can render no greater service than through the aim to develop among their participants a critical spirit, which means in part subjecting the practices and institutions of America to the closest scrutiny. "More and more our society and the world will need young men and women who have not only assimilated the past and made themselves familiar with the present, but who have also become articulate, informed, and thoughtful critics of both, and in this measure have qualified themselves to create the world and the future," Kenneth Keniston writes. "By teaching, embodying and expressing the critical spirit, the American university will continue to contribute to our society's capacity for self-understanding and self-renewal."[6]

The demand for student power begins in awareness of betrayal and hypocrisy and constitutes an affirmation of basic American values. It therefore compels a response from adults, who should address their attention to removing the more blatant and inhumane contradictions and trying to implement the values they profess. In addition, all should support the attempt by students to take control of their lives so that they may truly develop, grow and contribute to the necessary transformation of American society. All have a stake in helping men secure that freedom from arbitrary control and manipulation that is the essential precondition for human dignity, for human development and for education. There are other reasons to support changes in university life: the need to provide a model of a self-governing community capable of reconciling its claim to serve men with the bureaucratic structures necessitated by democratic education; the need to break the vicious cycle of the integration of men into an increasingly technologically determined society to make possible a future in which free men will want to live; the need to learn democracy through its practice. The challenges that confront this generation are perhaps as crucial and profound as any in history. We are, all of us, frightened—frightened of the future, frightened by our society, by many of our fellows, by the potential for evil we must recognize within ourselves. But, as Emerson said, "this time, like all times, is a very good time, if we but know what to do with it." And the university is only one place where the times are being tested, as men strive to gain the power that belongs to those who can say "I am my own man."

Those who would confront the issue of power squarely must recognize, then, that it infects every institution, from the family to the state, and it requires both personal and political change. A rebirth of power as freedom can only be carried out, Ronald Sampson writes, "by reflective, sensitive and brave individuals setting about the difficult task of reordering the nature of their own human relationships in the family, at work and in their general societies."[7] In these terms the unrest and uprisings in the past ten years among American Blacks, Chicanos and Indians, and the widespread concern among young people seeking new styles of life and work, are signs of the vitality and the strength of democratic sentiment. As more and more people ask questions about their personal responsibilities and seek to take control of their own lives, America may well experience a rebirth of the tradition of self-determination and voluntary cooperation that has given American democracy its distinctive character.

Yet, at the same time that men are seeking to reorder their personal relationships, they must also pay close attention to existing institutional life, facing directly the problem of concentrated economic and political power. To ignore the public arena in favor of the personal leaves the present wielders of power a free hand to do what they will, while it ignores as well the pressing need to reorder national priorities if real freedom is to be possible for the poor and oppressed both at home and in the

Third World. As many commentators have noted, Americans are caught in a double revolution, one in which the children of contemporary affluence seek a new quality of life and another in which the poor and the heretofore segregated minorities seek a share in that very affluence.[8]

The link between the two revolutions may well be found in the common concern of both to realize in practice the American promise of personal freedom, of that power that is the ability to act rather than be acted upon. The poor, locked into a social and economic system that thwarts them at every turn, seek some control over the conditions of their lives; the young, faced with the impenetrable bureaucracies of institutional life, seek a way to lead truly creative and responsible lives. Both groups would take control of and responsibility for their lives, but the educated youth of the middle class can do so by living in peripheral communities supported by the cast-off waste of the consumer society, a path not open, and not attractive, to the poor. Only if the facts of concentration and control of national resources are confronted and an appropriate political strategy is devised can the full promise of self-government be realized.

The beginning of such an effort is perhaps found in the very notion that provides the moral force for freedom as power, the notion of equality. There are very few men in our society who take seriously the contention so deeply rooted in the American tradition that men are equal as moral agents, each possessing the inherent right to make the crucial decisions that shape the direction and character of his life. Conservatives never accepted the idea, for it threatened their cherished values of order and deference, and it challenged their own power as well. While liberals profess acceptance of equality, they give far greater weight in practice to rationality and efficiency: the people's liberties should be respected but they should not be allowed to interfere with the planning and the technological changes that will in the long run serve their interests. Even many radicals, unsurpassed in their profession of faith in the people, seldom show much willingness to rely on popular judgement. Accordingly they frequently establish themselves as surrogates for the people, acting in their name but without their approval, sometimes through a violence that betrays their own elitist disdain for the tasks of organization, education and popular legitimation. "I love humanity; it's people I can't stand," Charles Schulz's Linus broods, and the words could stand as shorthand for the failure of our democracy.

The Brazilian educator Paulo Freire has seen this problem clearly. "Sectarianism" in politics, conservative, liberal, radical, expresses a common desire to grasp the historical process, identify with that process and act in its name. In the end such men deny freedom and equality in favor of the "truth" of history. As a result, Freire writes, "they end up without the people—which is another way of being against them." Instead Freire proposes that people commit themselves to the oppressed, determined to fight at their side, recognizing that the moral foundation is the right of each man to be a subject, not an object, of history, to grow and develop and to shape the future. Men and women must exercise this right themselves, and those who would "do the right thing" must be with them, not as teachers or as leaders, but as members of the oppressed. Solidarity with the oppressed, according to Freire, can be true only when they are regarded not "as an abstract category" but as "persons who have been unjustly dealt with, deprived of their voice, cheated in the sale of their labor." Too often even the best-intentioned reformers "talk about the people, but they do not trust them; and trusting the people is the indispensable precondition for revolutionary change."[9] The true radical, committed to the liberation of all men, is one who practices dialogue with all people, who believes that it is not the efficient expert or technician, or the charismatic politician, or the erudite scholar, or the revolutionary vanguard, who will lead men out of the wilderness, but that the people will come out themselves to seize control of their future or they will not come out at all.

This point of view has particular relevance to one of the most pressing issues confronting the United States in the 1970s: the need to discover means whereby the centralized state, still needed to check and eventually control the concentrated economic and social power, which has been created by technology in a capitalist system, can be reconciled with the even more critical obligation to provide institutions that allow individuals and groups to gain some real control over the decisions that affect their lives. For years liberals, radicals and socialists agreed on the need to increase the role of the federal government in national life in order to control, direct and humanize the power of national corporations. This task was made difficult in America by constitutional limitations on federal authority and the fragmentation of the legislative branch into sectional and self-interested blocs. Only the president enjoyed a national popular mandate; only his office effectively symbolized the national interest as against private and sectional interests. Accordingly the index of liberal reform in twentieth-century America was the presence or absence of strong presidents, and the heroes of the era have been men like the Roosevelts, Woodrow Wilson and John F. Kennedy, all talented and aggressive chief executives.

Only in recent years have events led to any serious questioning by reformers of this reliance upon the presidency. Most important of the causes of this re-examination has been the undeclared war in Viet Nam with its dramatic revelation of the erosion of constitutional limits on presidential power. Less noticed has been the impact of national unrest, particularly in urban ghettos. The long, complicated struggle for control of funds in the community action program of the War on Poverty was one sign of growing demands for a greater say by recipients of assistance in the development of their neighborhoods and cities. The riots, and the rise of the black power movement, provided further evidence of a broad-based rebellion on the part of the poor and disadvantaged against the paternalism and bureaucracy inherent in reforms carried out by government at all levels. In urban slums, on campuses, even on the farms, those who are the objects of liberal concern, who are supposed to be the beneficiaries of education, welfare and housing reform now demand a real voice in the administration of programs designed to meet their needs, for their freedom and dignity must be based upon real, tangible control over the forces and powers that dominate their lives.

This context of apparent contradiction between centralized control and social planning and personal and group dignity provides the framework of significance for the work of Saul

Alinsky. For thirty years Alinsky has been for liberals and conservatives alike, a gadfly, a disturber, often a sheer obstructionist. In all those years of liberal reform Alinsky stood apart, organizing the poor and the nearly poor to prevent or delay programs his enemies believed were for the good of Alinsky's followers. In the tension between centralized planning and decentralized participation, between government and the local community, between the rational calculation of the common good and popular determination of social goals, Alinsky has stood solidly and aggressively with the people.

A trained criminologist, Alinsky began his career as a self-styled "professional agitator" and community organizer in Chicago in the late 1930s. There he directed an effort by churches and unions to organize and unite the multiplicity of ethnic and religious groups in the stockyards area. The Back of the Yards Neighborhood Council was an "organization of organizations," a federation of most area ethnic, religious, fraternal, and economic associations that undertook projects of neighborhood improvement while at the same time acting as the voice of the whole community in dealing with city government. As a result of the council's work a deteriorating neighborhood was stabilized, inter-group tensions were alleviated, crime and delinquency were reduced and civic services vastly improved.

From this experience Alinsky went on to become a professional neighborhood or community organizer. Through the Industrial Area Foundation, Alinsky offered his services, and those of men he had trained, to cities and neighborhoods interested in combating internal disintegration and fragmentation and external manipulation and exploitation. His best-publicized effort prior to 1964 was in Chicago's Woodlawn area, a once upper-middle-class neighborhood near the University of Chicago that had become predominantly Negro and was beset by the poverty, crime and apathy long characteristic of big city slums. The Woodlawn Organization (TWO), which Alinsky helped establish, first attacked local merchants who exploited the area, then fought the city for better educational facilities and finally earned national headlines for its fight against local urban renewal schemes and against the expansion plans of the University of Chicago. Success in gaining a voice in urban renewal and slowing the pace and character of university expansion established TWO as a permanent fixture in the area, and after Alinsky's departure it continued to function as the nation's best example of an effective community organization.

Although in the minds of the American right wing Alinsky has long been synonomous with communism and subversion, he was also anathema to the liberal community, at least until the 1960s. The rise of black nationalism and black power, the publication of Charles Silberman's *Crisis in Black and White* and the urban riots all brought a change in Alinsky's image. His organizers were invited into several communities to help construct unified black coalitions. While the local power structure responded to these invitations with rage, others began to see him as a "riot preventer," whose techniques helped channel frustration into constructive programs for community betterment. After several of these efforts, however, tension developed between Alinsky and his predominantly white organizers and militant black leaders, so that at the end of the decade he withdrew from action in black ghettos to develop new work in corporation reform and middle-class, white community organizations.

Alinsky is not a philosopher or a systematic social theorist. He has frequently denied that he is propagating a doctrine, insisting instead that he and his aides are simply "technicians trying to organize people." Yet he quite clearly stands solidly within the American democratic tradition, applying that tradition creatively in the modern situation. Like the Founding Fathers, he is a tough-minded realist, aware of the need for organization and for militance to guard popular liberties. "All I stand for is real democracy," he has written, "and that means popular participation and militant organization. The have nots will not just be handed opportunity on a silver platter; they will have to take it by their own efforts," words that echo Paulo Freire's.

The core of Alinsky's Americanism is a literal, almost fundamentalist, democracy. Anticipating Staughton Lynd, Alinsky argued in the 1946 *Reveille for Radicals* that there existed a native radical tradition with a goal of full democracy and tactics that implied an ongoing threat of direct action. That tradition was based on a genuine, complete but realistic faith in mankind. The people, as individuals and collectivities, possess ultimate worth, the present is theirs to control, the future theirs to determine. Alinsky fully accepted the advent of urban industrial society, his Jeffersonianism was purged of any trace of the agrarian, but unlike his liberal counterparts who have dominated politics for over a quarter century, he rejected reform from the top down. Rather the people must determine themselves the pace and quality of social change; the world to be made must be made by and for the people themselves. The bureaucrat who administers a program of urban planning or renewal has no more right to decide the future of a city or any part of it than does the business executive or the university president. Decisions that affect peoples lives must be made by the people themselves.

If Alinsky's faith in the people and his insistence upon what would later be called participatory democracy seem familiar, it may be because they are staple items in liberal vocabulary, though the extent of their practice is highly questionable. More immediate and concrete was Alinsky's conviction that where he and the old left, and today he and the new left, part company is on the issue of power. "Liberals fear power or its application," Alinsky wrote, "They labor in confusion over the significance of power and fail to recognize that only through the achievement and constructive use of power can people better themselves."[10] The goal of all Alinsky's work, the strategy and tactics that have brought him notoriety, is to bring to the people real power, a real ability to control the forces and events that shape their lives. Integration or black power style segregation; urban renewal or urban preservation; political or direct action, all these questions are secondary; the big point for Alinsky is that when decisions are made, the people themselves should make them. "In the last analysis of our democratic faith," Alinsky writes, "the answers to all the issues facing us will be found in the masses of the people themselves, *and nowhere else.*"

The trouble with democracy in America, as Alinsky has seen it since the mid thirties, is that it is partial and incomplete. Many people: Blacks, poor whites in Appalachia, farm laborers,

Mexican Americans, have lacked the power to influence, much less control, legislation that directly affects them. Alinsky more than any single man has made the poor and their leaders aware of the indispensible need for organization. To those who are oppressed, left out, he says, "Look, you don't have to take this. There is something you can do about it. But you have to get power to do it, and you will only get it through organization. Because power just goes to two poles, to those who have money and to those who've got people. You haven't got money so your own fellow men are your only source of strength." Herein lies the ideology of the "peoples' organization," the contribution of Alinsky to American reform.

Many have noted the difficulties America faces because of the absence of any significant organized group on any level which represents the people, the public interest, the community. Alinsky early recognized this problem and the consequent need to build an organization to represent the community as a whole rather than any particular group within it.

> Every institution in the community now finds itself beset with other interest agencies competing for the attention, and in many cases certain loyalties, of the individual. No single institution today . . . whether religious, economic or social, has as many ties to the individual in as many different facets of his life, as they possessed in the past. Specifically, there were the old days when men looked to and accepted the authority and direction of their labor unions in other fields than the direct, specific area—and the same applied to their churches; but those were the old days. These are new people, with multiple minor loyalties to multiple smaller organizations—a life as fluid and mobile as the city itself . . . . The fracturing and almost pulverizing of the previous, simple, relatively organized unity of the individual, his community and his church demands today a unified approach of all of the community institutions working together on those areas of life outside of their particular domain of interest . . . . The community becomes the only feasible and pragmatic unit . . . . The Roman Catholic Church must bring its full resources to bear in programs designed to develop the mobilized power of the community in the struggle for order, hope, opportunity and dignity. The community represents that source of energy from which the power can be generated which is so essential for this job.[11]

Alinsky rejected the two major alternatives previously chosen by those who were concerned with the community. He regarded the rhetorical stress on the people, urging each man to act with disinterested civic-mindedness, altruism, unselfishness, as naive and paralyzing, for in such a situation those with power could divide and overcome the fragmented efforts of reform-minded individuals. But he also rejected the option of relying on the expert, whose work usually served the interests of the powerful and undermined popular democracy.

Instead Alinsky called for "peoples organizations" made up of the people not simply as civic-minded individuals but as members of groups. The peoples' organization is a super-organization, rallying men and women by cementing together all their existing and fragmented loyalties: religious, economic, ethnic, racial, social, all the competing loyalties of men in a pluralist society. If it is to speak for the community the organization must encompass all its elements. Building on existing institutions and associations, the new organization requires no break with tradition, no immediate severing of old ties: it enlists the people where they are. For Alinsky this is the only approach "that would be truly representative of the people and truly in keeping with the spirit of democracy. A Peoples Organization is built upon all these diverse loyalties, to the labor unions, to the social groups, to the national groups, to the myriad of groups and institutions which comprise the American Way of Life."

The initial point is participation and the experience of power to make decisions and be responsible for them, which implies overcoming fatalism, hopelessness and the alienation of people from one another, and actually living through the experience of acting together to achieve liberation, what Friere calls "conscientization," men becoming conscious of their oppression and their ability, acting together, to achieve their vocation to grow as men. Thus the specific program is subordinated to action, praxis, because, as Alinsky puts it, "after all, the real democratic program is a democratically minded people."

The tactic for organization, and its method as well, is conflict: the peoples organization is a "conflict group." Conflict is natural among a free people, for they naturally differ and clash in their pursuit of differing ends. It is the price of democracy and the cost of freedom. "Constant dissension and conflict is and always has been the fire under the boiler of democracy,"

Alinsky believes, an idea that has brought him into fierce battles with his fellow social scientists, preoccupied as they are with the social system, stability and conflict resolution. One, Philip M. Hauser, head of the department of sociology at the University of Chicago during its struggle with The Woodlawn Organization, charged that Alinsky's methods "actually impeded the achievement of consensus and thus delayed the attaining of Woodlawn's objectives."[12] From this perspective the will of the people who are the objects and the victims of social change only become important when they coincide with the will of the powerful, producing a consensus determined ultimately by the men at the top. "One thing we instill in all our organizers is that old Spanish Civil War slogan 'Better to die on your feet than to live on your knees,' " Alinsky replies to his critics. "Social scientists don't like to think in these terms. They would rather talk about politics being a matter of accommodation and consensus—and not this conflict business. This is typical academic drivel. How do you have consensus before you have conflict? There has to be a rearrangement of power and then you get consensus."

Alinsky's personal style of ridicule, occasional cynicism and refusal to deal seriously with theoretical issues has its weaknesses, but his approach exemplifies democracy in action. Participation, organization, conflict and action are necessary features of democratic existence. Without the power to implement an idea, it becomes in a sense meaningless. This is Alinsky's strongest point: he professes to speak for no particular vision of the good society, in whose name the people will be coerced and manipulated. Rather he works to implement the more fundamental right of the people to determine what the good society will be. "Regardless of what the situation is," he writes, "people will not be able to do anything constructive, anything in the truly democratic spirit for themselves and others, unless they have the power to cope with the situation, whatever it may be and wherever it occurs. So I just hold to that point—build the organization and cross each bridge as we come to it."[13]

What makes Alinsky a radical in America is not his ideas but his effort to implement them. Everyone professes to believe in democracy, but few are willing to pay its costs in terms of their own power and self-esteem. Instead they become cynical and hypocritical, professing reverence for the people, for their employees, their students, their subordinates, but insisting that they keep their place and accept the demands made upon them. "The fundamental issue which will resolve the fate of democracy is whether or not we really believe in democracy," Alinsky writes. "The democratic way of life is predicated upon faith in the masses of mankind, yet few of the leaders of democracy really possess faith in the people. If anything our democratic way of life is permeated by man's fear of man. The powerful few fear the many, and the many distrust each other." Liberals and Conservatives, Democrats and Republicans, "share in common a deep fear and suspicion of the masses of the people." Because Alinsky has taken the slogans of democracy seriously, because he has tried to get Americans to practice what they preach, he has been and remains anathema to both right and left, to all who share contempt for the people as they are and know better than the people themselves what they should become.

It should be clear by now that Alinsky occupies a central position in debates about social action. On the one hand he is a constant irritant to the liberal establishment, with its willingness to do things for the poor but its fear of the poor themselves. This feeling is mutual, for Alinsky's views were clear in his attack of the War on Poverty, which he called "a prize piece of political pornography . . . a huge political pork barrel, and a feeding trough for the welfare industry, surrounded by sanctimonious, hypocritical, phony, moralistic bastards."[14]

On the other hand Alinsky's relations with the new left and the black power movement are almost equally strained. In a debate published in the spring of 1968 Alinsky squared off against radical ministers and young Negro activists who called for revolution. Ivanhoe Donaldson told Alinsky: "Although I want to be free to get a job where I want, I don't really want those jobs . . . I really want to destroy those corporations because they represent the dehumanization of other people like myself around the world." Rev. Richard Shaull supported Donaldson: "To me the significant thing is that the people in

the ghetto and the Third World and the universities are beginning to discover that we are up against some sort of total system
of domination which has its roots in the very structure of our
society, and it is this that we must come to grips with."

Alinsky replied from thirty years of experience as a community organizer and, while his response was somewhat unfair
to the new left, it exposed the central problem, which contemporary radicals must confront if they are to have any
influence on the future.

> I happen to live—not utterly I suppose, but pretty much, 99%—in
> a pragmatic world, and with me the basic problem is always one
> of starting off in the world as it is. What can we do about it?
> Where? How? . . . You don't simply dismiss basic realities—you're
> not going to get up and say to people who are unemployed, jobs
> aren't important, housing isn't important, breaking into this area
> of life isn't important, what we need is a whole new world, the
> hell with the whole corporate structure . . . . Now basically, what
> you have to do if you're going to have change, is to have power,
> and in order to get power, you've got to get mass organization
> support, and if you're going to get mass organization support,
> you're going to start off with issues that are meaningful to
> people: jobs, housing, rights. From there you start moving on. If
> you don't do that, you're just more or less talking to yourself.
> This has been my big concern with black power . . . . I think
> black power is desperately needed. But I think there's going to be
> so much jazz going around about how we need to get rid of
> civilization, and we've got to go get ourselves a whole new society
> and so forth—this is utterly not communicating to the blacks, any
> more than to any other part of our society. So, as a consequence,
> it becomes a flow of rhetoric: noble ideals and noble aspirations
> which are out of this world. It becomes what I would call a form
> of political hippieness.[15]

If the rhetoric of liberation is to issue in the reality of freedom
from oppression contemporary radicals are going to have to
confront their own elitism and come to terms with the work of
men like Alinsky and Paulo Freire.

Discussion of the contemporary American scene has taken us
a considerable distance from the issues of Catholic identity. Yet
this has not been simply a digression but an effort to provide a
foundation for an argument regarding the relevance of the
Catholic tradition to the American situation and for a sketch of
a mission for the church in the American future. If, as has been

argued above, the decisive questions facing America today are not the abstract "issues" of racism, violence and war, but the concrete question of rekindling a sense of responsibility on the part of people for our collective life and providing concrete institutional forms for effective assumption of responsibility, then the vocation of the Christian in society may be a bit clearer. Surely such a situation is one to which the Catholic tradition in social and political thought can authentically address itself.

The encyclicals on social questions of Pope Leo XIII and Pius XI provided until recently the basis for most Catholic discussion of economic, social and political questions. These documents and their major interpretations contained a flaw, which always limited their utility, particularly in the United States. Catholic social thought was permeated by what Michael Novak called in another context "non-historical orthodoxy." The popes believed that there was an ideal Christian social-political order resting on divine intention that provided the standard for judging the world and the goal of its efforts. This ideal order derived from man's creation in God's image and his salvation through Christ, and centered on His Church, which was the custodian of his message and the dispenser of his grace. Intimately related to this church-centered view of history was the concept of natural law that defined man's rights and obligations and provided the basis for ordering social life. Deeply influenced by the Romantic reaction to the Enlightenment and the French Revolution, Catholic social thinkers sketched the content of the ideal order in terms of a glossed-over image of the Middle Ages. Universal association with the church and its discipline, a consensus on ultimate goals and values, a variegated, lively group life and a system of rights and obligations characterized the model of society that served as the Catholic alternative to modernity.

Lacking a positive sense of change and development, the church adhered to a view of the world largely unaffected by modern forces. Alienated from modern society, its leaders clung to outmoded concepts of economy and politics, forcing Catholics in democratic societies to adapt this reactionary pattern to the realities of their situation and in doing so often facing charges of compromise and betrayal from their own ranks. The church's failure derived from its hopeless effort to project a model of the world as it ought to be, an effort doomed from the start. More important it was an effort that led to the paternalism, authoritarianism and self-righteous arrogance scathingly diagnosed by Dostoevski. Yet the failure did not invalidate portions of the Catholic critique of modern industrial society. The church saw and condemned the fallacies of the free market and the idea of progress; it recognized and occasionally denounced the inhumanity of a system that elevated production and accumulation above the needs and the freedom of man. Most important, many Catholics held firmly to the venerable Christian belief that men should be the subjects of history and that they were responsible for their actions.

Concretely Catholic social thought contained two major emphases that continue to be of central importance. Negatively it condemned the tendency of liberalism to divide men from one another and, in the name of freedom, leave them open to the exercise of power by the self-interested. In destroying guilds and other associations, liberalism seemed to free men for progress, but, if they failed in the competitive arena, they had no defense to fall back on. Only the state remained as a locus of effective power, and, when democracy came, it frequently tended to totalitarianism, for men had nowhere else to turn for protection against economic forces beyond their control. Liberalism, beginning in emancipation from state control, ended by endowing the state with enormous irresponsible power over a mass citizenry lacking effective means of group action. Personal alienation and political tyranny were the result. In its reaction against liberalism the church often failed to act honestly or effectively on its critique, but it constantly denied the moral validity of such liberal individualism and capitalist economics.

Catholicism's hostility to the liberal state had as its positive side an emphasis on the need for a rich associational life, for a wide range of economic, social and cultural organizations intervening between individuals and the state. Man's social nature required such groups for realization of his diverse goals, and he needed them too for protection against impersonal forces controlled by the powerful. These groups should have many matters of collective importance in their hands. By the principle of subsidiarity the church argued that the state should encourage such bodies and confine itself to limited goals and objectives. Democracy had to be social and economic in order to be viable politically, liberal Catholics argued, which meant that trade unions, industrial democracy and educational and cultural freedom were required for man's freedom and satisfaction, however far church practice deviated from these principles.

In the encyclicals of Pope John XXIII the positive elements of the Catholic social tradition took on new importance, freed now from the hoary hand of Romanticism. Firmly locating himself in history, Pope John did not, like his predecessors, look back to a lost age of unity and simplicity but instead looked forward to an emerging world community bound together by communications, economic interdependence and a common fear of nuclear annihilation. That world required not Christian uniformity but an ability to live with differences in a pluralist environment. It needed therefore a world government able to act on behalf of mankind's common interests and profound change within nations that would make states responsible to their people. "Socialization," the proliferation of agencies and institutions through which men could indeed exert some control over the decisions that effected their lives, was the fundamental process by which men could maintain their dignity and responsibility amid the complexities of modern life.

Thus both Catholic social thought and American realities converge upon a common theme: the need for major institutional changes that will allow men and women to protect their rights, exercise their responsibilities and grow and develop in truly human fashion. The need is not primarily for public ownership of the means of production, for further technological innovation, for expanded education, but for the kinds of institutional changes that will assure that these and other innovations will serve the needs of real, breathing men and women. Responsiveness in institutions will follow holding those institutions responsible to the people they serve. Meaningful work for young people in the affluent society will accompany a serious movement to redirect human energies and social resources to the alleviation of misery and suffering rather than to the power and prestige of established nations and their leaders.

Only if America can develop new institutions of popular control suited to the age will its democracy survive. There are already signs of renunciation of the ideals of equality and individual freedom and responsibility not only in national practice but in the dominent orthodoxy of the learned professions, most notably among social scientists. Only radical and imaginative thought and dedicated work and suffering can stem the tide and renew the rich tradition of local and voluntary action, which is the safeguard of freedom. Christians are called to join that struggle because of their central concern with human freedom, with the power of each man to become fully human as his Creator intended. Catholic Christians have much in their tradition to further support an effort to develop voluntary bodies of all sorts to aid man in his quest for freedom and dignity. Around this effort may well cluster all the truly creative energies of the new Catholic Americans of the 1970s.

10
NEW DIRECTIONS
FOR AMERICAN CATHOLICISM

The preceding chapters have conveyed something of the turmoil and the confusion presently stirring within the American Catholic community. The problems of American Catholics both influence and are influenced by the problems of American society. On the one hand the breakdown in the unity of the Catholic population, the increased sophistication of Catholic intellectuals and the energy generated by the devotion and commitment of thousands of priests, nuns and young people have joined with other forces in the United States to undermine some of the most cherished customs and institutions of American society. Old definitions of Americanism, patriotism, social justice, have buckled beneath an onslaught launched by many groups, including a significant number of Catholics. Constituting 20 to 25 per cent of the population, Catholics are an important, strategically located segment of the American people; changes in their attitudes, structures and organization are bound to amplify through the society as a whole. On the other hand, for the same reasons they cannot be immune to changes in the broader society. The Negro revolution, the escalation of violence at home and abroad, the shattering of cold war cliches are all bound to make their influence felt on Catholics, displacing accepted versions of the society to which the church and its members sought to adapt and confusing accepted formulas for reconciling these dual loyalties.

Anyone who projects a new church for the new age is unforgivably arrogant. One of the great lessons of recent years is that freedom is indivisible. When the conciliar declaration on religious liberty, with its vindication of freedom of conscience for non-Catholics, was published, Harvard historian H. Stuart Hughes, echoing unwittingly the sentiments of conservatives, pointed out that once granted to those outside the fold, free-

dom of conscience could not be denied to those within.[1] The
evolution of the birth control debate to a point where many
Catholics follow their conscience and refuse to take the
church's comments seriously is a case in point. In social and
political thought there are similar lessons to be drawn. For years
Catholic pundits insisted that there was, contained in the social
encyclicals, a Catholic answer for every problem facing society.
If Catholics would only unite behind that program, they insisted, the social problem could be quickly solved. History has
proven otherwise, for nowhere have Catholics been able to agree
on any single positive feature of a political or social order.
Where agreement has been imposed: in inter-war Austria, in
Portugal or Spain, it has been done at the cost of the very
freedom of conscience the church has now resurrected. It
appears that the message of the Gospel cannot be translated
into a clearly defined picture of society as it ought to be. On
the basis of Christian revelation the church and its members
may categorically reject certain institutions and practices such
as war or racial discrimination as wrong and un-Christian, but it
cannot develop a positive program of political or social organization of the same dogmatic force. For example, the church
can authoritatively reject modern war as a violation of Christian
truth, but it cannot, as the church, provide the sole authoritative way of eliminating the arms race or ending a particular war.
Involved in such questions are economic, social, political,
psychological and sociological problems, which must be dealt
with on their own terms. Moreover, society, if it is to be free,
must resolve its conflicts through mechanisms of consent that
run counter to any attempt to impose a single solution based on
the teachings of a single church.

Of course the church has often defined the problem of
freedom in different terms. Traditional liberal Catholicism
accepted the idea of "a free church in a free state." This
formula meant that the state, based on the freedom of its
members, could allow freedom to the church to set its own
standards for membership and could allow it to function as a
corporate worshipping and teaching body without detriment to
itself. Freedom for the church meant allowing it to govern itself
as it saw fit, however much its internal life might diverge from

the democratic principles of the broader society. Now, the problem for the church goes deeper, for not only must it reconcile itself to a free society, as it attempted to do in the Decree on Religious Liberty, but it must at the same time come to terms with freedom within, as the demands of religious voluntarism are brought into the very confines of the church itself. Not for many centuries, if ever, has the Catholic church been willing in practice to admit that adherence to it was or should be a matter of free consent on the part of free men, nor that its decision-making processes should involve the participation of its lay, clerical and religious members. Rather it has insisted on controlling the cultural life of Catholics and where possible of the society as a whole in order to help form the conscience of men and to exert a beneficent, moderating influence on the human passions of society's members.

Perhaps the most important requirement for the immediate future is the truthfulness about which Hans Kung has written so eloquently: "that basic attitude through which individuals and communities, in spite of difficulties, remain true to themselves without dissimulation and without losing their integrity." A truthful church, according to Kung, would be a church free of coercion and pride, critical of worldy powers, prepared for suffering and humiliation, always exercising the "grace of ministry in the form of a servant: service of God as service of men and service of men as service of God."[2] It would be, in short, a free church composed of free men.

Some have tried to suggest what such a church would look like, but it seems that the situation is too fluid to allow successful model building. Rather, for the time being at least, Catholics must reconcile themselves to a developing plurality of structures related in varying ways to the hierarchy as a center of unity. The new openness and freedom in the sisterhoods for example has resulted in a proliferation of experimental groups attempting to find a means of fulfilling the demands of Christianity in a modern setting. Few insist that theirs is the only way; rather they are fully aware that they are just beginning, seeking new forms of community to allow them to reach their goal, which remains now as it has always been, service to their fellow man. An American Jesuit has suggested that similar changes are coming in the male orders. While he was unable to describe what the orders would look like in the future, he expressed his certainty that new forms would inevitably emerge and that the temper for the foreseeable future would be renewed dedication to the goal of service and a pragmatic and experimental approach to the means of its realization. The question of celibacy is likewise treated in these terms; not what is demanded by authority but what is required by the commitment to service. Priests who raise the question almost invariably insist that neither marriage nor celibacy is an end in itself, for the only absolute ends are Christ and mankind.

If one was asked to suggest a policy for the immediate future, then, he could do no better than answer with the hip phrase: "hang loose." This suggests an emphasis on freedom and movement at the expense of order and clarity. It means that the bishops should regard the present ferment as an opportunity rather than a threat, should look for potental rather than search out dangers. The old church may well have sinned on the side of order, authority, clarity of doctrine and of structure; the new church might compensate by moving in the opposite direction. No institution likes to pay the price of freedom: inefficiency, lack of respect for guidelines and formal authority, frequent aberrations and even irrationality. But the lesson of history is clear: the Catholic church preserved itself, its power and influence, at the cost of much of its dynamism and messianic drive. More than other institutions, the church must fear not deviation but rigidity, not rebellious attempts to reach the reality behind itself but its own natural tendency to identify itself with that reality. In the spirit of humility and self-examination of the years of Pope John, churchmen for the first time in recent history were willing to admit that the church might have erred. In that spirit they abandoned triumphalism and sought to remove any taint of pride. But the process is a continuing one, as it must be for any institution based on ideals and principles. The priest is not the church, the pope is not the church, and the church is not the Kingdom of God. Realization of that seems to suggest that what church leaders must do is hang loose, see how things work out, withhold criticism and condemnation save in the clearest violations of the spirit of

Christianity, encourage those who seek to live a sincere Christian commitment. If pope, priests, nuns and people took the message of Pope John seriously, if they thought of all problems in terms not of the preservation of truth but service to each other, to those outside the church and to Christ, then the energy released could well exert an influence on history as profound as that unleashed in the Roman empire almost two thousand years ago.

"Hanging loose" and letting Christians "do their thing" may not sound like an acceptable policy to men schooled in the traditional wisdom of the manuals of ecclesiology. How would such terms look in a seminary text on the church? Nevertheless one wonders whether it doesn't make sense. For one thing there isn't much choice. The only alternative seems to be an attempt to draw the line and reimpose norms and structure from the top, and there is a good deal of evidence to indicate that such action, if truly enforced, would drive many of the most energetic and valuable members of the church out of its confines. Self-interest alone dictates a tactic of waiting and seeing. Again, traditional ecclesiology has been found wanting even by the overwhelming majority of the world's bishops. The conciliar statement on the church was its most revolutionary, substituting ancient and imprecise scriptural imagery for the neoscholastic canonical definitions that dominated most recent discussion. No single question is more important in determining a Christian position on the issues of the day than "What is the Church." The conciliar decree answers the question in the marvelous metaphorical language of Scripture and the Fathers, and by doing so it opens rather than closes, emphasizes movement and process rather than order and structure, demands a life rather than a doctrine and inhibits attempts to show that this structure or that element of canon law is of itself the word of God. The over-all effect is to relativize such things, to make canon law a means not an end, to place all things under the question: How far do they help or hinder the living of the Christian life and the building of the Kingdom of God. The new theology, like "the signs of the times," seems to dictate a policy of "hanging loose," a policy of freedom based on responsibility to Christ and to mankind. A truthful church, Kung writes, "would allow scope for initiative, she would encourage small groups to operate as committed in an unconventional way in the secular world and to experiment without being controlled in everything."[3]

In concrete terms this policy means that bishops should not be overly concerned about the maintenance of their authority nor should they get hysterical about doctrinal orthodoxy. While being ready to point out the dangers of disunity and to present what they interpret as the consensus of the magesterium, they should do so in a fraternal and tolerant spirit. And these should be their secondary functions. More important they should take the model of service seriously, seeking to encourage those movements of their people that serve men in need and instructing all their flock in the centrality of the demand for service. Models of service themselves, they could well spend many years re-examining that huge system of schools, hospitals, orphanages, welfare centers, church buildings and real estate investments, asking of each whether it serves the people of God and the community at large, whether its functions might be better served by other institutions, whether its mere existence is sufficient justification for its continued existence. Finally they could devote their attention to the problem of freedom, the dimensions of which they have not yet appeared to notice. They can continue to ignore it only at their peril.

The church can afford to "hang loose" if it has confidence in itself and its people. It can afford to let the people carry the burdens of leadership and seek to point the way if it really believes in the possibilities of Christian action that it preaches. But can a similar policy be adopted in society at large. Can Catholics, can any Americans, afford to hang loose in the presence of poverty, violence and war. The answer here must be both yes and no; America can afford to allow experimentation, can even encourage such experimentation, because no more than the church does the nation possess a positive model of itself. Like the church the nation must commit itself to freedom and therefore to the absence of authoritative model building. But like the church the nation has some negative checks of powerful authority: poverty, racism and social injustice are un-Christian, and they are violations of the nation's highest ideals. Insisting on commitment to those ideals and encouraging efforts to realize them, America must have sufficient faith in her people to allow them to try. This means a more activist stance for the government of society than it does for the church's leaders, for the existence of large blocs of concentrated power committed to preserving the status quo will effectively prevent any significant or effective experimentation in the absence of strong governmental action. Nevertheless the government's regulating and taxing power must be exercised in a context of rapid decentralization aimed at providing new institutions through which all Americans can acquire a sense of power over their lives and responsibility for their communities and their nation.

As for the individual Catholic, his options are open. If he accepts the responsibility that is his as a Christian, he will know that the social sins of racism, violence and poverty are his responsibility. He will realize that now as always God is working his revolution in our history, and he must seek his vocation in cooperation with God's activity. Where is God at work in the world, where is his Kingdom breaking in? It is a tough question, which allows no more than a tentative and humble response. But Christians do know that God's reign will be characterized by unity, by peace and by love and that all men are called to God's service. Where men are making peace, where men are reaching out to each other in love and fraternity, where men are struggling for liberation from oppression so that they may be free to respond to God's call, there, it is possible to believe, the spirit of God is at work—and that is where the Christian should be. No men are perfect, and no human movements are pure; not all who claim to desire peace and freedom really do. Nevertheless the Christian responsibility is clear—to identify with the struggle, to join the forces of liberation, and, even when he must abandon a particular group because of its hypocrisy or its use of sinful means, he must continue the struggle, with others if possible, alone if necessary. Fully committed to securing God's Kingdom, clear and realistic in his assessment of present realities and possibilities, he stands on the frontiers, proclaiming the good news of God's promised future for man and risking all in his immersion in the contemporary struggle for its realization.

Such a description of the task of the individual Christian makes clear once again the inseparability of the "church question" and the "political question." Rebuilding the church is not so simple a task as many have imagined. It is not a part-time job distinct from such other areas of life as family, work and politics. The Christian vocation allows no part-time response but only a wholehearted commitment of energy, talent and love to the cause of Christ. Of course the church will always be a community of those responding to Christ's call and acknowledging his Lordship. But the message of the council and the recent popes makes clear that its mission includes more than worship and proclamation of the Gospel. The traditional functions of fellowship and service remain central, and these can only be carried out actively in the world and with a hope for a Kingdom for all men. Thus renewal of the church requires an active involvement in society.

Sociologist Robert Nisbet once pointed out that institutions do not discover or recover a purpose through discussion but through activity that all involved regard as important. Similarly Sidney Mead describes the American denomination as "a voluntary association of like-hearted and like-minded individuals, who are united on the basis of common beliefs for the purpose of accomplishing tangible and defined objectives."[4] These considerations suggest that the church will take shape not only around commitment to Jesus but around action in the world that its members regard as of greatest significance. For many in America today, as a matter of fact, reconstruction of the church is a distinctly secondary concern to the problems of war, racism and economic injustice. It is surely possible, then, that in common efforts to act politically to achieve goals consonant with Christian faith men will find the shape of the new church.

Yet, when one looks into the political arena the situation is complex and, at first glance, depressing. In the fall and winter of 1971-1972 the peace movement has fallen on dark days. The resumption of frequent bombing of North Viet Nam and Laos and the revelation of the terror warfare of the "electronic battlefield" met with no wave of opposition at home. The Nixon administration's handling of troop withdrawals and the question of prisoners of war evoked considerable public sympathy and support. Confident of public backing, the government came down hard on militant dissent, climaxed by the indictment of Philip Berrigan and five others for conspiracy to blow up heating tunnels in Washington and kidnap White House aide Henry Kissinger. At a meeting in Cambridge, Massachusetts a short time later a young theology student expressed the feeling of many when he said that if the Berrigan brothers were jailed for long terms, and their wing of the movement was destroyed, he would be near despair. Morally unable to join with either the militant advocates of violence or the liberal impotence of Clergy and Laymen Concerned about Viet Nam, he saw no option to that of nonviolent direct action and resistence, now in danger of destruction through government suppression. At meeting after meeting the alternatives were laid out: local political organizing, nonviolent action, mass demonstrations for the spring; letter writing to persuade Congress to end the draft or to impose a deadline for withdrawal of troops; or underground organizing aimed at direct, violent, terrorism to bring the war home, but none of the alternatives were advocated with either confidence or great conviction.

At this stage many were reflecting on some of the lessons of the past few years. For one thing it had become quite clear that the problems confronting the nation (and the world) are intimately related. A few years ago many antiwar people still believed that the war, racism, poverty and other issues were separable and could be faced each on its own terms. It is true that now there is a danger at the other extreme of asserting the unity of all issues under a single term like imperialism, racism or fascism. It is necessary to be intellectually honest and rigorous, to respect distinctions and adapt strategies and tactics to varying situations. Nevertheless, while analyses differ, it cannot be denied that all the immediate problems have roots deep in national life. The unresponsiveness and irresponsibility of institutions, the preoccupation of people with private goals and satisfactions and their sporadic and frequently irrational involvement in the public sphere and the demoralization of youth—and of many of the finest adults—all reflect a profound crisis of the American spirit and deep contradictions in the fabric of American life. Whether one concludes that what is needed is a complete overhaul of the political system, or a dramatic transformation of economic relationships, or a radical shift in consciousness, a spiritual conversion, the nation surely needs revolutionary change, not merely a series of reforms unrelated to any over-all systematic shift in national goals, values and institutions.

However, no one has yet presented a fully satisfactory statement of the sources of the problems or a plausible program for such change. To illustrate this point it is only necessary to look briefly at the segments of the American left. Liberals are concerned about the preservation of civil liberties and would like to terminate the war and direct attention to the problems of city, race and ecology. They are united by their conviction that the American system can work, that electoral politics remain the arena in which any fundamental change must take place, that America can survive a considerable amount of dissent and that the problems must be solved without jettisoning national ideals and institutions. Two important things can be said about American liberalism today. One is its total bankruptcy of ideas. Almost nowhere in the last few years has a particularly useful idea issued from the liberal community: no new ideas on Viet Nam, on the Middle East, on the economy, on pollution, on the political structure itself. Fearful of the silent majority, hung up on crime, drugs and race, demoralized by party divisions, anxious for personal advancement, they stand on the defensive before the charge of isolationism leveled at them by the Nixon administration and the charge of weakness and futility made by their enemies on the left. At home they offer only a neo-New Deal: more money, more centralization of power, more technological innovation in governmental affairs, more efficiency. Indeed, it is the Nixon administration that has proposed the major innovations of recent years: guaranteed income and revenue sharing, and neither of these represents anything like a beginning of America's renewal.

A second negative comment on the liberals is their obvious disorganization. Highly critical of Blacks and students for their organizational weaknesses, liberals have done little to pull their own ranks together. The useful efforts begun by liberal senators after Cambodia foundered with the approach of the 1970 elections. No organizational effort drew the Goodells, Hatfields and McCloskeys together with their opposite numbers in the Democratic party. Each remains dependent on his local support, none dares make a break that might jeopardize his future but offer some hope to concerned people in the community. The old alliances and coalitions stand in ruin, available in elections where alternatives are limited but almost impossible to mobilize for legislation or concerted action. Even where "New Politics" people have succeeded in ousting an incumbent or capturing a primary they have not yet proven that they can stay organized and affect significantly the direction of party politics. This last point is crucial: almost every major legislative accomplishment of the last 40 years has resulted from the backing of either the Southern racists oligarchs of Congress or the urban machine politicians and organized labor. If one writes off the South and the unions, as many on the left do, it is impossible to see how the reforms of which liberal politicians speak can ever be effected. Nevertheless, although bankrupt of ideas and devoid of power, liberals still deserve support because there is an absence of viable alternatives; their concern with civil liberties and their short-run goals offer some prospect of keeping the door open to the development of a more radical politics.

Since the split in the SDS there has existed no national organization to represent radicals. The disagreements that destroyed SDS: race, workers and women, have divided local radical communities into sects frequently at war with one another. Temporary alliances in the face of repression can be made and its spread may eventually reunite them, but for the moment the radicals are just as divided among themselves as are others on the left. Yet they retain great leverage in given situations. Alert to the presence of discontent, they are often able to give it a direction and leadership it desperately needs. (Indeed, the radical organizer common to every city often plays a role similar to that of the communist labor leader in the thirties.)

There has been a violent, terrorist movement, of that there

can be no doubt, though how highly planned, organized or coordinated it is is a matter of conjecture. While this is partly the ultimate fruit of failure, a sign of despair, it is also evident that it represents the fact that among a minority of young people there is a new intensification of commitment and dedication, a willingness coldly and calculatingly to "go all the way." Most important, it should be borne in mind that the revolutionary movement, if one wants to call it that, is a variegated and rich one. In the cities of eastern Massachusetts, for example, in addition to terrorist bombers of whom very few remain, there are many other serious radicals living in loosely linked collectives, working in educational and other jobs and spending what time they can spare organizing. They share in common an intense disgust with almost every phase of American society, a near total dedication to changing it and a conviction that the normal processes of change are useless at best. In long evening meetings they debate ideology, tactics and strategy, agreeing most of the time in their critique but seldom in their scheme of action. What is most striking about this group is that it operates on the clear understanding that significant change will take a long time and a great deal of work and that they are enlisted for the duration. Additionally they recognize the necessity for organization and for attention to theoretical analysis. Even in its absence, they often succeed in finding community with one another and doing humane, useful work. For all their faults of impetuosity, overseriousness and frequent incoherence, they are, most of the time, the most promising of the young.

The third component of the left is the Resistance, those who have banded together to resist the government and the "war machine." Shading at either end into the liberals and the revolutionaries, the people of the Resistance are frequently religious and always intensely dedicated. Often found living in small groups, they join with revolutionaries for theoretical analysis, joint projects and common defense. Just as internally diverse as other movement groups the resisters have moved slowly but steadily from being the "left wing of the peace movement" to being the "right wing of the revolution." Stung by repression and by their inability to arouse public opinion; uncertain whether to continue on the road of nonviolent direct action;

powerfully attracted by the model of the Black Panthers; despairing of their ability to bring about change by moving the national conscience, the resistance seems to move ever closer to the revolutionary option. What continues to distinguish this group, however, is its ethical and religious preoccupations and its emphasis on resistance to unjust authority and to the evil of war, rather than on positive revolutionary action. The two are related, for Christian and American radicals have found in their religion a firm foundation for resistance to the obvious sins of war, racism and poverty, but far less guidance in formulating a model of the good society or a strategy for bringing social and political change. Thus the Resistance movement, so attractive and courageous, contains in its radicalism and its alienated negativity, built-in limitations for large sectors of the population.

Radicals of all persuasions have, however, taken to heart the lessons of the 1960s in a way few liberals have, for they realize with increasing clarity that the nation's problems are intimately related to one another, deriving from common causes deep in American society and that, accordingly, the struggle for change is going to be long and difficult. Despite massive effort and considerable success in mobilizing large numbers of people, the peace movement has only been able to moderate conduct of the war in Southeast Asia. The civil rights movement, similarly, has attained only minimal gains despite its apparent success in stirring the conscience of America. Organizing a neighborhood, reforming a university's curriculum, building an underground church or a free school, researching and planning alternative approaches to housing, health care, waste disposal and transportation and undertaking a thousand other projects absorb enormous quantities of time and energy. If these micro-problems require long-term commitment, surely creating an economy "for use and not for profit" and a government that truly serves the people and a society that maximizes people's ability to shape their own lives, to grow and develop as free and responsible persons, these are tasks that will take the lifetime of this and subsequent generations. The truly relevant question then becomes not "how can I register my dissent from the war?" but "how can I use my life, my time, energy and talents in the service of my fellow man?" If it is truly revolutionary change the times demand, then long-term personal commitment is imperative, and men must construct together viable institutions for working for social change.

While it would be foolhardy to define that method, experience has brought its lessons. For one thing it is clear that there must be far more attention given to theoretical analysis of the causes of our public problems, which means close examination of the actual life of America and its institutions. Such analysis is imperative if rational planning of future work and action is to be possible, and these discussions must be tempered by awareness of the differing perspectives and value orientations existing in the movement and by loving exchange and criticism. While study and debate can prove sterile if unrelated to actual political work, that work likewise will be frustrating and ultimately unsuccessful if unrelated to a deepening appreciation of the over-all character of the historical situation, of the long-range goals that shape projects—and the strategies that relate organizing and issue oriented work to the goals and direction of the movement as a whole.

While coalitions of liberals and radicals are indispensible for the defense of civil liberties, for mass demonstrations and for the attainment of short-range objectives, little is to be gained by overlooking or playing down real theoretical and moral differences. Demands for uniformity will generate intergroup conflict, reduce already depleted membership and resources and eliminate the educational and recruiting potential of diverse organizations. Naturally each group feels it has the proper perspective on the situation, but the failures of the past and the gloomy prospects for the future should chasten such zeal and channel ideological fervor into dialogue with other groups. Within the broad spectrum of agreement on the need to end the war and ensure self-determination for people at home and abroad, men must work from where they are and grow in self-knowledge and mutual concern. Small groups of people sharing similar values and ideals can help each other overcome their fears, reinforce each other's commitment and aid each other in the quest for an authentic reconciliation of values with style of life and work. Closed in on themselves, such groups could become isolated and self-righteous. Working in fraternal solidarity with others in a movement that offers real hope for the future, they can overcome their own impotence. Open to the broader community beyond the movement, and working daily within it, members of movement groups will be reminded of their humanity, of the immensity of the task before them and of the need to relate not simply to people like themselves but to the infinite variety of men and women, with whom they yearn to live and work in freedom and love.

Concretely the form of such groups will vary considerably. At present there are issue-oriented organizations like the American Civil Liberties Union, Clergy and Laymen Concerned about Viet Nam and the National Welfare Rights Organization. The members of such groups characteristically work at normal jobs and live normal lives, devoting a few hours a week to the group. At the other extreme is the revolutionary commune, the Black Panther cell or the action collective, the members of which are completely devoted to the organization. While they may hold a job, there lives are committed to political work, which in turn dictates their style of life. Both types of organization have their weaknesses. The former fail to overcome the gap between the values their members uphold and the values that dominate their day to day life, while the latter demands a subordination or even elimination of alternative loyalties and a radical transformation of life style that can be destructive to individual personality. There is a very real need for a third type of organization that can avoid these difficulties, a need particularly acute for Christians and which the various resistance collectives are trying to fill.

Christians who in the last decade have become deeply alienated from the existing institutions in state and society very often feel that they are called to a fullness of life, to the integration in their personal lives of theory and practice. Again and again they affirm the importance of honesty and truthfulness, of the need to sincerely try to live according to the truths of faith, to authentically live a life for others. This quest for authenticity has drawn nuns and priests out of convents and rectories and into the streets and has led many lay people to feel a profound discontent with their jobs and their style of life.

Yet they are held back from the kind of break Daniel Berrigan urges them to make by family responsibilities, by dislike of available options or by group values and loyalties that do not accord with those of present organizations.

Perhaps the model that might help some is the working collective, a group of like-minded men and women, living and working in the world but bound together by common values and mutual concern, seeking to clarify their options through discussion, trying to live out their dedication through service to one another and through common efforts at social and political change. In such a group, the participants seek to relate their professional work to the goals and values they profess and to understand that work in its political context. Individuals working in business, government, education or elsewhere are able to strengthen themselves against the conformist pressures of these employing institutions. Perhaps they are able together to find ways in which their work can benefit the community. They then become agents of change within the institution of power, using their influence to oppose its selfishness and to nudge it in a different direction. Perhaps the member of the collective changes jobs, bringing his skill and experience to another position where he can better serve the cause of liberation of the oppressed and help construct new and responsible agencies of social service. In either case he is enabled through the collective to look beyond his own career and the needs of his own situation. Instead of turning his back on middle-class life, refusing to use his skills or influence to help open the door to change, he remains as long as possible where he is, softening the hostility of established institutions to the demand for popular control and responsibility, helping to turn them in the direction of service to society. If he fails, he searches for other ways to use his skills on behalf of the community, perhaps through the wide range of independent clinics and professional collectives springing up around the country.

Perhaps the collective phenomenon provides a model for the church. If a group of people were joined together to try to relate their work to common political goals, and they in turn understood these in the light of a common affirmation of Jesus Christ, their collective would indeed be nearly indistinguishable from a church. Like the church, the collective finds its meaning not in itself but in the goal it seeks, the new society it strives to create within the shell of the old. Just as the church is a herald and an anticipatory sign of the coming Kingdom of God, so the collective announces the living reality of man's hope for liberation and fulfillment, and it strives to manifest the reality of those hopes in its own internal life. The mutual aid and love that mark the members' relationships with each other testify to the sincerity of their convictions and to the nature of the hoped—for society of the future. Finally, if the collective is composed of Christians, they proclaim to all their faith in Jesus Christ as the Lord of History, that in his life and message the meaning of life is made present to man and that his promise of freedom and dignity lives through their union with him, drawing them and all men to his coming reign.

Thus the collective may be for some the new form of the church, providing a structure within which communities of men and women join together for worship, proclamation, fellowship and service. Acknowledging their unity with other Christian communities and with other groups working for the advent of God's Kingdom, the collective-church accepts the tension and ambiguity of the historical situation, posed on the threshold between past and future, between the here and now world of power and promise and the coming Kingdom of freedom and righteousness, and it acknowledges both with utmost seriousness.

The church, the local community of the faithful, might, then, take shape around politics. The response of Christians to the present crisis may indicate forms of life and action through which to express, share and deepen their commitment to Jesus as Lord and to forward his work in the world. The structure and form of the primary community might follow the function; that is to say, the desire of groups of Christians to work effectively against war, racism and injustice, might lead them to form collectives, and they might end by calling these collectives churches. Ten years ago such an idea would have seemed wildly heretical, clearly violating basic doctrines about the church. In those days it was believed that the form and function of the church were given and were not subject to revision because of changing historical situations. The purpose of the church was to serve as the ordinary means of salvation and it form was the hierarchical pattern of Roman Catholicism, a pattern divinely revealed and sanctioned. Pope, bishop, priest, religious, laymen, all had a role in this timeless structure. Sacraments, orders, liturgy, spirituality, everything in the church was clearly defined in relation to the primary task of bringing men to an other-worldly salvation. The motto of Pope Pius XI, "To Restore All Things in Christ" meant in practice extending as far as possible the saving influence of the church. To suggest that the church's shape and spirit might derive from the requirements of politics and social action would have seemed absurd.

Yet much has happened in the last decade, and nowhere is the revolution more sharply etched than in ecclesiology. Many observers felt at the time that the Vatican Council's document on the church was its premier accomplishment. Substituting the biblical images of the "people of God" for the traditional stress on order and authority, the council shifted the center of atten-tion from juridical structures to Christian vocation. In doing so it obviously upgraded the role of the laity, re-emphasized the positive role of the church in the world and relativized many ideas about the church heretofore considered sacrosanct. As E. E. Y. Hales has argued persuasively, Pope John XXIII had hoped that the council, by removing the dead weight of cen-turies, would release the church from its internal preoccupa-tions so that it could better get about its primary task of service to mankind.[5] While in many ways this goal was not reached, the council did succeed in re-establishing the ideal of the church as a servant community. Now it is clear that its internal life should be characterized by the loving service of its members to one another and its work in the world should be directed not to establishing its own dominance but to serving the real needs of the human community. These themes, so characteristic of Pope John's encyclicals, mark a subtle but important shift. From Leo XIII to Pius XII the social action of the church was derivative and secondary to the church's larger mission of saving men's souls. After the council social action came to be seen as intrinsic to Christian commitment: to be a member of the church is to belong to a community the fundamental purpose of which is to help men fulfill God's will for man, which is the Kingdom of God.

Already, prior to the council, theologians had been re-examining the idea of the church. Dietrich Bonhoeffer had asked the question which shook the foundation: How can the church survive in a religion-less world? And Bonhoeffer had provided a norm for response in his description of Jesus as a "man for others." Bishop John Robinson of the Anglican Church took up Bonhoeffer's question and answered that the church must define its own mission in the light of the promise of God's Kingdom. In the United States Harvey Cox said that the church in the secular city must be "where the action is," shaping its form to fit its mission of service to the broader community. Catholics Karl Rahner and Yves Congar, noting that the church had become a minority in the world, pointed in similar direction, insisting that there was no reason to believe that everyone would, or even should, belong to the church.[6] And Gustave Weigle, worrying over the religiosity of post war America, wrote that "When the majority believes and speaks well of the God of faith, we may legitimately begin to fear. In the words of the Supreme Master of Christianity, believers form his *little* flock. If they are a large herd, their shepherd may very well be someone other than the Lord."[7]

In these terms the council did not go far enough, for it never clearly faced up to the most radical question: "What is the church for?" but it did insist that the church takes its mission in light of the coming Kingdom of God. In the aftermath of the council, Protestant and Catholic thought converged on this point: that the mission of the church is related to the coming Kingdom. As Cox put it: "a doctrine of the church is a secondary and derivative aspect of theology which comes after a discussion of God's action in calling man to cooperation in the bringing of the Kingdom. It comes after, not before, a clarification of the idea of the Kingdom and is the appropriate response to the Kingdom in a particular era."[8]

Rahner, Edward Schillebeeck, Johannes Metz, Jurgen Moltmann and others took up the same theme, looking forward to the coming Kingdom as well as backward to the historical Jesus for their evaluation of the church. As Richard McBrien wrote, summing up post-conciliar ecclesiology at the end of the decade: "The Church is no longer to be conceived as the center of God's plan of salvation....The central reality is not the Church but the Kingdom of God....The Kingdom of God is the reign and rule of God in Christ and it comes into being wherever and whenever men love one another and accept one another's burdens in a spirit of compassion, concern, generosity, and sensitivity. All men are called to the Kingdom; not all men are called to the Church."[9]

All men, called to the Kingdom, are called to the struggle against dehumanization. The Christian makes this explicit, for he clearly affirms his faith in Christ as Lord. In this light the traditional functions of the church must be met creatively in each era. The church proclaims Christ's Lordship and his promise for the future. More, the church in its inner life provides a credible sign of the Kingdom. Its spirit of fellowship and love prefigures the Kingdom and gives evidence of the truth of its proclamation. And finally the church serves the Kingdom by joining in the struggle for human freedom and development.

In this context, the renovation of the form of the church out of the struggle against the Viet Nam war and domestic injustice seems more than fitting. If the Christian's primary vocation is to seek to realize God's Kingdom, and at the same time he is called to the explicit acknowledgment of God's promises for man, then he is a Christian called out to the church. It is only natural that he will shape and form his communities in terms of those responsibilities, so that his assessment of "where the action is" and the requirements of the political situation should be explicit elements in his creative effort to mold a congregation suited for service. Catholics who are liberals, radicals or revolutionaries, to say nothing of conservative Christians, differ not over this need to acknowledge Jesus as Lord or to constitute a credible sign of Christ's presence, but over the specific mode of service to man. As a result they are bound to have different needs to be met, different ideas about the nature and content of the church's diaconea. While preserving unity and fellowship with each other, they should be free to form communities they feel best suited to their historical situation.

Free to do so while retaining fellowship with other Christians, the American Catholic is at last on his own. No longer must he seek to make America Catholic or to make the church American. Instead, face to face with the real issue of human survival, human freedom and human hope, he may join actively in the struggle, secure in the realization that, at last, he is about a work that will fulfill the best aspirations of both Catholic and American traditions. Perhaps César Chavez, leader of the California farm workers, best summed up the call of the future for American Christians when he ended a month-long fast by calling his followers, and men everywhere, to renew their commitment to nonviolence. His words stand as the challenge of the 1970s for the new American Catholic:

> Those who oppose our cause are rich and powerful and they have many allies in high places. We are poor. Our allies are few. But we have something the rich do not own. We have our own bodies and spirits and the justice of our cause as weapons. When we are really honest with ourselves we must admit that our lives are all that really belong to us. It is my deepest belief that only by giving our lives do we find life. I am convinced that the truest act of courage, the strongest act of manliness is to sacrifice ourselves for others in a totally non-violent struggle for justice. To be a man is to suffer for others. God help us to be men.[10]

NOTES

PREFACE

1. H. Richard Niebuhr, *The Kingdom of God in America*, Harper Torchbook Edition (New York, 1959), p. xv.

CHAPTER 1

1. John F. Kennedy, Inaugural Address, *Public Papers of the Presidents of the United States: John F. Kennedy*, I (Washington, 1962), p. 1.

2. Walter Ong, S.J., *American Catholic Crossroads* (New York, 1959); *Frontiers in American Catholicism* (New York, 1961).

3. Michael Novak, *A New Generation: American and Catholic* (New York, 1964); Daniel Callahan, *The Mind of the Catholic Layman* (New York, 1963).

4. Donald Thorman, *The Emerging Layman* (Garden City, 1962); John Tracy Ellis, "American Catholics and the Intellectual Life," *Thought* XXX (Autumn 1955), pp. 353-386.

5. John Cogley, "The Catholic and the Liberal Society," *America* CI (July 4, 1959), p. 495.

6. Hans Kung, *The Council, Reform and Reunion* (London, 1962).

7. Gustave Weigel, S.J., "The Present Embarassment of the Churches," in John Cogley, editor, *Religion in America* (New York, 1958), p. 284.

8. Cogley, "Introduction," *ibid.*, p. 8.

9. Daniel Callahan, "Putting the Liturgy in its Place," *National Catholic Reporter* (August 9, 1967), and letters published in weeks following. *National Catholic Reporter* hereafter cited as NCR.

10. Andrew Greeley, "An Institutionless Church?," in his *The Hesitant Pilgrim: American Catholicism after the Council* (New York, 1966), pp. 50-58.

11. John P. Sisk, "The Sweet Dream of Harmony," *NCR* (August 31, 1966); "The Sweet Dream of Liberation," *NCR* (September 13, 1967).

12. Dorothy Dohen, *Nationalism and American Catholicism* (New York, 1967).

13. Will Herberg, "Religion and Culture in Present-Day America," in Thomas T. McAvoy, editor, *Roman Catholicism and the American Way of Life* (Notre Dame, 1960), p. 15.

14. Raymond Williams, "The Catholic Crisis," *Nation* CCIII (August 17, 1967).

15. Stanley Elkins, *Slavery* (Chicago, 1959); Richard Hofstadter, *The Age of Reform* (New York, 1955).

16. Max Weber, *Politics as a Vocation* (Philadelphia, 1965).

17. Thomas Merton, *Seeds of Destruction* (New York, 1964), pp. 120-121.

CHAPTER 2

1. On this subject see my article "Needed: A New History," *America* CXX (May 3, 1969), pp. 528-531.

2. Josef L. Hromadka, *Impact of History on Theology* (Notre Dame, 1970), p. 56.

3. Jürgen Moltmann, *Theology of Hope* (New York, 1965), pp. 117, 118.

4. American Historical Association, *Newsletter* VIII (March, 1970), p. 8.

5. C. Vann Woodward, *The Age of Reinterpretation*, pamphlet published by the Service Center for Teachers of History (Washington, 1961), p. 22.

6. Howard Zinn, "History as Private Enterprise" in K.H. Wolff and Barrington Moore, Jr., editors, *The Critical Spirit: Essays in Honor of Herbert Marcuse* (Boston, 1967), p. 172.

7. Social Science Research Council, *Theory and Practice in Historical Study*, Bulletin No. 54.

8. Staughton Lynd, "The Historian as Participant," unpublished MSS in author's possession.

9. Charles Beard, *The Nature of the Social Sciences*, quoted in Robert A. Skotheim, *American Intellectual Histories and Historians* (Princeton, 1966), pp. 100-101.

10. Hromadka, *Impact of History on Theology*, pp. 104-105.

11. Walter Ong, S.J., *Frontiers in American Catholicism* (New York, 1959), p. 53.

12. Pope John XXIII, Opening Speech to Vatican Council in Walter M. Abbott, S.J., editor, *Documents of Vatican II* (New York, 1966), p. 712; "Pastoral Constitution on the Church in the Modern World," *ibid.*, p. 201.

13. Michael Novak, *The Open Church* (London, 1964), Chapter 5.

14. See for example R. Adolf, *The Grave of God* (New York, 1967).

15. Daniel O'Connor, *Catholic Social Doctrine* (Westminster, 1956), pp. 7-8.

16. Novak, *The Open Church*, p. 55.

17. Ernst Troeltsch, *The Social Teachings of the Christian Church*, Harper Torchbook Edition (New York, 1962), II, pp. 993-994.

18. Karl Rahner, "The Present Situation of Christians: A Theological Interpretation of the Position of Christians in the Modern World," in *The Christian Commitment* (New York, 1963), pp. 3-37.

19. Emmanuel Cardinal Suhard, "Growth or Decline," in *The Church Today* (Chicago, 1953), p. 131.

20. Pope John XXIII, Opening Speech to Vatican Council, in Walter M. Abbott, S.J., editor, *Documents of Vatican II* (New York, 1966), p. 715.

21. Pope Paul VI, quoted in *New York Times*, September 12, 1965.

22. Herbert W. Richardson, *Toward an American Theology* (New York, 1967), p. ix.

23. Johannes Metz, *Theology of the World* (New York, 1969), p. 84.

24. Jürgen Moltmann, *Religion, Revolution and the Future* (New York, 1969), p. 132.

25. Jürgen Moltmann, "Hope and Planning," *Cross Currents* XVIII (Summer 1968), p. 318.

26. Johannes Metz, *Poverty of Spirit* (Westminster, n.d.), pp. 5-6.

27. Alexis de Tocqueville, *Democracy in America*, Mentor Book Edition (New York, 1956), p. 317.

28. *New York Times*, January 18, 1969.

29. C. Wright Mills, *The Sociological Imagination* (New York, 1959), p. 174.

30. Sidney Mead, "Church History Explained," *Church History* XXXII (March 1963), pp. 18-19.

31. *Ibid.*, p. 23.

32. Sidney Mead, "History and Identity," *Journal of Religion* LI (January 1971), pp. 3-4.

33. These comments and those that follow are developed in detail in my article "American Catholic Historiography: A Post Conciliar Evaluation," *Church History* XXXVII (March 1968), pp. 80-94.

34. Robert D. Cross, "Rewriting American Catholic History," *Commonweal* LXXIX (December 13, 1963), pp. 351-352.

35. Peter Guilday, "The Catholic Church in the United States," *Thought* I (June 1926), p. 7.

36. This theme is present in the work of most American Catholic historians, but is most clearly associated with Father Thomas T. McAvoy. While insisting that the minority thesis merely means that Catholics were not the most numerous and had religious differences with their neighbors, Father McAvoy regards recognition of these facts as the key to American Catholic self-understanding. See for example "American Catholics: Tradition and Controversy," *Thought* XXXV (Winter 1960), pp. 583-600; "The American Catholic Dilemma," *Review of Politics* XX (April 1959), pp. 456-60.

37. L.J. Trinterud, "The Task of the American Church Historian," *Church History* XXV (March 1956), p. 10.

38. Louis Hartz, *The Liberal Tradition in America* (New York, 1955); Richard Hofstadter, *The American Political Tradition* (New York, 1958); David Potter, *People of Plenty* (Chicago, 1954).

39. Andrew Greeley, "After Secularity: The Neo-Geimeinschaft Society: A Christian Postscript," *Sociological Analysis* (Summer Supplement, 1966), p. 121.

40. Henry F. May, "The Recovery of American Religious History," *American Historical Review* LXX (October 1964), pp. 79-92.

41. Walter Ong, S.J., *American Catholic Crossroads* (New York, 1959), Chapter 1.

42. John XXIII, *Mater et Magistra*, American Press Edition (New York, 1961), p. 50.

43. Sidney Mead, "Professor Sweet's Religion and Culture in America: A Review Article," *Church History* XXII (March 1953), pp. 33, 45.

44. Franklin H. Littell, "Toward a Theology of Church History," *Cross Currents* XX (Winter 1970), p. 57.

45. John Tracy Ellis, "American Catholicism in 1960: An Historical Perspective" in *Perspectives on American Catholicism* (Baltimore, 1963), p. 57.

46. Henry J. Browne, "A History of the Catholic Church in the United States," in Louis Putz, C.S.C., editor, *The Catholic Church, U.S.A.* (Chicago, 1956), p. 35.

47. Quoted by James H. Moynahan, *The Life of Archbishop John Ireland* (New York, 1953), p. 50; Dorothy Dohen, *Nationalism and American Catholicism* (New York, 1967). Bishop John Wright earlier expressed his concern over Catholicism's perhaps too uncritical Americanism and nationalism. See for example his introduction to Putz, *op. cit.*, pp. xi-xxiii.

CHAPTER 3

1. Martin Marty, *The Search for a Usable Future* (New York, 1969).

2. Sidney Mead, "Church History Explained," *Church History* XXXII (March 1963), p. 22.

3. Carl Braaten, "Toward a Theology of Hope" in Martin E. Marty and Dean G. Peerman, editors, *New Theology No. 5* (New York, 1968), p. 110.

4. J. Moltmann, *Theology of Hope* (New York, 1968), p. 119.

5. Henry Steele Commager, *The Search for a Usable Past* (New York, 1967), pp. x, 12, 22.

6. What follows is greatly influenced by David W. Noble, *Historians Against History* (Minneapolis, 1965).

7. Perry Miller, "Religion and Society in the Early Literature of Virginia," *Errand into the Wilderness* (Cambridge, 1956), Chapter 4.

8. John E. Smylie, "National Ethos and the Church," *Theology Today* XX (October 1963), 316.

9. H. Richard Niebuhr, *The Kingdom of God in America* Harper Torchbook Edition (New York, 1959), p. 17.

10. William Clebsch, "A New Historiography of American Religion," *Historical Magazine of the Protestant Episcopal Church* XXXII (September 1963), pp. 225-258.

11. William Warren Sweet, "The Frontier in American Christianity" in John T. McNeill *et al.*, editors, *Environmental Factors in Christian History* (Chicago, 1939), p. 391.

12. Winthrop Hudson, "How American is Religion in America," in Jerald C. Brauer, editor, *Reinterpretation in American Church History* (Chicago, 1968), p. 155.

13. Jerald C. Brauer, "Changing Perspectives on Religion in America," in his *Reinterpretation in American Church History* (Chicago, 1968), pp. 1-28.

14. Sidney Mead, "Reinterpretation in American Church History" in *ibid.*, Brauer, p. 185.

15. Sidney Mead, "The Nation With the Soul of a Church," *Church History* XXXVI (September 1967), pp. 262-283.

16. Robert Bellah, "Civil Religion in America" in Martin Marty, editor, *The Religious Situation: 1968* (Boston, 1968), pp. 331-355; Robert Handy, *A Christian America* (New York, 1971); Martin Marty, *Righteous Empire* (New York, 1970).

17. Henry F. May, "The Recovery of American Religious History," *American Historical Review* LXX (October 1964), pp. 79-92.

18. Sydney E. Ahlstrom, "The Problem of the History of Religion in America," *Church History* XXXIX (June 1970), pp. 228-229.

19. William Clebsch, "A New Historiography of American Religion," *Historical Magazine of the Protestant Episcopal Church* XXXII (September 1963), p. 231.

20. Rudolph Vecoli, "Prelates and Peasants: Italian Immigrants and the Catholic Church," *Journal of Social History* II (Spring 1969), p. 219.

21. Andrew Greeley, *The Catholic Experience* (Garden City, 1967) p. 291. See also my review article, "Andrew Greeley and American Catholicism," *Catholic World* CCVII (April 1968), pp. 36-38.

22. Philip Gleason, "The Crisis of Americanization" in Philip Gleason, editor, *Contemporary Catholicism in the United States* (Notre Dame, 1969), pp. 3-32.

23. Richard Lamanna and Jay Coakley, "The Catholic Church and the Negro," *ibid.*, pp. 147-194.

24. Vecoli,"Prelates and Peasants," p. 268.

25. Leslie Dewart, *The Future of Belief* (New York, 1966); Eugene Fontinelle, "Reflections on Faith and Metaphysics," *Cross Currents* XVI (Winter 1966), pp. 15-40; James Hitchcock, *The Decline and Fall of Radical Catholicism* (New York, 1971).

26. James Gillis, *This Our Day* (New York, 1933), p. 141.

27. Peter Guilday, *The Life of John England* (Westminster, 1954), p. 773.

28. "American Catholicism and the *Aggiornamento*," *Review of Politics* XXX (July 1968), pp. 275-291; revised in Chapter 14 of McAvoy's posthumously published *A History of the Catholic Church in the United States* (Notre Dame, 1969).

29. Michael Novak, *A New Generation: American and Catholic* (New York, 1964).

30. Daniel Callahan, *The Mind of the Catholic Layman* (New York, 1963).

31. John Courtney Murray, *We Hold These Truths* (New York, 1960), p. 9. Quotes are from pp. 12, 43, 41, 43, 73.

32. See for example Richard Hofstadter, *The American Political Tradi-*

tion (New York, 1955), preface, and Louis Hartz, *The Liberal Tradition in America* (New York, 1958).

33. Daniel Boorstin, *The Genius of American Politics* (Chicago, 1956).

34. James Cardinal Gibbons, *A Retrospect of Fifty Years*, I (Baltimore and New York, 1916), p. 230.

35. The controversy is traced in Thomas T. Love, *John Courtney Murray: Contemporary Church-State Theory* (Garden City, 1965).

36. Donald Thorman, *The Emerging Layman* (Garden City, 1965).

37. Thomas T. McAvoy, C.S.C., "The Emerging Layman—Emerging From What?," *Davenport Messenger*, November 4, 1965.

38. John E. Smylie, "National Ethos and the Church," *Theology Today* XX (October 1963), p. 314.

39. Will Herberg, *Protestant, Catholic, Jew* (New York, 1960), p. 263.

40. Ralph Gabriel, *The Course of American Democratic Thought* (New York, 1941).

41. Robert N. Bellah, "Civil Religion in America," *Daedalus* XCVI (Winter 1967), pp. 1-21.

42. Sidney Mead, "The Nation With the Soul of a Church," *Church History* XXXVI (September 1967), p. 275.

43. Philip Gleason, "Immigration and American Catholic Intellectual Life," *Review of Politics* XXV (April 1969), p. 151.

CHAPTER 4

1. R.R. Palmer, *A History of the Modern World*, 2nd ed. (New York, 1960), p. 603.

2. *Ibid.*, p. 604.

3. Emmanuel Cardinal Suhard, "Growth or Decline?," in *The Church Today: The Collected Writings of Emmanuel Cardinal Suhard* (Chicago, 1953).

4. Reinhold Niebuhr, *The Irony of American History* (New York, 1952), pp. 160, 162.

5. Richard Hofstadter, *Anti-Intellectualism in American Life* (New York, 1963), p. 136.

6. Walter Ong, S.J., "The Mechanical Bride," *Social Order* II (February 1952), p. 83.

7. James Cardinal Gibbons, *A Retrospect of Fifty Years*, II (Baltimore and New York, 1916), p. 190.

8. Quoted in Peter Guilday, *The Life and Times of John England*, II (New York, 1927), p. 375.

9. Thomas T. McAvoy, C.S.C., "The Formation of the American Catholic Minority, 1820-1860," *Review of Politics* X (January 1948), p. 17.

10. James Cardinal Gibbons, *A Retrospect of Fifty Years*, II, p. 20.

11. Bishop Robert J. Dwyer, "The American Laity," *Commonweal* LX (October 17, 1960), p. 15.

12. Philip Gleason, "The Crisis of Americanization," in Gleason, editor, *Contemporary Catholicism in the United States* (Notre Dame, 1969), pp. 3-32.

13. Victor R. Greene, *The Slavic Community on Strike: Immigrant Labor in Pennsylvania* (Notre Dame, 1968), p. 33.

14. Timothy L. Smith, "Immigrant Social Aspirations and American Education, 1880-1930," *American Quarterly* XXI (Fall 1969), p. 536.

15. Peter and Alice Rossi, "Some Effects of Parochial School Education in America," *Daedalus* XC (Spring 1961), p. 324.

16. Smith,"Immigrant Aspirations," p. 542.

17. Daniel P. Moynihan and Nathan Glazer, *Beyond the Melting Pot*, (Cambridge, 1963), p. 313; see also Timothy L. Smith, "Religious Denominations as Ethnic Communities: A Regional Case Study," *Church History* XXXV (June 1966), pp. 13-19; Rudolph Vecoli, "Prelates and Peasants: Italian Immigrants and the Catholic Church," *Journal of Social History* II (Spring 1969), pp. 217-268; Victor R. Greene, "For God and Country: The Origins of Slavic Catholic Self-Consciousness in America," *Church History* XXXV (December 1966), pp. 446-460.

18. John J. Burke to William Kerby, November 7, 1906, Kerby Papers, Catholic University of America.

19. James Cardinal Gibbons, *A Retrospect of Fifty Years* (Baltimore and New York, 1916), II, p. 213.

20. *Ibid.*, II, pp. 145-146 and 84-85.

21. Henry Steele Commager, *The American Mind* (New York, 1958), p. 193.

22. Timothy L. Smith, "New Approaches to the History of Immigration in Twentieth Century America," *American Historical Review* LXXI (July 1966), p. 1273.

23. Greene, *Slavic Community*, p. 51; Stephen Thernstrom, *Poverty and Progress* (Cambridge, 1964).

24. Quotations are drawn from Peter Guilday, editor, *The National Pastorals of the American Hierarchy* (Westminster, 1954).

25. Quoted in John Tracy Ellis, *The Life of James Cardinal Gibbons*, I (Milwaukee, 1952), p. 154; Archbishop John Ireland, *The Church and Modern Society* (Chicago, 1897).

26. Frederick J. Zweirlein, "The Triumph of the Conservative-Progressives in the Catholic Church in the United States," *Social Justice Review* LI (July-August 1958), p. 119.

27. John Tracy Ellis, editor, *Documents of American Catholic History* (Milwaukee, 1962), pp. 534-543. For a detailed discussion of these controversies see Robert D. Cross, *The Emergence of Liberal Catholicism in the United States* (Cambridge, 1958); Thomas T. McAvoy, C.S.C., *The Great Crisis of American Catholic History* (Chicago, 1957).

CHAPTER 5

1. Modernism in American and the impact of its condemnation are only beginning to be studied. A good start has been made in assessing the

effects of the condemnation in an essay by Michael Gannon, "The Intellec-
tual Formation of the American Priest," in John Tracy Ellis, editor, *The
Catholic Priest in the United States: Historical Investigations* (Collegeville,
Minn., 1971), pp. 293-383.

2. John L. Murphy, "Seventy-five Years of Fundamental Theology in
America," Part I, *American Ecclesiastical Review* CL (June 1964), p. 394.

3. This is a subject badly in need of investigation. For a start see
Thomas F. Curley, "Catholic Novels and American Culture," *Commentary* XXXVI (July 1963), pp. 34-42.

4. Thomas T. McAvoy, C.S.C., "The Catholic Minority After the
Americanist Controversy, 1899-1917," *Review of Politics*, XXI (January,
1959), p. 57.

5. *Tablet*, July 30, 1932.

6. Arthur M. Schlesinger, Jr., *The Vital Center* (Boston, 1946); *Partisan Review* XVII (February to May 1950).

7. Statistics are taken from the annual *Official Catholic Directory* for
the years cited.

8. John Cogley, "Old Soldiers Never Die," *Commonweal* (May 17,
1963), pp. 215-216; "Catholic Power and Black Power," *NCR* (February
12, 1969).

9. Quoted in John Tracy Ellis, "American Jewish-Catholic Relations:
Past and Prospect," *American Benedictine Review* XVIII (March 1967), p.
53.

10. John Higham, *Strangers in the Land* (New York, 1963); Richard
Hofstadter, *The Age of Reform* (New York, 1955).

11. Digby Baltzell, *The Protestant Establishment* (New York, 1966).

12. See my "American Catholics and Anti-Semitism in the 1930s,"
Catholic World CCIV (February 1967), pp. 270-276, from which the
material is drawn; *Social Justice*, November 20, 1936.

13. *Social Justice*, December 5, 19, 1938. April 11, 1938; Coughlin,
Why Leave Our Own? (n.p., 1939), p. 155.

14. *The Guildsman*, April 1941.

15. "Father Coughlin and the Press," *Commonweal* XXIX (December
16, 1938), pp. 5-6; Michael Williams, "Views and Reviews," *ibid.* XXVIII
(May 27, 1938), p. 129; "Testimony Against Anti-Semitism," *ibid.* XXX
(July 7, 1939), p. 265.

16. Quoted in *Tablet*, August 6, 1938. See also Wilfrid Parsons, S.J.,
"Popular Fronts and Catholicism," *Commonweal* XXVI (February 19,
1937), pp. 464-6.

17. *Tablet*, July 8, 1939; December 5, 1938. Resentment of this kind
was not confined to conservatives. John A. Ryan wrote in 1938: "The
great majority of Catholics are not Jew haters or Jew baiters, but many of
them are irritated when they find, in a few large cities, particularly greater
New York, Jews exhibiting indifference to the enormous outrages, assasi-
nations, etc., perpetrated by the Loyalist Government upon Spanish Catholics. Probably the best way of counteracting Catholic indifference to the
persecution of the Jews—insofar as it exists—would be a deliberate and

sustained effort by the leaders of Jewry to prove that they are not indifferent to the sufferings of Catholics at the hands of the Spanish Loyalists." Ryan to Philip Stevenson, November 30, 1938, Ryan papers, Catholic University of America.

18. John Tracy Ellis, "American Jewish-Catholic Relations: Past and Prospect," *American Benedictine Review* XVIII (March 1967), p. 55.

19. Moynihan and Glazer, *Beyond the Melting Pot*, (Cambridge, 1963), pp. 298-299. See also Richard Robbins, "American Jews and American Catholics: Two Types of Social Change," *Sociological Analysis* XXVI (Spring 1965), pp. 1-20.

20. See in particular Rodney Stark and Charles Glock, *Christian Beliefs and Anti-Semitism* (New York, 1966), appendix.

21. Robert McAfee Brown, " 'Secular Ecumenism': The Direction of the Future," in Donald R. Cutler, editor, *The Religious Situation: 1969* (Boston, 1969), pp. 395ff.

CHAPTER 6

1. Thomas T. McAvoy, C.S.C., "American Catholicism and the *Aggiornamento*," *Review of Politics* XXX (July 1968), p. 283.

2. Statistics are drawn from *The Official Catholic Directory* published annually by P. J. Kenedy and Sons.

3. Reinhold Niebuhr, "A Note on Pluralism" in John Cogley, editor, *Religion in America* (New York, 1958), pp. 47, 49.

4. "Looking Backward, Looking Ahead: Fortieth Anniversary Symposium," *Commonweal* LXXXI (November 20, 1964), p. 264.

5. John Cogley in his *Religion in America* (New York, 1958), p. 269.

6. See the articles collected in Frank L. Christ and Gerard E. Sherry, editors, *American Catholicism and the Intellectual Ideal* (New York, 1961).

7. Donald McDonald, *Catholics in Conversation* (Philadelphia, 1960), pp. 83-84.

8. Garry Wills, "A Farewell (Quite Fond) to the Catholic Liberal," *The Critic* XXIX (January-February 1971), p. 15.

9. Walter Ong, S.J., *Frontiers in American Catholicism* (New York, 1961), p. viii.

10. John Cogley, "Old Soldiers Never Die," *Commonweal* LXXIX (May 17, 1963), p. 215.

11. Daniel Callahan, *The Mind of the Catholic Layman* (New York, 1963), p. 175.

12. Hans Kung, "The Church and Freedom," *Commonweal* LXXVIII (June 21, 1963), pp. 343-353.

13. Andrew Greeley, "Sociology of Religion," *The Critic* XX (August-September 1962), p. 11.

14. Philip Scharper, "Speculations," *The Critic* XXIII (February-March 1965), p. 43.

15. Michael Novak, *The Open Church* (London, 1964), p. 337.

16. Michael Novak, *A New Generation: American and Catholic* (New York, 1964), p. 9.

17. Gary MacEoin, *New Challenges to American Catholics* (New York, 1965), p. 43.

18. Michael Novak, "American Catholicism After the Council," *Commentary* (August 1965), p. 52.

19. Karl Rahner, "The Present Situation of Christians: A Theological Interpretation of the Position of Christians on the Modern World," in *The Christian Commitment* (New York, 1963).

20. David J. O'Brien, "American Catholicism and the Diaspora," *Cross Current* XVI (Summer 1966), pp. 307-323.

21. John Leo, "Thinking It Over," *NCR* (September 28, 1966).

22. H. Stuart Hughes, "Pope John's Revolution: Secular or Religious," *Commonweal* LXXXIII (December 10, 1965), pp. 301-304.

23. John Leo "Thinking It Over."

24. Editorial, *Ave Maria* (September 24, 1966).

25. Sr. Marie Augusta Neal, *Values and Interests in Social Change* (Englewood Cliffs, 1968), p. 159.

26. Russell W. Gibbons, "Conflicts in Catholicism," *Nation* CXCV (December 8, 1962), p. 388.

27. Gary Wills, *Politics and Catholic Freedom* (Chicago, 1964).

28. *National Review* XVII (May 4, 1965).

29. Gibbons, "Conflicts in Catholicism," p. 389.

30. Will Herberg, "Open Season on the Church?," *National Review* XVII (May 4, 1965), p. 365.

31. Gibbons, "Conflicts in Catholicism," p. 310.

32. Andrew Greeley, *The Hesitant Pilgrim* (New York, 1966), p. xi.

33. John Tracy Ellis, "On Selecting American Bishops," *Commonweal* LXXXVI (March 10, 1967), p. 649.

34. Daniel Callahan, "Christianity Is, Finally, More Than Ethics," *NCR* (May 14, 1969).

35. Andrew Greeley in "Issues that Divide the Church," *NCR* (March 12, 1967).

36. Donald Thorman, *American Catholics Face the Future* (Wilkes Barre, 1968).

37. *Ibid.*, Chapter 13.

38. Douglas Roche, *The Catholic Revolution* (Toronto, 1968).

39. Karl Rahner, "The Present Situation of Christians: . . . " p. 23. For an interesting if overstated case against the reformers from the point of view of theology see James Hitchcock, *The Decline and Fall of Radical Catholicism* (New York, 1971).

40. Editorial, *Tablet*, April 1, 1933.

41. Quoted in John G. Deedy, "The Catholic Press: The Why and the Wherefore," in Martin E. Marty, editor, *The Religious Press in America* (New York, 1963), pp. 80-81.

42. John Cogley, "*Commonweal* and *NCR*," (June 18, 1969).

43. Peter Steinfels, "A Time to be Urbane, a Time to be Combative," *NCR* (July 2, 1969).

CHAPTER 7

1. Andrew Greeley, *The Catholic Experience* (New York, 1967).

2. Daniel P. Moynihan and Nathan Glazer, *Beyond the Melting Pot* (Cambridge, 1963), p. 229.

3. Peter Guilday, *Life of John England,* II (Westminster, 1954), p. 519.

4. Ralphael M. Huber, editor, *Our Bishops Speak* (Milwaukee, 1952), pp. 98-101.

5. Lee Benson, *The Concept of Jacksonian Democracy* (Princeton, 1961), p. 165.

6. Niebuhr to Felix Frankfurter, July—, 1960 in Frankfurter Papers, Library of Congress.

7. John Cogley, "Toward a New Politics," *Commonweal,* LXXVIII (April 5, 1963), pp. 37-38.

8. Garry Wills, *Nixon Agonistes* (New York, 1969), p. 546.

9. Staughton Lynd, *Intellectual Origins of American Radicalism* (New York, 1968), p. 173.

10. David J. O'Brien, "Eugene Genovese and the Student Left," *Liberation* XIV (October 1967), pp. 29-33.

11. Hayden V. White, "The Burden of History," *History and Theory* V (Spring 1966), pp.111-134.

12. Lynd, *Intellectual Origins,* p. 13.

13. Richard Shaull, introduction to Paulo Freire, *The Pedagogy of the Oppressed* (New York, 1970), p. iv.

14. Peter Steinfels, "Christian Democracy—R.I.P.," *Commonweal* LXXXI (December 1967), pp. 294-296.

CHAPTER 8

1. "Statement of Cesar Chavez in Support of Philip Berrigan *et al.,* February 20, 1971," Boston Defense Committee, privately circulated.

2. Daniel Berrigan to Rosemary Ruether, *NCR* (September 16, 1968).

3. Daniel Berrigan, "Letter to the Jesuits," April 10, 1970. Copy in author's possession.

4. Andrew Greeley, "The Berrigans-Phrenetic," *Holy Cross Quarterly* IV (January 1971), pp. 15-22.

5. As quoted in Daniel Berrigan, *The Trial of the Catonsville 9* (New York, 1970), p. 60.

6. Berrigan to Ruether, cited above.

7. "Letter to Jesuits."

8. "Taking Fr. Berrigan Seriously," *Commonweal* XCII (August 7, 1970), p. 380.

9. Daniel Berrigan and Robert Coles, *The Geography of Faith* (Boston, 1971), p. 129.

10. William Bosworth, *Catholicism and Crisis in Modern France* (Princeton, 1962), p. 156.

11. Leo XIII, "On Christian Democracy" in Etienne Gilson, editor, *The Church Speaks to the Modern World* (New York, 1954), pp. 327-328.

12. *Ibid.*, p. 328.

13. Quoted in Geunter Lewy, *The Catholic Church and Nazi Germany* (New York, 1966), p. 326.

14. Reinhold Niebuhr, "Religion and Politics" in Peter H. Odegard, editor, *Religion and Politics* (New Brunswick, 1960), pp. 107-108.

15. Lewy, *op. cit.*, p. 326.

16. Philip Berrigan, quoted in *Commonweal* XC (June 14, 1968), p. 373.

17. Daniel Berrigan, "On 'The Dark Night of the Soul,'" *New York Review of Books* (October 22, 1970).

18. "The Berrigan Case" *Commonweal* XC (January 1968), p. 373.

19. Daniel Berrigan, *The Trial of the Catonsville 9* (New York, 1970), pp. 30-31.

20. Daniel Berrigan, "How to Make a Difference," *Commonweal* XCII (August 7, 1970), p. 385.

21. *Ibid.*, p. 386.

22. Karl Marx, quoted in *Karl Marx: Selected Writings in Sociology and Social Philosophy*, edited by T. B. Bottomore and Maximilien Rubel (London, 1963), pp. 40-41.

23. Richard Hinners, "Christianity and Marxism," unpublished essay in author's possession.

24. Speech of Rev. Patrick McDermott, Worcester, Massachusetts, March 28, 1971.

25. John P. Sisk, "The Sweet Dream of Harmony," *NCR* (August 31, 1966). Sisk, "Sweet Dream of Liberation," *ibid.* (September 13, 1967).

26. Quoted in William Miller, "The Radical Idea of the Catholic Worker," unpublished manuscript.

27. Thomas Merton to Dorothy Day, July 12, 1962, Catholic Worker Papers, Marquette University.

28. Peter Riga, *Crisis in Catholic Thought* (Milwaukee, 1962).

29. James Douglass, "The Gospel's Revolution Against Violence," *Catholic Worker* (December 1969).

30. John Cogley, "Radical Catholics: After the *Catholic Worker*," *NCR* (October 30, 1968); Jack Cook, "Cogley and the Relevance of Radicalism," *Catholic Worker* (November 1968).

31. Peter T. Rohrbach, "From Teresa of Avila to Eldridge Cleaver: The Odyssey of a Radical Priest," *Catholic World* (June 1970), pp. 114-119.

32. Thomas Merton, *Seeds of Destruction* (New York, 1955), p. 46.

33. Michael Novak, *Theology for Radical Politics* (New York, 1969), p. 122.

34. John Cronin, *Catholic Social Action* (Milwaukee, 1948), p. 102.

35. Raymond Williams, "The Catholic Crisis," *Nation* CCIII (August 17, 1967).

36. Brian Wicker, "The Aims and Hopes of Britians's New Catholic Left," *Critic* XXVI (October and November 1967), p. 64. Wicker has summed up the state of the movement in *First the Political Kingdom* (Notre Dame, 1967).

37. *The Slant Manifesto: Catholics and the Left* (London, 1966), p. 49.

38. Richard Hinners, "Christianity and Marxism," unpublished essay in author's possession.

39. Karl Rahner, "The Present Position of Christians: A Theological Interpretation of the Position of Christians in the Modern World," in *The Christian Commitment* (New York, 1963), p. 7.

40. Brian Wicker, "Law, Love and Politics," *Commonweal* (November 25, 1966), p. 220.

CHAPTER 9

1. John Kenneth Galbraith, *Economics and the Art of Controversy* (New Brunswick, 1965).

2. *The Writings of Thomas Jefferson* (Washington, 1903), III, p. 320.

3. Edward N. Robinson, "Comment" in Charter G. Dobbins and Calvin B. T. Lee, editors, *Whose Goals for American Higher Education?* (Washington, 1968), pp. 128-129.

4. Staughton Lynd, *Intellectual Origins of American Radicalism* (New York, 1967), p. 13.

5. William Arrowsmith, "The Idea of a New University," *Center Magazine* III (March 1970), p. 47.

6. Kenneth Keniston, "Responsibility for Criticism and Social Change" in Dobbins and Lee, *Whose Goals for American Higher Education?* (Washington, 1968), p. 163.

7. Ronald Sampson, "Power: The Enshrined Heresy," *Nation* (January 4, 1971), p. 17.

8. Kenneth Keniston, "You Have to Grow Up in Scarsdale to Know How Bad Things Really Are," *New York Times Magazine,* April 27, 1969.

9. Paulo Freire, *Pedagogy of the Oppressed* (New York, 1970), p. 23.

10. Saul Alinsky, *Reveille for Radicals* (Chicago, 1946), p. 29.

11. Saul Alinsky, "The Urban Immigrant" in Thomas T. McAvoy, C.S.C., editor, *Roman Catholicism and the American Way of Life* (Notre Dame, 1960), p. 146.

12. Saul Alinsky, *Reveille for Radicals,* pp. 11, 79.

13. Patrick Anderson, "Making Trouble is Alinsky's Business," *New York Times Magazine* (October 9, 1966).

14. Daniel P. Moynihan, *Maximum Feasible Misunderstanding* (New York, 1969).

15. "Conversations or Revolution," pamphlet reprint of dialogues carried in *NCR* (Lent 1968), pp. 7-10.

CHAPTER 10

1. H. Stuart Hughes, "Pope John's Revolution: Secular or Religious?," *Commonweal* LXXXIII (December 1965), pp. 301-304.

2. Hans Kung, *Truthfulness* (New York, 1968), pp. 20-21.

3. *Ibid.*, p. 27.

4. Robert Nisbet, "Crisis in the Universities," *The Public Interest*, no. 10 (Winter 1968), pp. 57-58; Sidney Mead, *The Lively Experiment* (New York, 1963), p. 104.

5. E.E.Y. Hales, *Pope John and His Revolution* (New York, 1966).

6. Dietrich Bonhoeffer, *Letters and Papers from Prison* (New York, 1962); J.A.T. Robinson, *The New Reformation* (New York, 1965); Harvey Cox, *The Secular City* (New York, 1965); Karl Rahner, *The Christian Commitment* (New York, 1963); Yves Congar, *The Wide World My Parish* (Baltimore, 1961).

7. Gustave Weigel, *The Modern God* (New Haven, 1959), p. 94.

8. Harvey Cox, *The Secular City*, (New York, 1965), p. 125.

9. Richard McBrien, *Do We Need the Church?* (New York, 1969), *passim*.

10. Quoted in Peter Matthiessen, *Sal Si Puedes* (New York, 1969), pp. 195-196.

INDEX